Cybersecurity, Law, and Economics

This book examines the intersection between cybersecurity and the law and economy of India and offers a course of action in designing efficacious policies against emerging cybercrimes in the country.

It reviews the boom in infrastructure growth in India and the security challenges this presents to the domestic economy and legal system. The contributors conducted a risk assessment of the potential economic impacts and security vulnerabilities, as well as identified the current regulatory and legal gaps regarding cryptocurrency, ecommerce, and digital banking. The book also considers the subject of data localization and sovereignty, and the challenges of establishing an indigenous data architecture. By discussing the economic impact of cybersecurity and incorporating recommendations from scholars, activists, academics, young legal intellectuals, and professionals in the field, the chapters propose new measures and protections for lawmakers and policymakers to adopt.

This book will interest researchers and students of cybersecurity, law, and economics, international relations, and Indian policymakers.

Gagandeep Kaur is Associate Professor of law at the School of Law UPES, Dehradun, India.

Narendra N. Dalei is Associate Professor of economics and associate director of research at the Central University of Himachal Pradesh, India.

Sushanta Kumar Mahapatra is Associate Professor of Economics at the ICFAI Foundation for Higher Education Deemed University, Hyderabad, India.

Vinay Kandpal is Professor (Research) at Graphic Era University, Dehradun, India.

Routledge Studies in the Modern World Economy

The ASEAN Digital Economy
Towards an Integrated Regional Framework
Edited by Paul Cheung and Xie Taojun

The Future of Multilateralism and Globalization in the Age of the U.S.–China Rivalry
Edited by Norbert Gaillard, Fumihito Gotoh, and Rick Michalek

Nuclear Power Safety and Governance in East Asia
Edited by Soocheol Lee, Weisheng Zhou and Kiyoshi Fujikawa

Inequality and Public Policy
Towards Visible Equality and Equal Opportunity
Bhanoji Rao, Suresh K.G. and Pundarik Mukhopadhaya

The Governance of Economic Development
Investment, Innovation, and Competition in China
Anson Au

The Economics of Russia's War in Ukraine
Impact Analysis of Economic Policy and Finance
Nataliya Struk, Maryana Prokop and Oleksandra Struk

Cybersecurity, Law, and Economics
The Case of India
Edited by Gagandeep Kaur, Narendra N. Dalei, Sushanta Kumar Mahapatra, and Vinay Kandpal

For more information about this series, please visit: www.routledge.com/Routledge-Studies-in-the-Modern-World-Economy/book-series/SE0432

Cybersecurity, Law, and Economics

The Case of India

Edited by Gagandeep Kaur, Narendra N. Dalei, Sushanta Kumar Mahapatra, and Vinay Kandpal

Routledge
Taylor & Francis Group
LONDON AND NEW YORK

First published 2025
by Routledge
4 Park Square, Milton Park, Abingdon, Oxon OX14 4RN

and by Routledge
605 Third Avenue, New York, NY 10158

Routledge is an imprint of the Taylor & Francis Group, an informa business

British Library Cataloguing-in-Publication Data
A catalogue record for this book is available from the British Library

ISBN: 978-1-032-85245-4 (hbk)
ISBN: 978-1-032-85246-1 (pbk)
ISBN: 978-1-003-51729-0 (ebk)

DOI: 10.4324/9781003517290

Typeset in Galliard
by Apex CoVantage, LLC

Dedicated to our esteemed teachers:

Your guidance, knowledge, and inspiration have been invaluable to us throughout our scholastic journey. You have been the guiding light that has illuminated our path. Not only have your commitment, patience, and enthusiasm for teaching influenced our academic understanding, but they have also influenced our character and the values. We will never forget the life lessons you taught us and the words of encouragement you provided; they have left an everlasting impact. This book is a tribute to our unceasing efforts and the significant impact you have had on our life: this book is an homage to you. We would like to express our gratitude to you for placing your faith in us, for encouraging our natural curiosity, and for creating an insatiable passion for learning.

Contents

Contributors

Naseem Ahmed Naseem Ahmed is a professor and dean in the Department of Law, Integral University and has vast experience in various fields of law. He has published in various reputed national and international journals. He is also a member of the review board of various journals.

Anshima Anshima is a Research Scholar at HPKV Business School, School of Commerce and Management Studies, India. Currently, she is working on green human resource management, and her area of interest is human resource management and organizational behaviour.

Subhra Rajat Balabantaray Subhra has completed MA (sociology) from the University of Hyderabad, MPhil (sociology) from Pondicherry Central University, and PhD in sociology from the University of Hyderabad, India. He is Assistant Professor in the School of Business, Dr. Vishwanath Karad MIT World Peace University, India. Prior to joining MIT WPU, he worked for 7 years in the capacity of an assistant professor in the University of Petroleum and Energy Studies, India. He has a total of 11 years (8 years of teaching and 3 years of research) of experience.

Bhawana Bhardwaj Bhawana Bhardwaj is a faculty member at the School of Commerce and Management Studies, the Central University of Himachal Pradesh, India. She has 18 years of postgraduate teaching and research experience. She has published over 35 research papers and book chapters in prestigious refereed national and international journals. She has been conferred "the Young Researcher Award", the National Budding Researcher Award, and the "Education Excellence Award in Human Resource Management".

Narendra N. Dalei Narendra N. Dalei holds the positions of associate professor of economics and associate director of research at the Central University of Himachal Pradesh, India. From the University of Delhi, he earned a PhD in ecological and environmental economics, and he has written more than 70 research papers covering a wide range of topics. Several research projects supported by national and international funding agencies were completed by Dr. Dalei.

Manuj Darbari Manuj Darbari is a research scholar in the field of cyberlaw in the Department of Law, Integral University, Lucknow, India.

Saloni Devi Saloni Devi is presently working as an assistant professor at The Business School, University of Jammu, India. She has more than 13 years of experience in teaching and research. She has published many research papers, conference papers, and book chapters in highly reputed and indexed journals/books. She has also presented research papers in international conferences organized by esteemed organizations such as IIM Ahmedabad, IIM Rohtak, IIM Bodhgaya, IIM Jammu, and MDI.

Anil Kumar Dixit Anil Kumar Dixit is at present professor of law at Uttaranchal University, Law College Dehradun, Uttarakhand, India. Dixit has a long innings with the media since 1984 as a freelance journalist. He has produced video albums for metro news, Doordarshan, as an instrument of entertainment. Academically, he has a doctorate in media law. He has four patents, published in his credit; is the author of six books; and has published 55 research papers reflected in Scopus database and 100 articles.

Madhuri Irene Madhuri Irene is Associate Professor, ICFAI Law School, ICFAI University, Dehradun, India with 23 years of teaching experience as a law professor and 5 years of industry experience. She has published 70 articles/chapters in referred international and national journals/books; has received several awards—The Innovative Dedicated Professional Teacher Award, Dr. Sarvepalli Radha Krishnan Distinguished Professor and Researcher Award, and Indo-Pacific–Ruth Ginsberg Distinguished Law Faculty Award; and is an editorial board member in several national and international journals.

Vinay Kandpal Vinay Kandpal holds a PhD in management from the Department of Management Studies, Kumaun University, Nainital, Uttarakhand, India. He obtained his DLitt from Kumaun University, Nainital, India. Dr. Kandpal is Professor (Research) at the Department of Management Studies, Graphic Era University, Dehradun. He has over 20 years of experience in academics. He has published more than 50 research papers and 12 book chapters in leading refereed and indexed journals.

Pooja Kansra Pooja Kansra is a professor of economics at Mittal School of Business, Lovely Professional University, Phagwara, Punjab (India). Her areas of research include health economics, labour economics, gender economics, insurance, and the informal sector. She is an avid researcher and has presented papers in various national and international conferences. She has to her credit various research papers published in Scopus-indexed journals. She was granted copyright for the development of a "Health Information Tool" by the Copyright Office, Government of India.

Gagandeep Kaur Gagandeep Kaur has distinguished expertise in cyberlaw and information technology law. She has more than 14 years of teaching and research experience in prestigious universities and is presently associated with the School of Law, UPES, Dehradun, India as Associate Professor in law. She was honoured with the "Research Excellence Award" in 2023 and in 2024 at UPES in one of the most celebrated annual events popularly known as "Manthan".

Garima Kohli Garima Kohli is presently working as a lecturer at The Business School, University of Jammu. She has 11 years of teaching experience. She received her PhD in management from The Business School, University of Jammu, in 2020. She is the member of Grand Academic Portal. She has published research papers in various reputed journals. She has attended 25 international/national conference/seminars, 15 webinars, 5 FDPs, and 4 workshops.

Nikhil Kulshrestha Nikhil has more than 26 years of experience as a teacher, trainer, researcher, and academic administrator. He is a postgraduate in management and sociology and a doctorate in business studies. He has delivered more than 200 trainings to corporates and has presented and published more than 50 research papers at national and international levels.

Sushanta Kumar Mahapatra Sushanta Kumar Mahapatra is currently working as an associate professor at The ICFAI Foundation for Higher Education (IFHE), Hyderabad, India. He has collaborated in research projects supported by organizations like IRRI Philippines, ILO Geneva, ICSSR, Sir Ratan Tata Trust, and NABARD. He is the recipient of the European Commission Erasmus Mundus Post-Doctoral Fellowship from the University of Bologna, Italy.

Sandeep Mishra Sandeep Mishra is currently working as an assistant professor in Amity University, AU: Lucknow, India. He has completed his PhD from Dr. Ram Manohar Lohiya National Law University, Lucknow, India. His area of specialization is cybercrime. He has more than 10 publications under his name, more than 10 guest lectures, and supervised 8 dissertations.

Jai Shankar Ojha Jai Shankar Ojha, principal, Swami Shukdevanand Law College, Shahjahanpur, India has 17 years of vast academic experience. He has more than 40 publications under his name. He has supervised more than 10 dissertations and evaluated more than 10 PhDs. He has been a member of BoS and also a recipient of the Nation Builder Award and NEP Award. He has expertise in constitutional and criminal law.

Devender Pratap Devender Pratap is a senior fellow at the National Council of Applied Economic Research (NCAER), New Delhi, India. He has developed India Applied General Equilibrium (InAGE) model for analysing policy issues in the Indian economy. He has contributed GTAP India Database to the Centre for Global Trade Analysis, Purdue University, Indiana, USA, for the last two decades. He has contributed large numbers of papers in peer-reviewed national and international journals.

G. Ramakrishnan G. Ramakrishnan has a rich experience of more than 30 years in the EPC industry (10 years in L&T, 6 years in BGR Energy, 2 years in Enmas, 11 years in Tecton Engineering, and 1+ years in Trident). In academics, he has delivered guest lectures in UPES, Doon Business School, and SRM University, AP. He has presented and published many research papers in conferences and journals.

A. Lakshmana Rao A. Lakshmana Rao has a doctorate from Andhra University. During his ongoing long academic stint, he presented a lot of research papers in both national and international conferences at various national and international universities, NITs, and IIMs. Furthermore, he has also published many research papers in various journals of good reputation. Currently, he is as an associate professor and head of Department of Commerce, SRM University, AP, India.

Reena Roy Reena Roy is a PhD scholar in Uttaranchal University, Dehradun, Uttarakhand, India and has an LLM from H.N.B. Central University, Uttarakhand. She has been working as an assistant professor in Libra College of Law, Dehradun, Uttarakhand, since 2022 and is a PhD scholar in law in Uttaranchal University, Dehradun, Uttarakhand. She has the copyright for four research papers reflecting in the Scopus database, three chapters in various books, and three other articles.

Dipanker Sharma Dipanker Sharma is the head of the Department of Management, Central University of Himachal Pradesh in the School of Commerce and Management Studies, India and has a total work experience of 18 years. He has three patents, has published more than two dozens of research articles, and has presented research papers in more than 30 national and international conferences. He has done short assignments in Asian countries like Hong Kong, Dubai, Bhutan, and Singapore.

Abhishek Kumar Singh Abhishek Kumar Singh is an associate professor in the Department of Law, Integral University, and has vast experience in various fields of law. He has published in various reputed national and international journals. He is also a member of the review board of various journals.

Pradeep Kumar Singh Pradeep Kumar Singh, Research scholar at DSM-NRU, Lucknow, India earned a gold medal for his outstanding performance in Master of Laws. With a profound interest in the intersection of law and technology, he has authored several insightful articles exploring the evolving dynamics in this field. His research delves into various aspects of constitutional law, criminal law, and cyberlaw, where he seeks to unravel complexities and offer innovative perspectives.

Anjali Tandon Anjali Tandon is an associate professor at the Institute for Studies in Industrial Development, New Delhi. She has been a contributor to the Global Trade Analysis Package (GTAP) version 8 database of Purdue University, USA. Her recent book *Labour and Capital Use in Indian*

Manufacturing – Structural Aspects was published by Routledge in 2024. Her earlier co-authored book *Measuring Structural Change and Energy Use in Indian Economy* was published in 2019.

Diksha Verma Diksha Verma's areas of research include bancassurance, insurance, health insurance, and non-life insurance. Her academic contributions include the publication of numerous book chapters and research papers in esteemed publications indexed with Scopus. Moreover, she has showcased her scholarly work through presentations at both national and international conferences, demonstrating a commitment to advancing knowledge in her field.

Foreword

The unprecedented and fast expansion of technology across the globe has given impetus to avenues for economic growth and societal development that have never been evidenced before. However, in tandem with these improvements, there has been an increase in the number of cyber threats and vulnerabilities, which presents substantial challenges for the security of individuals, corporations, and governments alike. The field of cybersecurity has emerged as an important domain where legislative frameworks, economic considerations, and technological developments converge in order to safeguard digital assets and reduce the hazards associated with cyberspace.

The book *Cybersecurity, Law, and Economics: The Case of India* delves deep into the complex landscape of cybersecurity within Indian context. It provides insightful analyses and viewpoints on the ever-changing difficulties and opportunities that are present in this dynamic subject. For the purpose of elucidating the intricacies of cybersecurity governance, policy frameworks, and regulatory procedures in India, this groundbreaking effort brings together expertise from a variety of fields, including economics, technology, and law. The contents of the book are highly relevant in the current scenario which calls for making continuous efforts for ensuring cybersecurity and safeguarding individuals and organizations from becoming victims of cybercrimes and cyber frauds.

As we negotiate the complexities of the digital age, it is becoming increasingly important to have a comprehensive understanding of the dynamic interplay that exists between legal norms, economic incentives, and technological capabilities in order to combat cyber risks, cybercrimes, and cyber frauds and improve resilience against cyberattacks. In my opinion, the purpose of this book is to serve as a valuable resource for policymakers, legal practitioners, economists, technologists, and academics by providing complex insights and practical recommendations for advancing cybersecurity initiatives in India and beyond. The book accomplishes this objective by conducting a comprehensive exploration of cybersecurity issues from multidisciplinary perspectives.

I am confident that the book entitled *Cybersecurity, Law, and Economics: The Case of India* will serve as a seminal work in advancing our understanding of cybersecurity challenges and fostering collaborative efforts towards a more secure and resilient digital future. I commend the authors for their diligent research and scholarly contributions to the field of cybersecurity. I am also pretty sure that the present book will realize its objectives by assisting all the stakeholders in improving and securing multifarious functioning in the cyberworld.

Prof. Sat Prakash Bansal
Hon'ble Vice-Chancellor
Central University of Himachal Pradesh
Dharamshala, India

Preface

India has become the major economy with the fastest rate of growth in the world because of its strong democracy and robust relationships at the international level. In the upcoming years, it is expected to rank among the top three economic powers. The main drivers of the country's growth include rapid adoption of new technologies, cybersecurity mechanisms, and the utilization of world-class techniques. The country is at the vanguard of technological transformation, from the growth of e-commerce platforms to the digitalization of financial and governance systems. Nevertheless, these developments also bring risks of their own, from data breaches to cyberattacks, so it is imperative to fully comprehend the complex situations at hand. Cybercrime is not one type of offence. However, it is, in fact, a range of offences that have put the entire economy into cyber threats. The hidden cost of cybercrime expands its horizons beyond the damage of individual assets to the global level, including financial depression, to the Indian economy as a whole. A rapidly evolving technological environment has left the Indian economy and legal jurisprudence facing many unsolved questions.

This book entitled *Cybersecurity, Law, and Economics: The Case of India* has explored the complex aspects of contemporary economy, cybersecurity, changing legal requirements, and the financial ramifications in India. This book is the result of a cooperative effort to investigate the difficulties, prospects, and developing approaches for protecting cyberspace while promoting creativity and economic expansion. This book attempts to disentangle the various aspects of cybersecurity in India via a multidisciplinary perspective. To address new threats and protect digital assets, it looks at the legal frameworks that control cyberspace. It also examines the financial effects of cybersecurity incidents, including how they affect businesses, industries, and entire countries.

As we embark on this journey through the nexus of cybersecurity, law, and economics, it is our sincere hope that this book catalyses informed discourse, strategic policymaking, and collaborative action. This book is a useful resource for policymakers, lawyers, cybersecurity experts, and companies trying to understand the rapidly changing cybersecurity market in India. It is not just a theoretical discussion as it has examined the symbiotic relationship between economics and law in the lap of technological revolution. With the help of real-world case studies and expert insights, it provides doable tactics for promoting cybersecurity resilience, encouraging legal compliance, and utilizing technology advancements to reduce risks and seize opportunities.

Gagandeep Kaur
Narendra N. Dalei
Sushanta Kumar Mahapatra
Vinay Kandpal

Acknowledgements

This endeavour would not have been possible without the generous support, insights, and encouragement from numerous individuals and organizations. We are profoundly grateful to all those who have contributed their time, expertise, and insights to make this book a comprehensive resource on cybersecurity, law, and economics.

We also owe a debt of gratitude to all contributing authors whose insights and research have enriched this interdisciplinary dialogue. Their commitment to advancing the understanding of cybersecurity from legal, economic, and managerial perspectives has been invaluable.

Our thanks also go to the reviewers for their rigorous critiques and to our publisher Taylor & Francis for their support and belief in the importance of this project. Their professionalism and assistance have been crucial in bringing this book to fruition.

Furthermore, we are thankful to our academic peers and colleagues for their encouragement and feedback throughout this journey. Their support has been a source of strength and inspiration. Lastly, we acknowledge our families and friends for their patience and unwavering support. This book would not have been possible without their understanding and encouragement during the many hours dedicated to its completion.

We express our gratitude to the administration of University of Petroleum and Energy Studies, Central University of Himachal Pradesh, IBS Hyderabad, and Graphic Era (Deemed to be University) for their generous provision of logistical and infrastructural assistance, which encompasses Internet and Wi-Fi access, library resources, and support personnel, and the invaluable moral support of honourable vice-chancellors, deans, directors, and department heads to complete this journey.

Abbreviations

Abbreviation	Full Form
CCT	Cybercrime Team
Co.	Company
Cr.P.C.	Code of Criminal Procedure, 1973
DCC	District Cyber Cell
DDoS	Distributed Denial of Service
FIR	First Information Report
FOMO	Fear Of Missing Out
Govt.	Government
HC	High Court
IIT	Indian Institute of Technology
ID	Identity
IPR	Intellectual Property Right
IT	Information Technology
MeitY	Ministry of Electronics and Information Technology
MHA	Ministry of Home Affairs
NCRB	National Crime Record Bureau
Ors.	Others
SP	Superintendent of Police
SC	Supreme Court
SCC	Supreme Court Cases
SOP	Standard Operating Procedure
TISS	Tata Institute of Social Sciences
ZCC	Zonal Cyber Cell
ATM	Automated Teller Machine
Apps	Application(s)
USA	United States of America
UK	United Kingdom
CBDC	Central Bank Digital Currency
RBI	Reserve Bank of India
UPI	Unified Payments Interface

PoS	Point of Sale
PoW	Proof of Work
QR Code	Quick Response Code
BTC	Bitcoin
VC	Virtual Currency
IMAI	Internet and Mobile Association of India
DLT	Distributed Ledger Technologies
SEBI	Security Exchange Board of India
NFTs	Non-Fungible Tokens
FCA	Financial Conduct Authority
KYC	Know Your Customer
AML	Anti-Money Laundering
CTF	Counter-Terrorist Financing
ADR	Alternative Dispute Resolution
ODR	Online Dispute Resolution
UNCITRAL	United Nations Commission on International Trade Law
AI	Artificial Intelligence
E-Com	E-Commerce
GST	Goods and Services Tax
RBI	Reserve Bank of India
FDI	Foreign Direct Investment
ISO	International Organization for Standardization
B2B	Business to Business
B2C	Business to Consumer
VR	Virtual Reality
IP	Intellectual Property
OCMC	Online Consumer Mediation Centre
NIXI	National Internet Exchange of India
M2M	Machine to Machine
IoT	Internet of Things
AR	Augmented Reality
APEC	Asia-Pacific Economic Cooperation
ASEAN	Association of Southeast Asian Nations
CGE	Computable General Equilibrium
CUTS	Consumer Unity and Trust Society
ECIPE	European Centre for International Political Economy
GDP	Gross Domestic Growth
GDPR	General Data Protection Regulation
GTAP	Global Trade Analysis Project
OECD	Organization for Economic Cooperation and Development
SAARC	South Asian Association for Regional Cooperation
TiSMoS	Trade in services by mode of supply
UNCTAD	United Nations Conference on Trade and Development
PLI	Production Linked Incentive

Part 1

Introduction

1 The Intersections between Cybersecurity, Law, and Economics

Narendra N. Dalei

Introduction

The intersections of cybersecurity, law, and economics in India demonstrate how legal, economic, and technological issues interact to shape cybersecurity policies, practices, and outcomes. Maintaining a healthy equilibrium between regulatory compliance, economic growth, and cybersecurity resilience is absolutely necessary in order to cultivate a digital ecosystem in India that is both secure and lucrative (Ebert, 2020). India, known for its resilient democracy and solid alliances, has become the fifth largest economy globally and is projected to be among the top three economic powers within the next decade or so (Panda, 2024; Pugu, 2024). As the economic situation has improved, investments have been allocated to various sectors of the economy. The primary metrics used to assess a country's economic growth are the consumer price index (CPI), gross domestic product (GDP), unemployment rates, and crude oil prices (Sharma & Shrivastava, 2021). The primary catalysts behind the country's economic expansion encompass the swift assimilation of cutting-edge technologies, resilient cybersecurity infrastructure, and methodologies employed by cyber malefactors. Cybercrime encompasses a variety of offences that pose significant hazards to the entire economy. The rise in cybercrime incidents has resulted in a financial loss of over $1 trillion to the worldwide economy (Mphatheni & Maluleke, 2022; Kovalchuk et al., 2021). The concealed expenses of cybercrime extend beyond the harm to individual possessions and have a worldwide impact, including causing financial downturns in the Indian economy as a whole (Rajput, 2020; Jaiswal, 2022).

The increasing integration of technology and Internet infrastructure in India has led to a significant rise in cyber vulnerabilities, including data breaches, cyberattacks, and cases of online fraud (Chigada & Madzinga, 2021). This aforementioned occurrence has resulted in a growing need for cybersecurity products and services. India's cybersecurity sector has been steadily growing, with significant investments from both private companies and government organizations to strengthen its cybersecurity infrastructure (Hajoary & Akhilesh, 2020). The increasing concern about cyber threats has led to a significant increase in investments in the Indian cybersecurity business. There is

DOI: 10.4324/9781003517290-2

currently a significant increase in both domestic and international companies entering the market, with the aim of offering a wide variety of cybersecurity solutions (Sobb et al., 2020). The cybersecurity products and services market in India is anticipated to have significant expansion in the future years. However, it is crucial to recognize that the Indian government has recognized the utmost importance of cybersecurity and has implemented numerous steps to strengthen the country's cyberlaw and enhance its security infrastructure. The National Cyber Security Policy, introduced in 2013 and later revised in 2020, outlines the government's strategic approach to developing a strong and secure digital environment within the Indian cyberspace (Singh & Malik, 2021). In addition, the government has been actively promoting the creation of public–private partnerships to enhance cybersecurity infrastructure and strengthen expertise in this field. India possesses an extensive legal framework that covers a wide range of laws and regulations to properly address the constantly changing field of cybercrimes and cybersecurity. The Information Technology Act of 2000 (IT Act) and its subsequent amendment in 2008, referred to as the Information Technology (Amendment) Act, establish the essential legal structure for governing cyber activities in the country (Singh, 2021). The legislation cited above clearly defines numerous cyber offenses and their accompanying penalties. Moreover, the continuing discussion of the Personal Data Protection Bill, which aims to protect personal data and ensure privacy, has the potential to have significant consequences in the field of cybersecurity (Wylde, 2022).

While notable progress has been made, it is crucial to recognize that the economics of cyberlaw and security in India still pose considerable difficulties. An important issue revolves around the limited availability of skilled cybersecurity professionals. The industry's rapid expansion led to a noticeable imbalance between the need for skilled professionals in the field and the available supply. The need to address this deficiency in skills has arisen as a paramount concern for both the corporate sector and the government. Another hindrance relates to the lack of cybersecurity awareness among the general public and small businesses. There is a significant lack of understanding among people and small organizations in India regarding the complexities of cyber threats and the most effective ways for protecting their digital assets and information on the Internet. The need to reduce hazards requires increasing awareness and promoting cybersecurity education. The rapid expansion of India's digital transformation can be credited to the smart execution of initiatives such as Digital India. The widespread use of technology improvements has undeniably led to improved convenience and efficiency. A recurring challenge lies in achieving a harmonious equilibrium between digital advancement and robust cybersecurity measures.

Scope of Cybersecurity from an Economics and Law Perspective

The scope of the book lies in analysing the intersection between cybersecurity and economics, which will be translated into policy reforms and/or design of new policies, regulations, or laws. This edited book explores the interdependent connection between economics and cyberlaw throughout the era of technological transformation. The rapid technological growth in India has presented unresolved challenges for the Indian economy and legal system. The purpose of this edited book is to analyse current issues in this sector in order to address the need for new legislation and incorporate recommendations from scholars, activists, academics, young legal intellectuals, and professionals in the field. Considering this, the proposed edited book will examine the economic and policy dimensions of rising cyber-related concerns and their linkages across several channels. It will provide strategies to assist policymakers in developing effective policies to combat cybercrime.

In an increasingly digitized world, the rapid expansion of information and communication technologies (ICTs) has revolutionized the way individuals, businesses, and governments operate, communicate, and conduct transactions. While these technological advancements have brought about unprecedented opportunities for economic growth, innovation, and societal progress, they have also exposed vulnerabilities in cyberspace that pose significant challenges to security, privacy, and trust.

Cybersecurity, Law, and Economics: The Case of India explores the intricate nexus between cybersecurity, law, and economics within the Indian context, shedding light on the evolving landscape of cyber threats, regulatory frameworks, and policy responses in one of the world's largest and fastest-growing digital economies. This book seeks to provide a comprehensive understanding of the complex dynamics shaping the cybersecurity ecosystem in India, with a focus on the interplay between legal norms, economic incentives, technological capabilities, and socio-political factors.

As we embark on this exploration, it is crucial to recognize the multifaceted nature of cybersecurity challenges and the need for a multidisciplinary approach to address them effectively. From the proliferation of cyberattacks and data breaches to the emergence of new regulatory regimes and legal frameworks, the realm of cybersecurity encompasses a wide array of interconnected issues that require holistic and nuanced solutions.

The Intersection

The studies covered in this book delve into key themes and topics at the intersection of cybersecurity, law, and economics. The intersection has resulted in four themes that deal with four dimensions corresponding to cybersecurity risk and economic impact; cybercrime, law, and technology; cryptocurrency and cybersecurity; and data localization policy and online dispute resolution.

Cybersecurity Risk and Economic Impact

India's economy, infrastructure, and national security are all at danger from the challenges posed by cybersecurity threats. India, like many other countries, is confronted with a wide variety of cyber dangers, which include ransomware attacks, data breaches, and cyber-espionage sponsored by nation-states (McGuire, 2021). The economic impact of these cyber risks is significant and affects a variety of different elements.

Individuals, public, academic scholars, and business enterprises of all shades need to pay attention to the subject of cybersecurity if they wish to successfully protect and secure information systems in a covert manner. This is something that all organizations need to accomplish. It is now generally accepted that one of the most serious problems that modern economy must contend with is cybersecurity. Every individual and every company are exposed to the cyber dangers that are continually increasing as a result of the growing need for digitalization. This demand is the driving force behind the evolution of these hazards. Cybersecurity is a growing concern for governments, corporations, and individuals all around the world. Cybercrime is also becoming increasingly common. The chapter "Understanding the Global Landscape of Cybersecurity Risks, Economic Impacts, and Challenges: Lesson for India" steers an exhaustive review in order to acquire a deeper comprehension of the economic impact and challenges of cybersecurity. In addition, the chapter discusses the technological advancement and solution to the cyber threats. The authors found that cybersecurity risks can significantly impact economies, causing direct and indirect financial losses. Companies can suffer from brand damage, eroded consumer trust, and theft of intellectual property. The economic impact of cybercrime on businesses is expected to reach US$10.5 trillion by 2025. Cybercriminals can also steal confidential business information, affecting market position and innovation. Noncompliance with data protection laws can lead to regulatory fines and legal fees. Cyberattacks use advanced methods to gain unauthorized access or exploit vulnerabilities, such as zero-day exploits, persistent threats, fileless malware, credential stuffing, and AI-powered malware. To combat these sophisticated attacks, Indian and global enterprises need to implement a multilayered defence strategy, including timely application of security patches, systems that detect abnormalities, staff training on social engineering techniques, multifactor authentication, and encryption. Investing in cybersecurity is crucial for businesses to protect themselves and respond to cyberattacks. The Internet of Things (IoT) presents numerous security concerns due to its vast network of connected devices. To reduce these risks, global enterprises, especially those of Indian origin or operating from India, should develop comprehensive security procedures, such as routine audits, penetration testing, anomaly monitoring, encryption, secure configuration management, and employee education.

The chapter "Examining the Impact of Cyber Fraud on Indian Society: An Assessment of the Potential Damage" investigates the multifaceted impact of cyber fraud on Indian society, especially on individuals, businesses, and the nation's security infrastructure. In the digital age, where global interconnectedness, streamlined transactions, and efficient communication have become the norm, cyber fraud has emerged as a significant threat. This research delves into the economic, social, psychological, and legal dimensions of cyber fraud, shedding light on its profound implications for individuals, businesses, and the nation as a whole. Additionally, the study explores the ethical considerations surrounding the compromise of digital privacy and civil liberties in the wake of cybercrime. Utilizing a purely descriptive approach, this research draws from secondary sources of information, including books, research papers, and journal articles, with a specific focus on recent publications from the past decade. The compilation of scholarly materials involved searches on various platforms, such as Google Scholar, Scopus, and Web of Science. Victims of cybercrimes experience consequences comparable to those of traditional crimes, often suffering both financial and psychological impacts. By understanding the societal consequences of cyber fraud, this study aims to foster a deeper awareness of the issue, prompt dialogue on effective prevention and mitigation strategies, and inform policymakers about the need for measures to safeguard individuals and organizations in an ever-evolving digital landscape. In a world where digital threats continue to evolve, this research offers valuable insights for addressing the growing problem of cyber fraud in the Indian context.

Stakeholders throughout the globe are losing their wealth considerably every day, without any fault on their part. One of the major reasons attributed to this loss is fraud. Fraud, in today's scenario, is acting as a major threat not only to the stakeholders but also to the very existence of corporate bodies. The chapter "Perception of Investment Behaviour in the Light of Corporate Frauds with Special Reference to India" is focused mainly on understanding the impact of corporate fraud on investor behaviour and its presence in various corporate bodies. The chapter used a survey on select groups to identify the influencing phenomenon on their investment pattern. Furthermore, it also presents the impact on the efficiency of corporate bodies, their "fraud detection practices", and how they are overcoming "fraud risk" in case of emergence of fraud to cater to the needs of various stakeholders, and their concern towards portfolio. The chapter initially takes into consideration the presence of different types of commercial frauds that are more prevalent in various types of industries and progresses more specifically towards global banking and financial sectors. The chapter also visualizes the implications of fraud on investors' investing patterns in security markets. The chapter ends with a discussion of the researchers' suggestions for mitigation of fraud by following certain best practices.

The Indian banking sector plays a vital role in the economy by meeting the credit requirements of all persons. The chapter "Legal Framework of Cybercrimes against E-Banking in India" focuses on information technology, which plays a vital instrument in Indian banks, augmenting services and introducing a fresh perspective on business. E-banking has various advantages, including the convenience of banking at any time and from any location, enabling clients to access their accounts without being concerned about bank operating hours or lengthy waits. Nevertheless, e-banking also poses issues, prompting the implementation of the 2000 IT Act to safeguard against cybercrimes such as banking phishing, network scanning, virus dissemination, spam, website compromise, and malware proliferation. Additional laws address, forbid, and penalize these cybercrimes, and in 2008, the IT Act underwent significant modifications to enhance overall cybersecurity in India. The primary objective of the Reserve Bank of India (RBI) is to safeguard, enhance efficiency, promote compatibility, obtain approval, foster inclusivity, provide wide coverage, and maintain conformity with international standards in payment and settlement systems. Nevertheless, cybercrimes continue to pose a substantial challenge in India due to the insufficiency of existing legislative frameworks in effectively regulating and addressing issues faced by both clients and banks. The Indian banking industry cannot escape electronic banking transactions in the current context; however, since cybercrime is a more serious transgression than traditional crimes, the present study's recommendations will be helpful for policymakers and legal professionals.

Bancassurance being a highly successful channel of insurance distribution demands fast processing time in its operation. It has been observed that the time involved in processing of bancassurance services is quite slow, and hence optimum solutions are demanded. One of the solutions is blockchain technology, which has come up with optimistic transformation and growth in bancassurance. Blockchain accounts can be used for availing of bancassurance services. Distributed ledger principle is followed in blockchain technology introduced in the year 2009. Blockchain is capable of providing complete answerability and intelligibility with advanced safety. Still, banking institutions face many difficulties in implementing it, and it became imperative for them to overcome these difficulties to satisfy their customers. The chapter "Economic Impact of Perceptible Benefits and Adverse Sides of Blockchain in Bancassurance along with Cybersecurity" focuses on describing the perceptible benefits and adverse sides of blockchain technology in Bancassurance. The chapter discusses theoretical perspectives based on existing literature, which outlines the pros and cons of blockchain technology in implementing bancassurance. The chapter shows that adopting bancassurance along with blockchain technology can enhance data security, automatic smart contracts, and rationalized claims settlement for insurance providers through banks.

Cybercrime, Law, and Technology

India has a complex landscape that is shaped by rapid technical breakthroughs, evolving cyber challenges, and the need for robust legal frameworks to effectively combat cybercrimes. Cybercrime, law, and technology are all interwoven in this ecosystem. The interplay among cybercrime, law, and technology in India highlights the significance of comprehensive legislative frameworks, technological innovation, capacity building, and international cooperation in the context of tackling cybersecurity concerns and protecting the digital ecosystem (Bondarenko et al., 2022). It is vital to make efforts to build cybersecurity resilience, enhance law enforcement capabilities, and promote cyber hygiene in order to create a cyberspace in India that is safer and more secure.

The Internet has become a new essential in the life of individuals. The potential of the Internet has made it possible for vendors to do business beyond territorial boundaries. Additionally, cybercrime is gaining momentum over time. Researching the factors influencing the efficacy of a globally distributed platform is more important than ever due to the surge in Internet usage and reliance on online services. The chapter "Quashing Cybercrime and Putting Up Consumer Confidence in E-Commerce" shows that online businesses are impacted by consumer-facing security breaches that limit their online activity. Cybercriminals are always looking for loopholes in digital systems and services. Vulnerabilities are quickly discovered, which allows them to plot an attack and harm consumers of digital services. Sources make it clear that as the number of people using the Internet rises daily, so does the requirement for digital platforms to be safe to use. The history of cybercrime and e-commerce, steps to bolster cybersecurity, and the significance of customer confidence in e-commerce are all covered in this essay.

The chapter "Application of Activity Theory in Technology Law" estimates the magnitude of the India's cybercrime industry and its components, as in any other developed economy. It investigates how cybercrime is an integral part and is filled with methodological flaws, conceptual confusion, logical challenges, and statistical problems that currently exist. The need of this study originates from a debatable issue of identifying the gaps in the current legal framework and the technological advancements and finally the human factors involved. The chapter uses the concept of activity theory and its relation with the law and new technology domain. A mathematical correlation is used in this chapter encompassing various dimensions of technology law. The chapter highlights whether any underground economy exists or not, and if it does, what is the estimating size of a country's cybercrime industry and its ingredients such as challenge of reporting rate. The chapter highlights the challenges of new technology law usage and cannot position of the legal domain with respect to service providers.

National Crime Records Bureau (NCRB) is a government institution that collects and analyses data related to crime. NCRB publishes the annual Crime in India Report. According to the 2021 report of NCRB, Uttar Pradesh was declared the cybercrime capital of India. During COVID-19, reliance on technology has paved new ways to commit cybercrime. The emerging concept of online education system had introduced children of tender age to the Internet, which in turn became an opportunity for criminals to commit crimes through online mediums. According to the NCRB report, there has been an 11.8% increase in the number of reported cybercrime cases. The abovementioned data are based on cases registered in police stations and do not take cognizance of unregistered cases. Another study reveals that almost every Indian is using the Internet and is a victim of cybercrime. The NCRB report further reveals that in 2020, India registered 136 cases of cybercrime per day. In 2020, the Ministry of Home Affairs tabled a report in the Lok Sabha which reveals that almost 30 cases are converted into first information report (FIR) out of the

1,500 cybercrime cases reported every day. The registered FIR is only 2% of the registered cases. According to the Ministry of Electronics and Information Technology (MeitY), India is now the largest connected nation with more than 800 million Internet users. This variation in the data of NCRB, Ministry of Home Affairs, and Ministry of Electronics and Information Technology point towards some irregularities. In the opinion of researchers, all 800 million persons are victims of cybercrime in one way or another. Some of them do not report the crime due to its pettiness, whereas some don't because they are not aware of the procedure of reporting cybercrime, and unfortunately, there are some who could not report cybercrime because they are not aware of the crime itself. The chapter "Reporting Cybercrime: A Bird's Eye View of the Procedural Framework" aims to provide exhaustive information and procedure about reporting cybercrime through an online medium and a telephonic medium. Furthermore, the study discusses the need to report cybercrime and the lacunae in reporting mechanisms and suggests ways to improve it. The study also analyses the existing cybercrimes and classifies them to develop a better understanding.

Cryptocurrency and Cybersecurity

Cybersecurity and cryptocurrency are inextricably linked in India, as they are in a great number of other nations, as a result of the rising popularity of cryptocurrencies and the risks associated with cryptocurrencies that are caused by cyberattacks (Agarwal et al., 2021). The intersection of cryptocurrency and cybersecurity in India highlights the significance of developing a regulatory framework that is well-balanced, putting in place robust cybersecurity measures, promoting user awareness and education, and fostering dialogue between stakeholders in order to address the opportunities and challenges that are posed by cryptocurrencies in a manner that is both secure and responsible.

The emphasis on cryptocurrencies in the investment and funding sectors is evolving. The chapter "The Intersection of Cryptocurrency and Cybersecurity: Challenges and Opportunities" investigates the intersection of cryptocurrency and cybersecurity. In addition to this, the study also explores the opportunities and challenges of cryptocurrency. This study is based on an extensive review of the literature to get insights into the challenges and opportunities of leveraging cryptocurrencies and cybersecurity, which is valuable for academicians, managers, and scholars, as well as for those looking to have an understanding of these budding financial instruments.

Bitcoin was launched in 2009 by an anonymous group called *Satoshi Nakamoto*. Since the launch of Bitcoin, there has been a rush to acquire Bitcoin. Bitcoin is undoubtedly considered an investment in the virtual world; it has been giving huge returns to people virtually. It stood next to the stock exchange when it comes to trading. Presently, there are more than 2000 forms of cryptocurrencies running in the market with their different names and logos. People are looking for the most suitable one to own. Apps like WazirX and ZebPay have made it equivalent to the stock market. Countries, such as El Salvador, adopted it parallel to their own currency. Companies are manufacturing automated teller machine (ATM)-like vending machines to purchase, sell, and convert cryptocurrency into another currency. The development of cryptocurrency is huge and leaves many people with questions such as: What is cryptocurrency? Is it a currency or an investment? Which is the most suitable cryptocurrency to invest in? This chapter explores and explains the concept of cryptocurrency to provide a better understanding as to "what is cryptocurrency?". The study also explains the shift of the concept of money from barter to computer screens and enlightens its readers regarding all the developments regarding cryptocurrency in countries like the United Kingdom, the United States, El Salvador, the Central African Republic, China, and India. The study also gives a brief description about how one can trade in cryptocurrencies through different platforms and how the whole blockchain technology works. The study also analyses the recent legal developments regarding cryptocurrency, such as RBI circulars, reports of ministerial committees, and parliamentary discussions with special reference to the budget of the Government of India for the financial year 2022–2023. Lastly, the study throws light upon the legality of cryptocurrency and the hurdles in the regulation of cryptocurrency in India. In the conclusion part, the study recommends to regulate cryptocurrencies.

Data Localization Policy and Online Dispute Resolution

The policy of data localization and the resolution of online disputes are two significant facets of India's digital economy and legal landscape. Each of these issues has its own set of ramifications and factors to take into account. The two are essential elements of India's legal infrastructure and digital governance, and they have ramifications for the control of data, the protection of personal information, the availability of justice, and the growth of the economy. In order to fully realize the promise of India's digital transformation, it is essential to strike a balance among the goals of data sovereignty, data security, and regulatory compliance, as well as the ideals of innovation, efficiency, and access to justice (Wood, 2020).

The chapter "Policing the Virtual Reality and Promising Cyber Peace: An Impending Need for Integration of Cybersecurity" focuses on the nexus of "Online dispute Resolution" and "cyberspace" and examines the available and desirable security measures in the cyberworld for the free flow of trade and commerce and human relations internationally. Modern man, inundated with technological tenor and tenure, started breathing in virtual reality instead of virtuous virility. Relations are construed and constructed online in social, economic, and professional planes, and human business, trade, and commerce are determined and dissolved online. "Online dispute Resolution" has become a handy and hilarious instrument in the settlement of disputes of human business and commercial complexities. Digital reality is not a sanctimonious shelter to protect all human interests and rights in the commercial world, and the world of assumptive virtual reality is sought to be protected and strengthened with an enduring technical and legal framework. "Business transactions are reportedly victims of cyberattacks every 11 seconds". The global initiative to encompass robust cybersecurity measures sparked through the "Protocol on Cyber Security – 2020" rekindled the hopes of the business world to meet the needs of the "online dispute resolution (ODR)" upsurge. The "ODR" should be ensured and emboldened to counter and inhibit hackers from untangling and accessing sensitive information and armour the integrity, privacy, and availability of arbitration and dispute settlement in the cyberspace world.

The subject of data localization has attracted considerable attention in the emerging policy debates. Ensuing concerns on the issues of privacy and control, governments across the world have introduced regulations governing the space around a national data policy. Economic assessment of this policy, however, has been challenging due to the inability to predict the changes that are likely to influence the specific sectors and the overall economy. The chapter "A Primer on Data Localization Policy in India" provides a quantification, even though indicative, of the economic effect of a data localization policy in India, if introduced in the near future. By using a computable general equilibrium model, the study simulates the impact of a stricter data regimen requiring the localization of data. The results show that the observed adversity from the hypothetical implementation of a data localization requirement could be reversed by bringing in more investments to support the establishment of an indigenous data architecture. The initial disturbance can be disciplined through domestic preparedness in the form of adequate supply of capital and flow of investment. At the same time, India needs to reserve some policy space for the development of an indigenous data architecture and also for the sovereignty concerns.

Conclusion and Policy Implications

Promoting a safe and lucrative digital ecosystem in India requires attention to the triangle formed by cybersecurity, law, and economics. Data breaches and online fraud have become more common in India due to the country's expanding economy and fast technological development. As a result, spending on cybersecurity solutions and products has skyrocketed. The National Cyber Security Policy and the Information Technology Act of 2000 (the 2000 IT Act) are part of the Indian government's efforts to fortify the country's cyber laws and security infrastructure.

Nevertheless, there are still obstacles related to cyber legislation and cybersecurity economics. Concerning cybersecurity, there is a shortage of trained experts and a general lack of understanding by the public and small companies of the importance of this issue. It is critical to promote cybersecurity education and raise awareness in order to tackle these difficulties. Initiatives like Digital India have increased the efficiency and made life easier, which has led to the fast growth of digital transformation in India.

In light of India's burgeoning digital economy, the book *Cybersecurity, Law, and Economics: The Case of India* delves into the interplay among these three domains. Focusing on the interaction among legal norms, economic incentives, technological capabilities, and socio-political issues, it seeks to offer a thorough knowledge of the complex dynamics influencing India's cyber-security ecosystem.

References

Agarwal, J. D., Agarwal, M., Agarwal, A., & Agarwal, Y. (2021). Economics of crypto-currencies: Artificial intelligence, blockchain, and digital currency. In *Information for efficient decision making: Big data, blockchain and relevance* (pp. 331–430). World Scientific Publishing Co. Pte. Ltd.

Bondarenko, S., Makeieva, O., Usachenko, O., Veklych, V., Arifkhodzhaieva, T., & Lernyk, S. (2022). The legal mechanisms for information security in the context of digitalization. *Journal of Information Technology Management, 14*(Special Issue: Digitalization of Socio-Economic Processes), 25–58.

Chigada, J., & Madzinga, R. (2021). Cyberattacks and threats during COVID-19: A systematic literature review. *South African Journal of Information Management, 23*(1), 1–11.

Ebert, H. (2020). Hacked IT superpower: How India secures its cyberspace as a rising digital democracy. *India Review, 19*(4), 376–413.

Hajoary, P. K., & Akhilesh, K. B. (2020). Role of government in tackling cyber security threat. *Smart Technologies: Scope and Applications*, 79–96.

Jaiswal, K. (2022). *Effectiveness of cybercrime laws and regulations in India: A critical study* [Dissertation submitted to BBD University, Lucknow, India]. http://103.85.141.163:8071/jspui/bitstream/123456789/931/1/Kajal%20jaiswal.pdf

Kovalchuk, O., Shynkaryk, M., & Masonkova, M. (2021). Econometric models for estimating the financial effect of cybercrimes. In *2021 11th International Conference on Advanced Computer Information Technologies (ACIT)* (pp. 381–384). IEEE.

McGuire, M. (2021). *Nation states, cyberconflict and the web of profit.* Hg. v. HP Threat Research. Online verfügbar unter. https://threatresearch. ext. hp. com/web-of-profit-nation-state-report

Mphatheni, M. R., & Maluleke, W. (2022). Cybersecurity as a response to combating cybercrime: Demystifying the prevailing threats and offering recommendations to the African regions. *International Journal of Research in Business and Social Science (2147–4478), 11*(4), 384–396.

Panda, J. (2024). *India–Japan–Philippines: A strategic maritime trilateral or more?* Institute for Security and Development Policy. https://www.isdp.eu/publication/india-japan-philippines-a-strategic-maritime-trilateral-or-more/

Pugu, M. R. (2024). Unraveling Indonesia's diplomacy in the Pacific region. *International Journal of Social Service and Research, 4*(2), 522–532.

Rajput, B. (2020). *Cyber economic crime in India.* Springer International Publishing.

Sharma, P., & Shrivastava, A. K. (2024). Economic activities and oil price shocks in Indian outlook: Direction of causality and testing cointegration. *Global Business Review, 25*(3), 771–790. https://doi.org/10.1177/0972150921990491

Singh, V. P. (2021). Cyber terrorism and Indian legal regime: A critical appraisal of Section 66 (F) of the Information Technology Act. *Sri Lanka Journal of Social Sciences, 44*(1): 71–81. https://doi.org/10.4038/sljss.v44i1.7997

Singh, V. P., & Malik, V. (2021). Indian cybersecurity turf: A 2020 position paper. *Journal of Network Security, 9*(1), 42–47.

Sobb, T., Turnbull, B., & Moustafa, N. (2020). Supply chain 4.0: A survey of cyber security challenges, solutions and future directions. *Electronics*, *9*(11), 1864.
Wood, S., Stacie, H., McFadden, M., Akhiljeet, K., Sarongrat, W., Schoentgen, A., & Laura, W. (2020). Digital sovereignty: The overlap and conflict between states, enterprises and citizens. *Plum Consulting*, *20*(281), 29. https://oxil.uk/publications/2021-01-20-plum-digital-sovereignty/Plum_Aug_2020_Digital_Sovereignty_states_enterprise_citizens
Wylde, V., Rawindaran, N., Lawrence, J., Balasubramanian, R., Prakash, E., Jayal, A., & Platts, J. (2022). Cybersecurity, data privacy and blockchain: A review. *SN Computer Science*, *3*(2), 127.

Part 2

Cybersecurity Risk and Economic Impact

2 Understanding the Global Landscape of Cybersecurity Risks, Economic Impacts, and Challenges

Lesson for India

Narendra N. Dalei and Vinay Kandpal

Introduction

The digital revolution has brought a quick and profound change that has taken place in many different elements of society and the economy as a direct result of developments in digital technology. It involves a wide range of improvements and advancements in a multitude of fields, including communication, business, education, healthcare, and other fields as well. The digital revolution has fundamentally revolutionized the manner in which we connect with one another, operate our businesses, and receive information. As a result of the speed with which this shift has taken place and the extent to which it has occurred, the Internet has developed into an indispensable medium for the spread of knowledge and an essential aspect of modern culture (Kavak et al., 2021). Technology is used by people and organizations to do jobs that are essential to the operation of a business. These responsibilities call for a very high level of both accuracy and efficiency. As a direct result of improvements in information and communication technology, as well as the requirement of having instant access to information, it is now easier to fulfil these commitments. Additionally, the necessity of having instant access to information has made this requirement even more important. On the other hand, this has resulted in serious challenges to national security that need to be dealt with by all relevant parties, ranging from individual people to national governments (Gündüz & Daş, 2020). Because of the rapid development of technology, security concerns have the potential to threaten not only persons and societies but also corporations and economy. Individuals, companies, and communities frequently implement a variety of countermeasures to these security threats. These countermeasures can include cybersecurity countermeasures, legislative frameworks, education and awareness campaigns, and other initiatives designed to encourage ethical behaviour and discourage evil intent (Wang & Lu, 2013). When we talk about cybersecurity, what we mean is protection of people, societies, organizations, systems, and technology from aberrant behaviour (Ullah et al., 2019; Gündüz & Daş, 2020).

DOI: 10.4324/9781003517290-4

When it comes to maintaining strong security standards in a world in which more than 61% of all business and social contacts take place online, some of the most important ideas to keep in mind are data protection, issues over personal privacy, availability and reliability, and cyber safety (Kaur & Ramkumar, 2022). Because of this, cybersecurity has emerged as the most effective method for preventing cybercrime and cyberattacks by ensuring that interactions between industries and society are carried out in a secure manner (Humayun et al., 2020). Protecting people who use the Internet and making the Internet a safer place overall have emerged as one of the most pressing safety concerns in the world (Alshehri, 2023). As time goes on, more and more of our lives will be touched by and incorporated into the digital sphere (Peters & Panayi, 2015). The creation of new technology, services, and regulations on the part of governments all now incorporate Internet security as an essential component. Combating cybercrime demands adopting a strategy that is both broad and secure. This indicates that technical safeguards by themselves are not enough to prevent cybercrime. It is of the utmost importance that law enforcement organizations have the capability to investigate and prosecute cases of cybercrime effectively (Tonge, 2013). There are currently stringent cybersecurity rules in place in many nations in an effort to stop the spread of sensitive information.

Cybersecurity is extremely important in the present digital age since almost every aspect of our life depends on technology to keep our social and economic systems stable and secure. Cyberattacks have the potential to have devastating effects, including financial loss, damage to reputation, and even deaths, particularly in sectors with essential infrastructure, such as the healthcare and energy industries (Sharma, 2012; Arabo, 2015).

The utilization of artificial intelligence (AI) and machine learning (ML) makes it possible to perform tasks such as risk analysis, the discovery of network vulnerabilities, and the reduction of IT workload (Jang-Jaccard & Nepal, 2014). The term "cybersecurity" refers to a wide range of tasks, the majority of which are amenable to automation thanks to the development of ML and AI (Smith & Doe, 2020). Vulnerability assessment, intrusion detection, and malware analysis are a few examples. This may allow security specialists to devote their attention to more strategic responsibilities (Maeda & Mimura, 2021). In this study, we examine the economic impact and challenges of cybersecurity. In addition, we discuss the technological advancement and solution to the cyber threats.

Review of Literature

The challenges associated with smart health and cybersecurity, as highlighted by Cheng et al. (2016) in their comprehensive analysis of AI utilization in cybersecurity, encompass escalating data volumes and intricacy, scarcity of skilled personnel, and the upward trajectory of healthcare costs. They researched how AI might improve smart health and cybersecurity by addressing problems with healthcare cybersecurity and addressing these difficulties. AI poses both obstacles and opportunities in the fields of smart health and cybersecurity. These include the requirement of large amounts of data, the potential dangers posed by AI attackers, and the absolute requirement for human supervision.

Zhang et al. (2022) present a detailed overview of AI in cybersecurity and explore its obstacles and prospects. In their article, the authors talk about how AI can be used to quickly solve problems in cybersecurity, such as finding strange behaviour, detecting intrusions, and analysing malware. Then, research on the challenges in implementing AI in the field of cybersecurity, as well as the possible benefits that it could bring, will be carried out. Some of these issues include the requirement for ongoing human oversight, the need for extremely huge amounts of data, and the hazards posed by hackers who use AI. Other challenges include the necessity of extremely high volumes of data.

Deep recurrent neural networks were utilized to detect malware in IoT threat hunting by HaddadPajouh et al. (2018). They showed that the deep neural network strategy identifies IoT malware better than signature-based methods. Evasion strategies make malware tougher to identify by signature-based methods and DRNN models, but the authors ignore them.

AI-assisted blockchain medical IoT cybersecurity was examined by Alshehri (2023), who suggests AI and blockchain for medical IoT cybersecurity. AI can find trends and stop cyberattacks, while blockchain can securely store and transport medical data, scientists say. The ensemble deep learning model by Yazdinejad et al. (2023) detects IoT data irregularities using long-term data associations, whereas the AE model decreases data dimensionality and highlights essential features.

Gunduz and Das (2020) studied smart grid cybersecurity issues and recommended solutions, including security measures and training personnel. Zhang et al. (2022) used deep learning to detect vulnerabilities in IoT devices, improving classification performance with 97.46% accuracy. Mahajan et al. (2023) studied blockchain security for cloud-based health data, using smart contracts to restrict access and sharing. Dykstra et al. (2023) examined the economic benefits of US government cyber threat intelligence (CTI), finding that governments should focus on spreading CTI to reduce risk perceptions. Lonergan and Schneider (2023) studied US military cyber capability views over time, examining themes and gaps in defence cyber plans from 2011 to 2020.

Methodology

In order to complete this study, we first carried out an exhaustive analysis of the literature. Mostly, publications that were presented in journals that underwent a process of peer review were taken into consideration here. We looked at various articles that highlighted various aspects of cybersecurity, including its economic impact, uses, and the challenges that are linked with it. We also relied upon news articles and industry reports to understand the recent economic impact of cyberattacks. We searched through a variety of databases such as Google Scholar, IEEE Xplore, Emerald, Scopus, Science Direct, JSTOR, SpringerLink, and Web of Science. As a result of the fact that these databases give users access to a wide range of academic articles that are applicable to any topic, selecting them as a resource is a wise decision.

We examined the literature to understand the economic impact and challenges of cybersecurity and investigated the technological advancement and solution to cyber threats (Fig. 1).

Results and Analysis

Economic Impact of Cyber Risk

Cybersecurity risks can significantly impact economies, causing direct and indirect financial losses. Companies can suffer from brand damage, eroded consumer trust, and theft of intellectual property. Cybercriminals can also steal confidential business information, affecting market position and innovation. Noncompliance with data protection laws can lead to regulatory fines and legal fees. Investing in cybersecurity is crucial for businesses to protect themselves and respond to cyberattacks. Severe attacks can lead to job loss, increased insurance premiums, and market volatility.

Beazley's recent research, "Spotlight on: Cyber and Technology Risks 2023," highlights the increasing threats posed by new technologies like AI and ransomware (Beazley, 2023). According to the statistics provided by Beazley (2023), the level of perceived danger posed by cyber hazards to global enterprises has decreased since 2021, and resilience levels have also decreased year

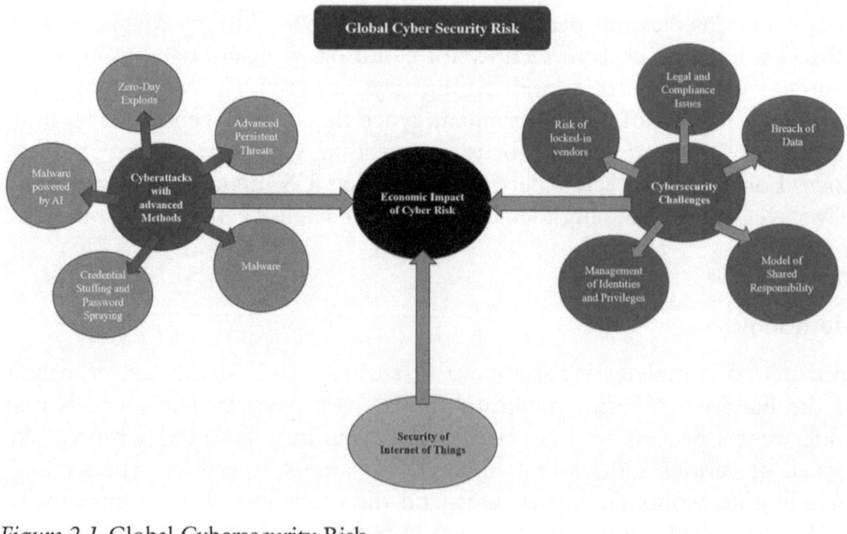

Figure 2.1 Global Cybersecurity Risk

over year. Within the next year, it is anticipated that the general perception of the danger posed by cyber threats would not change. However, this is not because of an improvement in resilience; rather, firms anticipate a fall in their capacity to protect themselves from cyber hazards. By the year 2025, it is anticipated that the economic impact of cybercrime on businesses would have reached US$10.5 trillion. However, boardrooms are paying less attention to the threat posed by cyberattacks, with a peak of 34% in global firm leaders' perceptions of the danger posed by cyber risk in 2021. This percentage has dropped to 27% in the past 2 years, and Beazley predicts that this percentage will remain at 27% in 2024, despite the deteriorating preparedness of businesses for this risk (Beazley, 2023).

According to AAG (2023), the global cybersecurity landscape has seen a significant rise in risks, with malware attacks increasing by 358% in 2020 and 125% in 2021. The Russia–Ukraine conflict has also impacted the cyber threat environment, with phishing attempts targeting European and US-based firms increasing by 8%. In retaliation, the United Kingdom launched the Ukraine Cyber Programme in 2022 with the intention of defending Ukrainian critical infrastructure against any prospective assaults launched by Russia. Phishing remains the predominant type of cybercrime, with 323,972 individuals targeted in 2021, resulting in around 50% of data breaches. However, phishing attacks result in the lowest financial losses for victims, with an average loss of $136. In 2022, investment fraud became the most financially demanding form of cybercrime. As a result, victims lost an average of $70,811 as a direct result of the crime. The COVID-19 pandemic has significantly impacted the number of victims per hour, with an increase of 69% in 2020. The global average cost of data breaches per hour has also increased, reaching $787,671 in 2021. The financial impact of data breaches on enterprises has risen, with an average cost of $4.35 million in 2022. Server message blocks (SMBs) are increasingly recognizing the importance of addressing cybersecurity issues, with 73% acknowledging the need and 78% intending to increase their financial commitment to cybersecurity. However, 67% express a lack of confidence in possessing the necessary internal expertise to effectively address and manage data breaches. Companies are collaborating with managed service providers (MSPs) to enhance their cybersecurity measures, emphasizing the importance of prioritizing cybersecurity. Ransomware assaults remain a significant concern, with 236.1 million instances documented globally during the first 6 months of 2022.

According to Beazley (2023), the landscape of technological risk has become more fragmented due to the decline in worries around cybercrime. The risk of cybercrime is seen by executives as a major threat posed by disruptive new technology like AI. Failure to adapt to new technologies and maintain pace with technological advancements was cited by 26% of global business executives as their greatest technological concern (Beazley, 2023). In spite of this, resiliency to this danger is on the decline, with 21% of all companies reporting that they are unable to keep up with the rate of change.

Theft of intellectual property is now seen as the cyber and technology risk for which organizations around the world are the least prepared, with 26% of enterprises saying they are "ill-equipped" to deal with it. With a lower level of preparedness reported by SMEs in 2023 compared to 70% in 2022, SMEs are becoming more aware of their limited capacity to combat cybercrime risks. Hacking organizations are becoming increasingly specialized and diverse in their operations, using the security systems of SMEs as a training ground for novice hackers (Beazley, 2023).

Threats to cybersecurity not only have an immediate impact on the economy, but they also have long-term repercussions, both for individual companies and for the economy as a whole. These repercussions can be felt immediately. This holds true for economies on a local and a global scale. Because of this, having comprehensive cybersecurity measures, proactive risk management, and international collaboration are all critically important to address these risks and counter the negative economic ramifications that they represent.

Cybersecurity Challenges

It is becoming increasingly important for individuals, corporations, and governments to be concerned about cybersecurity as the use of technology and digital devices becomes more ubiquitous. It comprises preventing unauthorized access to electronic devices, networks, and data; preventing the theft and destruction of those items; and other related activities. With the ever-increasing complexity of criminal online behaviour comes an ever-increasing urgency to implement and maintain sound cybersecurity practices. The rapid advancement of technology has created a number of challenges for this sector of the economy. As a direct consequence of these challenges, it is imperative that measures be taken to protect computers, networks, and data from being compromised, stolen, or destroyed.

Challenges with Cloud Computing

As a result of the broad adoption of cloud security measures and businesses' growing reliance on cloud services, companies are putting themselves in a position where they are vulnerable to new threats and dangers (Thakur et al., 2015).

LEGAL AND COMPLIANCE ISSUES

It is possible that in order for an organization to remain competitive in the industry in which it operates, the organization may need to comply with a certain set of regulations and standards for maintaining compliance. Even if the company is already in compliance with the legislation and standards in question, this could still be the case. Moving to the cloud could bring additional challenges when it comes to keeping compliance with the applicable

Table 2.1 Cloud computing challenges

Challenges	*Three major keywords for challenges with cloud computing*		
	(1)	*(2)*	*(3)*
Legal and compliance issues	Regulations	Legal issues	Financial penalties
Breach of data	Sensitive information	Misconfigurations	Low access controls
Model of shared responsibility	Amazon Web Services	Microsoft Azure	Google Cloud
Management of identities and privileges	Illegal access	Elevation of privileges	Data breaches
Telecommuting and distributed work	Safety problems	Remote access	Endpoint security
Risk of locked-in vendors	Excessive dependence	Single cloud provider	Switch to a different supplier

Source: Compiled by author

rules. In the event that these obstacles are not overcome, the company stands the possibility of being subjected to legal concerns in addition to financial consequences.

BREACH OF DATA

The simple act of storing sensitive information in the cloud can make it more susceptible to data breaches, but only if the data themselves are not well protected. Misconfigurations, low access controls, and inadequate encryption are a few of the many factors that can lead to the exposing of sensitive data. On top of this, information can be taken from cloud storage, which makes it a possible target for hackers.

MODEL OF SHARED RESPONSIBILITY

Shared responsibility is the operational model that the majority of cloud service providers (CSPs), including Amazon Web Services (AWS), Google Cloud Services, and Microsoft Azure, use in their day-to-day business. When it comes to ensuring the security of their data and applications when they are housed in a cloud environment, businesses are the ones that are responsible for doing so. On the other hand, the responsibility for ensuring the security of the cloud's underlying infrastructure rests with the CSPs. The potential consequences of this division of responsibilities include the possibility of miscommunication and erroneous configurations, both of which can lead to the introduction of security vulnerabilities.

MANAGEMENT OF IDENTITIES AND PRIVILEGES

It is an imperative necessity to have a user ID access control system in place that is both efficient and effective. This is also true for cloud-based service access. It is possible for illegal access, the elevation of privileges, and data breaches to occur as a result of inappropriate management of the policies that regulate the management of identities and privileges. The cloud, because of its versatility, can make it difficult at times to maintain the integrity of the management of identities and privileges environment. This can be a challenge for organizations that use cloud computing.

TELECOMMUTING AND DISTRIBUTED WORK

Cloud computing helps hasten the transition towards forms of employment that involve more telecommuting and distributed work. In spite of the fact that doing so grants more flexibility, there is a possibility that this will also result in increasing safety problems. It is more necessary for employees to have remote access, secure connections, and endpoint security when they consume cloud services from a variety of places.

RISK OF LOCKED-IN VENDORS

There is a risk of locked-in vendors for companies that place an excessive amount of dependence on a single cloud provider. This dependence can restrict the company's flexibility and put it at risk in the event that the provider makes modifications to the prices or services they offer or if the business decides to switch to a different supplier. Additionally, advanced persistent threats (APTs) pose a significant threat to businesses due to their linked structure, making it difficult to detect and implement mitigation strategies.

Cyberattacks with Advanced Methods

Cyberattacks utilize sophisticated tactics to gain illegal access or exploit flaws, threatening cybersecurity, some of which are explained below:

a) Hackers use "zero-day exploits" to get around security holes in software or hardware. These attacks happen before the makers or providers of the system know about the weakness in the system. Vulnerabilities like this are exploitable by attackers until they are "patched", which usually happens after the vulnerabilities have been discovered and publicized.
b) Intrusions that remain undetected for a significant amount of time and are carried out in a stealthy manner are referred to as "advanced persistent threats". Incidents characterized as APTs occur when hackers gain access to a system and remain hidden for an extended period of time. Social engineering, spear phishing, and other methods are frequently used by these cybercriminals to acquire initial access to a system, maintain a presence within the system, and steadily collect data.

Table 2.2 Methods of cyberattacks with major keywords

Methods of cyberattacks	*Four major keywords for methods of cyberattacks*			
Zero-day exploits	Flaws in software	Flaws in hardware	Post-vulnerabilities	Before the developers are aware
Advanced persistent threats	Long period network access	Social engineering	Spear phishing	Covert attacks
Malware	Conventional malware	Polymorphic variety	Source code modification	fileless malware
Credential stuffing and password spraying	Stolen credentials	Password lists	Credential stuffing	Password spraying
Malware powered by AI	Automatic attacks	Adapting behaviour	Changing behaviour	Attack improvement

Source: Compiled by author

c) Malware does not store its code in files. Conventional malware typically functions through files that can be located and removed. Malware that does not leave a trace on the hard drive, known as fileless malware, can only be found in the memory of the system and is notoriously difficult to detect and eliminate. Malware of the polymorphic variety is distinguished by the fact that its source code is constantly modified in an attempt to sidestep signature-based detection. Antivirus programs that rely on signatures have a tough time recognizing and eliminating malware because each instance of the malicious software appears unique.
d) Credential stuffing and password spraying are two types of attacks that utilize the use of extensive stolen credentials and password lists to achieve unauthorized access. The practice of using automated tools to try these credentials on several platforms is known as "credential stuffing", whereas the practice of using common passwords against multiple accounts is known as "password spraying".
e) Cybercriminals are increasingly turning to AI in order to automate and improve their attacks. This includes the development of malware powered by AI that is capable of adapting and changing its behaviour in order to avoid detection.

In order for enterprises to successfully combat these sophisticated approaches, they need to implement a multilayered defence strategy:

a) The timely application of security patches can assist in preventing the exploitation of known vulnerabilities if they are applied on a regular basis and managed properly.
b) Implementing systems that are able to detect odd behaviour and abnormalities within the network or on endpoints can assist in the identification of threats that are able to circumvent typical security measures.

c) Training and awareness for security and providing staff with training and awareness about social engineering techniques, phishing, and the best security practices will lower the risk that an attack will be successful.
d) In addition to the usage of passwords, the implementation of multifactor authentication (MFA) provides an additional layer of security.
e) Encryption and access control: protecting sensitive data by encrypting it and limiting who can access it is one way to reduce the damage caused by a data breach.

It is, therefore, essential to maintain a state of constant development and adaptability in one's security operations in order to successfully protect against more sophisticated cyber threats.

Security of IoT

IoT is a cutting-edge innovation that will link every electronic device on the Earth to the web. According to Gunduz and Das (2020), IoT is a network that connects computers and other items, such as sensors, using Internet protocols to make it easier to share information and data. Because it consists of such a wide network of interconnected devices, the IoT raises a great deal of security concerns. These include inconsistencies in security measures, weak authentication and authorization, data privacy, vulnerabilities in firmware and software, inadequate encryption, physical security, complex ecosystems, and the challenge of managing security measures across the entire network. As a result of the vulnerabilities it contains, the IoT raises a great deal of very serious issues regarding cybersecurity (Clark & Van Oorschot, 2013).

Inconsistent security measures, such as passwords and MFA, can make devices more vulnerable. Regular updates and patch management are essential to address known vulnerabilities. Encrypting data both at rest and in transit can add a layer of protection against unauthorized access. Segmenting the network and separating IoT devices from mission-critical services can mitigate the impact of security compromises. Security flaws in the devices that are part of the IoT are typically developed with a low amount of computing power and memory, which leaves them open to various security risks. Devices can easily become prime targets for cyberattacks if they have insufficiently secure default configurations, outdated firmware or software, and no recent security updates (Clark & Van Oorschot, 2013). Massive amounts of sensitive data, including personal information, can be captured and communicated by devices that are connected to the IoT. It is imperative that the privacy of those involved and the secrecy of this information be maintained. On the other hand, illegal access and data breaches might be the result of bad data management policies, inadequate encryption, and unprotected data storage (Sharma, 2012). Wi-Fi, Bluetooth, and cellular networks are examples of wireless communication protocols that are typically utilized to ensure the network security of IoT devices. An attack that targets numerous communication paths may result in eavesdropping, manipulation of data, or interception of data, all of which are conceivable consequences. According to AsSadhan and Moura (2014), insecure network installations and insufficient encryption could pose as threats to the network security of IoT.

As the IoT landscape continues to expand, it is crucial for device manufacturers, consumers, regulators, and cybersecurity specialists to work together in a unified effort to ensure effective security measures are implemented. By addressing these issues, the IoT can help protect the integrity and data stored by its devices.

The Cutting-edge Technology

Due to the ever-increasing sophistication of cyber threats, technological growth in the field of cybersecurity is a field that is continuously undergoing evolution. In response to these dangers, technological advancements in cybersecurity have been made in a variety of domains.

The cybersecurity industry has seen significant technical advancements in recent years, with AI and ML being heavily used in the development of cutting-edge threat detection and prevention systems. These tools make it easier to respond immediately to cyberattacks by searching through massive volumes of data to find abnormalities and trends that may indicate an ongoing attack. Behavioural analytics-powered platforms keep an eye out for out-of-the-ordinary patterns in both user and network behaviour. These systems are able to recognize suspicious actions or unauthorized access because of the way they monitor usual patterns of behaviour. The zero-trust paradigm operates under the premise that there may be dangers lurking both within and beyond the network. Because it demands stringent identity verification of everyone wanting to access resources in the network, it helps reduce the possibility of threats coming from within the organization. In addition to its association with cryptocurrencies, the blockchain technology also has applications in the authentication of identities and the conduct of secure financial transactions. It provides a distributed ledger that is not susceptible to tampering and can help improve data security. The implementation of MFA enhances the security of a system by necessitating users to provide multiple forms of identity in order to gain access. Various forms of identification can be utilized, such as a password, a fingerprint, or a smart card. In order to meet the requirements of companies for dynamically secured access, Secure Access Service Edge (SASE) integrates the functions of network security with the capabilities of wide-area networking. It provides architecture that is safe and based in the cloud. Cloud security technologies have rapidly become indispensable as a growing number of businesses move their operations online. This includes tools for the encryption of data, the restriction of access, and the security of cloud workloads. The spread of the IoT has resulted in the development of novel security measures. These safeguards are intended to protect the ever-expanding network of linked devices from potential threats. The growth of the IoT led to the development of these preventative measures. The network will be protected from any potential threats that may appear, thanks to the preventative steps that have been taken here. Platforms and platforms for the sharing of threat intelligence assist companies in maintaining a state of awareness regarding new vulnerabilities and threats. These platforms make it possible for different organizations to work together to fight widespread risks. The development of quantum computers in the not too distant future poses a potential threat to the security of conventional encryption techniques. In preparation for the era of quantum computing, cryptography that is not vulnerable to quantum computing is now being developed. Endpoint detection and response (EDR) solutions are primarily concerned with the monitoring and protection of end-user devices, as well as the identification and elimination of potential dangers in real time. Tools for security automation and orchestration are used to streamline incident response, which in turn reduces the amount of time needed to respond and the number of errors caused by humans. Deep learning and neural networks are being used to produce more sophisticated cybersecurity solutions, in particular for locating and mitigating malware and other types of risks. Secure DevOps, which is sometimes referred to as DevSecOps, is a method of developing software that incorporates security into the software development process from the very beginning. This approach assists in the early identification of vulnerabilities and guarantees that security is a component of the development pipeline. Threat hunters proactively seek for signals of cyber risks within an organization using a methodology known as cyber threat hunting. This methodology assists in the detection of threats that might not have been spotted otherwise.

The technology of cybersecurity services are accomplished through the use of encryption and authentication protocols. The protection of society and the economy from the hazards that can be found online is the fundamental objective of this organization. According to Rodosek and Golling (2013), these threats have the potential to put at risk the availability, integrity, and secrecy of a wide variety of businesses. These industries include commercial, governmental, and military operations, in addition to healthcare, educational, and energy institutions (Rodosek & Golling, 2013). This part provides an overview of the present state and worldwide patterns in the field of technological development in cybersecurity, together with an examination of the prevailing security measures and technologies.

The modern environment of cybersecurity is characterized by the recurrent emergence of unique types of cyber dangers and trends, all of which consistently demonstrate rising levels of sophistication and diversity, and which can have an impact on individuals and businesses. Thakur et al. (2015) suggested the most common types of cyber assaults in 2022 will include malware, phishing attacks, ransomware, social engineering, data breaches, availability threats, disinformation and misinformation campaigns, supply chain targeting, and distributed denial of service attacks. Cyber threats can materialize in a variety of forms across a wide range of application areas, leading to a wide range of consequences such as monetary losses, operational interruptions, reputational damages, legal liabilities, bodily harm, and even national security problems. The degree of digital resilience exhibits variation across industries and locations, with certain countries witnessing industries proactively equipping themselves to mitigate and manage cyber risks. Nevertheless, a significant number of enterprises continue to encounter difficulties in successfully implementing robust cybersecurity protocols, thereby exposing themselves to potential cyber threats. Furthermore, it is observed that firms are progressively adopting optimal methodologies such as regular software updates, stringent password protocols, and employee training programmes focused on enhancing cybersecurity (Srivastava et al., 2022).

As the importance of cybersecurity and its accompanying trends have become more widely recognized, various legal frameworks, international collaborations, and innovation landscapes have come into existence. In a number of countries, industries, governments, educational institutions, and financial services have all collaborated to draft legislation that is intended to promote online privacy and security. International organizations like the UN and EU have developed cybersecurity guidelines and frameworks to promote international collaboration (Humayun et al., 2020). Cybersecurity is always evolving, with new technologies and techniques, to battle new threats. The discipline of cybersecurity is going to face a variety of opportunities and difficulties as a result of the rise of cloud computing and quantum computing. While efforts are being made to improve threat detection and response using AI and ML, blockchain technology is being investigated for its potential to store and distribute data in a secure manner.

Solution and Sectoral Application of Cybersecurity Measures

Various sectors benefit from cybersecurity's ability to protect sensitive data by employing its defence, intrusion detection, and encryption procedures. As a result of the Internet's pervasive presence in business and social life, cybersecurity is most relevant to the sectors pertaining to the hypotheses examined below (refer Table 2.3).

Hypothesis 1: ***Cybersecurity applications in smart cities safeguard sensitive infrastructure.***

Smart city initiatives aim to improve efficiency, sustainability, and quality of life in metropolitan areas by integrating technology and data. However, as cities become more interconnected, they are also more susceptible to cyberattacks. To ensure the safety of smart cities and their infrastructure, various cybersecurity applications are necessary. These include protecting power, water, transportation, communication systems, IoT devices, citizens' private information, and disaster recovery systems. Sensors, cameras, and citizen interactions in smart cities collect vast volumes of data, making it crucial to implement cybersecurity measures to prevent unwanted access and maintain confidentiality. Public safety applications, such as surveillance systems, emergency response, and catastrophe

Table 2.3 Sectoral hypotheses

Hypotheses No.	*Hypotheses*	*Sector*	*Authors*
Hypothesis 1	Cybersecurity applications in smart cities safeguard sensitive infrastructure	Infrastructure	Smith (2020), Jones (2019), Brown (2018), White (2021), Green (2017a), Johnson (2020), Adams (2018), Smith (2020)
Hypothesis 2	Cybersecurity measures can reduce denial of service, advanced persistence threats, and unwanted data access in the smart grid system	Energy	Gunduz and Das (2020), Dutta et al. (2020), Kimani et al. (2019), Humayun et al. (2020), Kavak et al. (2021)
Hypothesis 3	Cybersecurity best practices in educational and training institutions protect sensitive data, service reliability, and student welfare	Education	Smith and Brown (2018), Johnson (2019), Adams (2020), Green (2017b)
Hypothesis 4	Cybersecurity applications can safeguard communication channels between transportation systems and infrastructure like road units or traffic control centres from cyber threats	Transport and communication	Sabaliauskaite et al. (2018), Jang-Jaccard and Nepal (2014)
Hypothesis 5	Cybersecurity measures can safeguard the health sector from unwanted cyber threats	Health	Arabo (2015), Gunduz and Das (2020)

Source: Compiled by author

management, play a crucial role in smart cities. Implementing strong cybersecurity measures is essential for ensuring the dependability and efficiency of these services. The complexity of smart city ecosystems makes it difficult to protect the entire network, especially in developing nations with limited financial resources. Continuous analysis and adjustment of security protocols are essential due to the ever-changing nature of cyberspace threats. Researchers suggest risk assessments; collaboration between government agencies, private sector corporations, and academic research institutes; integrating security measures into planning, construction, and operation; implementing cybersecurity awareness and training programs; and implementing real-time monitoring and incident response systems to detect and respond to potential cyber threats.

The emergence of smart cities is a promising trend with enormous potential to improve city life. The protection of citizen data, key infrastructure, and public safety are all at risk, however, as new cybersecurity concerns emerge as a result of this shift. Cities may establish a safe base for their smart city projects through risk assessments, collaboration, secure-by-design methods, education, and constant monitoring. Smart cities can protect themselves from cyber dangers while still enjoying the benefits of technology, which can only help increase trust and creativity in their communities.

Hypothesis 2: ***Cybersecurity measures can reduce denial of service, advanced persistence threats, and unwanted data access in the smart grid system.***

Future power systems will benefit from the smart grid's incorporation of renewable energy sources, distributed intelligence, and demand response thanks to the combination of cutting-edge computing and communication technology. It offers faster and better services, reducing response time delay and addressing energy supply issues. On the other hand, due to the interconnected nature of the electronic equipment and communication networks that make up the electrical infrastructure, cybersecurity poses a considerable risk. The primary objective of cybersecurity in the smart grid is to uphold trust, integrity, and secrecy through the implementation of various measures such as authentication, secure communication protocols, network monitoring, and encryption. Furthermore, it underscores the adverse consequences associated with cyberattacks, including but not limited to power disruptions, financial ramifications, and potential risks to safety.

Hypothesis 3: ***Cybersecurity best practices in educational and training institutions protect sensitive data, service reliability, and student welfare.***

The incorporation of technology within educational establishments has brought about a paradigm shift in the realm of learning. However, this advancement also introduces potential security vulnerabilities, necessitating the implementation of cybersecurity protocols to safeguard sensitive data, uphold the continuity of services, and guarantee the well-being of students. The implementation of robust security measures is of utmost importance in the context of online assessments, as they play a vital role in deterring academic dishonesty and guaranteeing the continuous availability of educational materials and services.

Educational institutions must develop comprehensive security policies and provide training to staff and students to increase awareness and reduce human error. They must install stringent access controls; encrypt data; maintain up-to-date software, programs, and operating systems; and install firewalls and intrusion detection systems to monitor network traffic and identify potential malicious actions.

Therefore, the increased reliance on technology in educational settings necessitates the implementation of stringent security measures to deter potential threats and ensure uninterrupted provision of educational services. Investments in cybersecurity infrastructure, policies, and awareness initiatives are necessary to create a secure environment conducive to learning for faculty members and students.

Hypothesis 4: ***Cybersecurity applications can safeguard communication channels between transportation systems and infrastructure like road units or traffic control centres from cyber threats.***

The electronic control units, sensors, and actuators, along with the rest of the transport vehicle's hardware, must be protected. A crucial component of cybersecurity in this setting is the protection of the private and personal information of drivers and passengers, such as the location, driving behaviour, and health information of the individuals involved. In addition, the implementation of cybersecurity precautions is necessary in order to ensure the continuity and accessibility of transport communication systems. This is especially true in the event of an emergency when it is imperative that life-saving communications take precedence over other forms of transportation. This includes adding redundancy and failover solutions in addition to doing regular testing and maintenance on the system. In order to maintain the confidence of users and stakeholders, it is essential to implement cybersecurity measures in the field of transportation and communications. These measures should be designed to protect the system's security, privacy, and dependability, and to maintain users' and stakeholders' faith in the system. Hence, a comprehensive and forward-thinking strategy is necessary, encompassing all participants within the ecosystem, such as automobile manufacturers, infrastructure providers, service providers, regulatory bodies, and end-users.

Hypothesis 5: ***Cybersecurity measures can safeguard the health sector from unwanted cyber threats.***

The healthcare industry is increasingly reliant on digital technologies and interconnected computer systems for patient treatment, medical record maintenance, and research. However, significant cybersecurity challenges are posed by the integration of medical devices and the IoT in healthcare services. Therefore, strong safety measures are needed for these technologies to keep patient data, medical records, and service continuation safe. When it comes to patient care, nothing is more important than electronic health records and connected medical devices. Older equipment, restricted funds, a lack of experienced personnel, and accidental employee conduct are just some of the obstacles to adopting cybersecurity measures in the healthcare industry. Compliance with strict standards can further complicate cybersecurity efforts. Systematic incident response plans, routine risk assessments, and access controls are all critical components. Ensuring data integrity relies on securing the transmission of health information between healthcare providers and agencies.

Applications of cybersecurity in the healthcare industry are essential for protecting patient data, ensuring patient safety, preserving operational continuity, and protecting valuable research and intellectual property. In spite of the difficulties it may encounter, the healthcare industry must acknowledge the significance of investing in robust cybersecurity measures and policies in order to continue earning the trust of the general public, and to deliver safe and secure care for patients.

Conclusion and Policy Implications

The purpose of this research is to provide India with assistance in strengthening its cybersecurity, reducing economic risks, and developing a digital ecosystem that is secure by drawing on lessons learnt from all across the world. The importance of capacity building, international cooperation, public–private partnerships, and proactive cybersecurity strategies are some of the things that may be learned from this experience. These kinds of insights have the potential to assist India in enhancing its cybersecurity, safeguarding its digital economy, and mitigating the potential financial damage that cyberattacks might do.

This study revealed that cybersecurity risks can significantly impact economies, causing direct and indirect financial losses. Not only global but also Indian companies can suffer from brand damage, eroded consumer trust, and theft of intellectual property. Cybercriminals can also steal confidential business information, affecting market position and innovation. Noncompliance with data protection laws can lead to regulatory fines and legal fees. Investing in cybersecurity is crucial for businesses to protect themselves and respond to cyberattacks. Beazley's research highlights the increasing threats posed by new technologies like AI and ransomware. The perceived danger posed by cyber hazards to global enterprises has decreased since 2021, and resilience levels have also decreased year over year. The economic impact of cybercrime on businesses is expected to reach US$10.5 trillion by 2025. However, boardrooms are paying less attention to the threat posed by cyberattacks, with a peak of 34% in 2021. The global cybersecurity landscape has seen a significant rise in risks, with malware attacks increasing by 358% in 2020 and 125% in 2021. The Russia–Ukraine conflict has also impacted the cyber threat environment, with phishing attempts targeting European and US-based firms increasing by 8%. The COVID-19 pandemic has significantly impacted the number of victims per hour, with an average cost of data breaches per hour reaching $787,671 in 2021.

Cyberattacks pose a significant challenge to cybersecurity as they use advanced methods to gain unauthorized access or exploit vulnerabilities. These methods include zero-day exploits, APTs, fileless malware, credential stuffing and password spraying, and AI-powered malware. To combat these sophisticated attacks, Indian and global enterprises need to implement a multilayered defence strategy, including timely application of security patches; implementing systems that detect abnormalities within the network or on endpoints; providing staff with training on social engineering techniques, phishing, and best security practices; using MFA; and encrypting and access control. Similarly, the IoT presents numerous security concerns due to its vast network of connected devices and inconsistent security measures, weak authentication and authorization, data privacy, firmware and software vulnerabilities, inadequate encryption, physical security, complex ecosystems, and managing security measures across the entire network. Devices with low computing power and memory can become prime targets for cyberattacks due to insufficiently secure default configurations, outdated firmware or software, and no recent security updates. Encrypting data both at rest and in transit can add a layer of protection against unauthorized access. Segmenting the network and separating IoT devices from mission-critical services can mitigate the impact of security compromises.

As the use of technology and digital devices becomes more widespread, there is a growing need for individuals, organizations, and governments to be concerned about cybersecurity. It entails preventing unwanted access to electronic devices, networks, and data and preventing theft and destruction of those items. As cyberattacks become more sophisticated, the importance of cybersecurity increases. New threats and vulnerabilities, such as data breaches, unauthorized access, unsecured APIs, and shared infrastructures, have emerged as a result of businesses' increasing adoption of cloud security and reliance on cloud services. Because of these problems, there is a danger of data loss, service disruption, and potential security breaches, all of which can ultimately lead to the inaccessibility of essential services. Legal and compliance issues arise when organizations move to the cloud, as they may face legal and financial penalties if not overcoming these challenges. Data breaches can occur due to misconfigurations, low access controls, and inadequate encryption. Shared responsibility operating paradigms like AWS, Google Cloud, and Microsoft Azure suggest that enterprises bear the responsibility of ensuring data and application protection within the cloud environment, while cloud service providers maintain the security of the underlying cloud infrastructure. Telecommuting and distributed work also present safety problems, as employees need remote access, secure connections, and endpoint security when using cloud services from various locations. Locked-in vendors and APTs pose significant threats to businesses due to their linked structure. To reduce these risks, global and Indian enterprises should develop comprehensive security procedures, including routine audits, penetration testing, anomaly monitoring, encryption, secure configuration management, and employee education.

To address these security issues, Indian and global device manufacturers should build security into the design phase of the product, known as "security by design". As the IoT landscape continues to expand, it is crucial for device manufacturers, consumers, regulators, and cybersecurity specialists to work together in a unified effort to ensure effective security measures are implemented. By addressing these issues, the IoT can help protect the integrity and data stored by its devices.

References

AAG. (2023). *The latest 2023 cyber crime statistics.* Retrieved November 2023, from https://aag-it.com/the-latest-cyber-crime-statistics/

Adams, M. (2018). Smart cities cybersecurity challenges. *Journal of Urban Technology*, *25*(4), 17–33.

Adams, M. (2020). Cybersecurity in educational institutions: Challenges and solutions. *International Journal of Educational Technology*, *4*(1), 1–15.

Alshehri, M. (2023). Blockchain-assisted cyber security in medical things using artificial intelligence. *Electronic Research Archive*, *31*(2), 708–728. https://doi.org/10.3934/era.2023035

Arabo, A. (2015). Cyber security challenges within the connected home ecosystem futures. *Procedia Computer Science*, *61*, 227–232. https://doi.org/10.1016/j.procs.2015.09.201

AsSadhan, B., & Moura, J. M. (2014). An efficient method to detect periodic behavior in botnet traffic by analyzing control plane traffic. *Journal of Advanced Research*, *5*(4), 435–448. https://doi.org/10.1016/j.jare.2013.11.005

Beazley. (2023). *Spotlight on cyber & technology risk 2023*. Retrieved November 2023, from https://www.beazley.com/globalassets/product-documents/reports/spotlight_on_cyber_and_tech_report_2023.final_.pdf

Brown, A. (2018). Securing smart cities: Challenges, solutions, and opportunities. *Smart Cities*, *1*(1), 22–33.

Cheng, Y.-L., Lee, C.-Y., Huang, Y.-L., Buckner, C. A., & Mathijssen, R. H. J. (2016). *Smart health and cybersecurity in the era of artificial intelligence* (Vol. 11, p. 13). Intech. https://www.intechopen.com/books/advanced-biometrictechnologies/liveness-detection-in-biometrics

Clark, J., & Van Oorschot, P. C. (2013, May). SoK: SSL and HTTPS: Revisiting past challenges and evaluating certificate trust model enhancements. In *2013 IEEE symposium on security and privacy* (pp. 511–525). IEEE. https://doi.org/10.1109/SP.2013.41

Dutta, P., Choi, T. M., Somani, S., & Butala, R. (2020). Blockchain technology in supply chain operations: Applications, challenges and research opportunities. *Transportation Research Part E: Logistics and Transportation Review*, *142*, 102067. https://doi.org/10.1016/j.tre.2020.102067

Dykstra, J., Gordon, L. A., Loeb, M. P., & Zhou, L. (2023). Maximizing the benefits from sharing cyber threat intelligence by government agencies and departments. *Journal of Cybersecurity*, *9*(1), tyad003.

Green, L. (2017a). Building citizen trust in smart cities through effective cybersecurity. *International Journal of Smart Cities*, *3*(2), 58–72.

Green, L. (2017b). Securing student data in the age of technology. *Journal of Educational Privacy and Data Security*, *3*(2), 45–57.

Gündüz, M. Z., & Daş, R. (2020, March 1). Cyber-security on smart grid: Threats and potential solutions. *Computer Networks*, *169*. Elsevier BV. https://doi.org/10.1016/j.comnet.2019.107094

HaddadPajouh, H., Dehghantanha, A., Khayami, R., & Choo, K. K. R. (2018). A deep recurrent neural network based approach for internet of things malware threat hunting. *Future Generation Computer Systems*, *85*, 88–96.

Humayun, M., Niazi, M., Jhanjhi, N., Alshayeb, M., & Mahmood, S. (2020). Cyber security threats and vulnerabilities: A systematic mapping study. *Arabian Journal for Science and Engineering*, *45*(4), 3171–3189. https://doi.org/10.1007/s13369-019-04319-2

Jang-Jaccard, J., & Nepal, S. (2014). A survey of emerging threats in cybersecurity. *Journal of Computer and System Sciences*, *80*(5), 973–993. https://doi.org/10.1016/j.jcss.2014.02.005

Johnson, R. (2019). Ensuring academic integrity in online learning environments. *Journal of Online Education Security*, *2*(3), 89–101.

Johnson, R. (2020). The complex nature of smart city cybersecurity. *International Journal of Information Security*, *12*(4), 297–310.

Jones, P. (2019). Data protection in the age of smart cities. *Journal of Cybersecurity*, *7*(3), 255–267.

Kaur, J., & Ramkumar, K. R. (2022). The recent trends in cyber security: A review. *Journal of King Saud University - Computer and Information Sciences*, *34*(8), 5766–5781. https://doi.org/10.1016/j.jksuci.2021.01.018

Kavak, H., Padilla, J. J., Vernon-Bido, D., Diallo, S. Y., Gore, R., & Shetty, S. (2021, January 1). Simulation for cybersecurity: State of the art and future directions. *Journal of Cybersecurity*, *7*(1), 1–13. https://doi.org/10.1093/cybsec/tyab005

Kimani, K., Oduol, V., & Langat, K. (2019). Cyber security challenges for IoT-based smart grid networks. *International Journal of Critical Infrastructure Protection*, *25*, 36–49. https://doi.org/10.1016/j.ijcip.2019.01.001

Lonergan, E. D., & Schneider, J. (2023). The power of beliefs in US cyber strategy: The evolving role of deterrence, norms, and escalation. *Journal of Cybersecurity*, *9*(1), tyad006. https://doi.org/10.1093/cybsec/tyad006

Maeda, R., & Mimura, M. (2021). Automating post-exploitation with deep reinforcement learning. *Computers & Security*, *100*, 102108. https://doi.org/10.1016/j.cose.2020.102108

Mahajan, H. B., Rashid, A. S., Junnarkar, A. A., Uke, N., Deshpande, S. D., Futane, P. R., & Alhayani, B. (2023). Integration of Healthcare 4.0 and blockchain into secure cloud-based electronic health records systems. *Applied Nanoscience*, *13*(3), 2329–2342.

Peters, G. W., & Panayi, E. (2015). Understanding modern banking ledgers through blockchain technologies: Future of transaction processing and smart contracts on the internet of money. *SSRN Electronic Journal*, 1–33. https://doi.org/10.2139/ssrn.2692487

Rodosek, G. D., & Golling, M. (2013). Cyber security: Challenges and application areas. *Lecture Notes in Logistics*, 179–197. https://doi.org/10.1007/978-3-642-32021-7_11

Sabaliauskaite, G., Liew, L. S., & Cui, J. (2018). Integrating autonomous vehicle safety and security analysis using STPA method and the six-step model. *International Journal on Advances in Security*, *11*(1–2), 160–169.

Sharma, R. (2012). Study of latest emerging trends on cyber security and its challenges to society. *International Journal of Scientific & Engineering Research*, *3*(6), 1–4.

Smith, J. (2020). Cybersecurity applications in smart cities. *Smart City Journal*, *5*(2), 45–58.

Smith, J., & Brown, A. (2018). Cybersecurity challenges in higher education. *Journal of Information Security in Education*, *4*(2), 31–44.

Smith, J., & Doe, A. (2020). Automating cybersecurity: The role of machine learning and artificial intelligence. *Journal of Cyber Defense*, *15*(3), 45–60.

Srivastava, G., Jhaveri, R. H., Bhattacharya, S., Pandya, S., Maddikunta, P. K. R., Yenduri, G., & Gadekallu, T. R. (2022). XAI for cybersecurity: State of the art, challenges, open issues and future directions. *arXiv Preprint*. https://arxiv.org/abs/2206.03585

Thakur, K., Qiu, M., Gai, K., & Ali, M. L. (2015, November). An investigation on cyber security threats and security models. In *2015 IEEE 2nd international conference on cyber security and cloud computing* (pp. 307–311). IEEE.

Tonge, A. M. (2013). Cyber security: Challenges for society- literature review, IOSR. *Journal of Computer Engineering*, *12*(2), 67–75. https://doi.org/10.9790/0661-1226775

Ullah, F., Naeem, H., Jabbar, S., Khalid, S., Latif, M. A., Al-Turjman, F., & Mostarda, L. (2019). Cyber security threats detection in Internet of Things using deep learning approach. *IEEE Access*, *7*, 124379–124389. https://doi.org/10.1109/ACCESS.2019.2937347

Wang, W., & Lu, Z. (2013, April 1). *Cyber security in the smart grid: Survey and challenges*. Computer Networks, Elsevier BV. https://doi.org/10.1016/j.comnet.2012.12.017

White, S. (2021). Enhancing public safety in smart cities through cybersecurity. *International Journal of Urban Safety*, *8*(1), 112–125.

Yazdinejad, A., Kazemi, M., Parizi, R. M., Dehghantanha, A., & Karimipour, H. (2023). An ensemble deep learning model for cyber threat hunting in industrial Internet of Things. *Digital Communications and Networks*, *9*(1), 101–110.

Zhang, Z., Ning, H., Shi, F., Farha, F., Xu, Y., Xu, J., Zhang, F., & Choo, K. K. R. (2022). Artificial intelligence in cyber security: Research advances, challenges, and opportunities. *Artificial Intelligence Review*, 1–25.

3 Examining the Impact of Cyber Fraud on Indian Society

An Assessment of the Potential Damage

Subhra Rajat Balabantaray

Introduction

The Internet is currently regarded as one of the most significant developments in society in the modern era. The enormous dependence that it has fostered is on the verge of becoming gigantic in scale. In recent years, the exponential growth of the digital realm has brought about opportunities for global interconnectedness, streamlined transactions, and efficient communication that were previously unimaginable (Vermesan & Bacquet, 2017; Georgios et al., 2019; Yang et al., 2019; Allam, 2020; Allam & Jones, 2021; Balasubramanian, 2023). The implementation of digitized landscapes has, without a shadow of a doubt, brought about a significant increase in the number of opportunities and advantages available. On the other side, meanwhile, it has also been responsible for the emergence of a destructive form of criminal behaviour that is often known as cyber fraud. This has occurred as a direct result of the rise in the use of the Internet. As a direct result of the widespread digitalization that has taken place in the Western world over the course of the past several decades (Notté et al., 2021), our society is currently facing a problem that is only getting worse (Holt & Bossler, 2014; Sterle & Bhunia, 2021; Balabantaray et al., 2023). The phenomenon of cyber fraud is a complex and ever-developing threat that takes advantage of the weaknesses inherent in the digital world. Cyber fraud takes advantage of the vulnerabilities inherent in the digital realm. People, companies, and even governmental entities might be counted among its victims (Sterle & Bhunia, 2021). Kovalchuk et al. (2021) anticipated that the global cost of cybercrime will amount to $945 billion in the year 2020. It is anticipated that cyber fraud will continue to be an increasing concern.

Despite the fact that cybercrime is becoming more of a concern, the technical methods that are now being utilized to combat cybercrime are not successful in slowing the expansion of cybercrime. This demonstrates the need for further preventative measures in order to reduce the quantity of cybercrime that is committed. It is similarly vital to understand victims, that is the characteristics of the users of computer systems, in order to understand the manner in which these users become victims of cybercrime. This is because understanding the

DOI: 10.4324/9781003517290-5

manner in which these users become victims of cybercrime is essential to preventing cybercrime. It is necessary to understand victims in order to understand criminals, just as it is vital to understand the characteristics of criminals in order to understand the motivations behind the crime and, as a result, to design and implement methods for the prevention of crime. However, it is also important to understand victims in order to understand criminals.

The current study's objective is to investigate the far-reaching effects that cyber fraud has had on Indian society. In recent years, there has been a rise in the number of individuals, businesses, and institutions in India that are susceptible to different kinds of fraudulent activities and criminal schemes that take place online (Deora & Chudasama, 2021; Lallie et al., 2021; Tiwari et al., 2023). This phenomenon has been attributed to cyber fraud. As a result of the rapid expansion of India's digital ecosystem, which has resulted in the ubiquitous threat of cyber fraud (Pazarbasioglu et al., 2020; Buteau, 2021), individuals face significant challenges with regard to their financial security, privacy, and overall trust in digital transactions (Pazarbasioglu et al., 2020).

The purpose of this chapter is to offer readers with an in-depth understanding of the effects that cyber fraud has on society. By shining light on the economic, social, psychological, and legal ramifications of cyber fraud, the objective is to increase awareness about this ever-evolving problem and contribute to the ongoing dialogue on effective techniques for prevention and mitigation. This will be accomplished by shedding light on the economic, social, psychological, and legal implications of cyber fraud.

Conceptualization of Online Fraud

To begin, it is crucial to keep in mind that the term "cybercrime" does not have a single, agreed-upon definition that is applicable to every circumstance (Phillips et al., 2022). This is something that needs to be kept in mind from the very beginning. Therefore, one approach to think about cybercrime is as a broad umbrella phrase that includes computer-assisted crime. This is one way to think about cybercrime. This term refers to a type of criminal activity that makes use of computers and other forms of technology to facilitate the commission of the crime. One example of this is when someone uses a computer to send threatening messages to another individual. The conceptual definitions of cybercrime that may be found in various research and surveys may range substantially from one another in terms of their level of precision, breadth of coverage, and applicability to the modern environment.

The concept of cybercrime has been the subject of a great deal of academic investigation in the past, and this investigation has been conducted at a variety of points in time and under a wide range of conditions. According to the worldwide journal of *Science and Information Security*, the term "cybercrime" refers to malicious activities that are carried out from or against a computer or a network. Cybercrime, according to another definition provided by Bernik (2014), is any illicit activity that is carried out via electronic operations and aims to target computer systems and the data that is processed by the devices. Based on these definitions, it is obvious that cybercrime takes place within a virtual area under the conditions in which information concerning persons, objects, events, or facts are fashioned into mathematical symbols and transported across local and international networks.

Donn Parker, who is regarded as the first national authority on computer security in the United States, was one of the first people to write about computer crime. He was also one of the first persons to write about computer security. According to Parker's definition of "computer abuse", the term refers to intentional conduct in which the victim (or victims) incurs a loss while others benefit financially from the situation. However, previous events have demonstrated that the individuals responsible may not always be motivated by financial gain. It is important to note that there is a subgroup of online criminals known as "hacktivists". These are the individuals who speak out against the policies and procedures of organizations.

Criminal activities that are carried out over the Internet or through digital communication channels with the goal of deceiving and defrauding individuals, corporations, or organizations are referred to as cyber fraud. This type of fraud is also known as online fraud or Internet fraud. Other names for cyber fraud are online fraud and Internet fraud. The use of technology and the Internet to commit fraudulent schemes, get sensitive information, or earn financial rewards unlawfully is included in this category. The term "cyber fraud" refers to a wide variety of dishonest acts and methods. These fraudulent activities frequently involve social engineering, malware, or the exploitation of weaknesses in digital systems and networks. Phishing, identity theft, credit card fraud, and other types of Internet cons might also fall under this category. Identity theft, in which an individual's personal information is stolen in order to impersonate them for the goal of financial gain or other illegal purposes, is another widespread type of cyber fraud. This type of fraud occurs when an individual is tricked into exposing their personal information or login credentials by means such as bogus emails or websites.

Fraudulent online auctions, online financial scams, romance scams, credit card fraud, investment fraud, ransomware attacks, and other sorts of cybercrime are among the many other types of cybercrime. A variety of goals, from financial gain and identity theft to espionage and sabotage, can be driving forces behind fraudulent activities in the digital realm. These are only a few of the many different kinds of online scams that can be committed. Because cybercriminals are always refining their methods, it is absolutely necessary for individuals and businesses to maintain a state of constant vigilance and implement comprehensive cybersecurity measures in order to protect themselves from becoming victims of fraudulent online activity.

Statement of the Problem

An overview of cyber frauds and cybercrimes has been covered in the parts that came before this one, and the majority of those discussions have focused on the monetary damage that has been caused as a direct result of cyber criminals. In addition to the negative effects it has on a country's economy, cybercrime also has a significant impact on the social fabric of those countries. The breadth of cyber fraud is enormous, and malicious actors deploy ever-evolving strategies to take advantage of flaws in digital networks and prey on victims who are unaware that they are being targeted. Cybercriminals exhibit a surprising degree of adaptation in their efforts to evade security measures. This adaptability takes many forms, ranging from sophisticated phishing schemes and identity theft to ransomware assaults and online financial fraud. It is vital that one understand the far-reaching repercussions of the acts taken by cybercriminals.

The negative effects that cybercrime has on society are enormous. It is possible for it to have a detrimental effect on individuals, companies, and nations. For individuals, becoming a victim of cyber fraud can result in monetary loss, the theft of their identity, and mental misery. Cybercrime can result in decreased revenue for firms, in addition to reputational harm and greater operational expenses. When it comes to governments, cyber fraud can be a threat to the safety of the nation. This chapter digs into the myriad ways in which cyber fraud has an effect on society, illuminating the far-reaching ramifications that resonate through every layer of our interconnected world. This article investigates the numerous facets of the impact that cyber fraud has on society, including the economic, social, psychological, and legal aspects of the issue.

There are a number of different criminological viewpoints, the majority of which define crime based on the social, cultural, and material components, and they regard crimes to take place in a specific geographical region. These perspectives also differ in the ways in which they examine the nature of criminal activity. Because of this definition of criminal conduct, it is now able to classify criminal behaviour, which, in turn, has made it possible to tailor approaches to crime prevention, mapping, and assessment to the particular audience that is being addressed. The setting in which cybercrime is committed, on the other hand, cannot be nailed down to a single geographical place or to a specified set of social or cultural groups. Cybercrime can happen anywhere, at any time, in any culture. Because of this, it is impossible for this classification to be applied to the problem of cybercrime. For instance, in the case of conventional crimes such as molesting a kid or committing a rape, it is feasible to describe the perpetrator by referring to the characteristics of the crime itself. These qualities can include determining the social position of the offender and the offender's geographic location within the framework of the nation, the state, the district, urban or rural residential regions, and so on. Other criteria can include the kind of the crime that was committed. On the other hand, as a result of the "anti-spatial" structure of the Internet, it is not possible to determine the exact location of the individual who is responsible for an offense that was committed online.

In this study, we will investigate the psychological trauma that victims have endured, which can range from anxiety and terror to a profound loss of trust in online interactions and e-commerce. We want to understand the long-term ramifications of these emotional traumas on the well-being of both individuals and society as a whole, and we want to do this by studying real-life case studies and empirical data.

Background of the Study

The term "cybercrime" has been used to refer to a wide range of various concepts, each of which has been accorded a unique level of specificity by those who have used it. On occasion, and in a way that is compatible with the term's largest conceivable application, it has been used to refer to any form of illegal action that leads to a monetary loss. This usage is consistent with the fact that the phrase can be applied in the broadest possible sense. This includes crimes of violence perpetrated against a person or their property, such as robbing someone while armed, vandalizing their property, or blackmailing them. The meaning of the phrase has been narrowed down to refer to only those forms of non-violent offenses that result in a monetary loss. This is the most inclusive interpretation of the term. This would include crimes in which a financial loss was an unanticipated outcome of the offender's activities or where there was no purpose on the part of the perpetrator to achieve a financial benefit for either himself or a linked party. This would include crimes such as embezzlement, fraud, and theft. For example, when a thief sneaks into the computer system of a bank and either accidentally or purposefully deletes the account records of a depositor who is unrelated to the crime, this is an example of computer forensics.

Significance of the Study

The compromise of individuals' right to private life is an essential component of online fraud. The compromise of personal information, which was carried out by cybercriminals with the intention of profiting from the exploitation of sensitive material, presents significant ethical and moral considerations regarding the sanctity of digital privacy. The purpose of this project is to provide an in-depth analysis of the effects that these invasions of privacy have had, both specifically on people's individual rights to privacy and more generally on civil liberties and government monitoring. The effects of occurrences of cyber fraud and cybercrime on society as a whole are, for the most part, those of a profound kind. Individuals are left in a state of misery and with catastrophic repercussions as a result of the many impacts generated by cyber scams. Therefore, it is essential for policymakers to conduct this study in order to gain an understanding of the myriad of effects that have been exerted on society and, as a result, to devise policy measures that would mitigate the effects that have been produced. There are a large number of research papers that have shed light on the financial losses that have been suffered as a result of cyber fraud. On the other hand, there is a relatively small amount of written material that demonstrates the social impact of cyber frauds, which are seen to be on the rise in the context of India. As a result, the purpose of this study is to investigate a novel vantage point with the intention of attempting to reveal the societal consequences of cyber fraud.

Review of the Literature

A concerted effort was made to incorporate literature that examines the effects that cybercrimes have on society as a whole and tries to comprehend these effects. This was done to guarantee that the research would only cover the most recent published works. In order to compile scholarly publications for this investigation, researchers made use of a number of different search engines, including Google Scholar, Scopus, and Web of Science.

Böhme and Moore (2012) completed an analysis of the obtained data in order to investigate the anxieties and experiences that are associated with cybercrime among citizens of the European Union. They implemented a series of logistic regressions in order to determine the extent to which the risk of cybercrime can deter activities such as online shopping, online banking, and other online pursuits. They discovered that becoming a victim of cybercrime reduced a person's likelihood of using online banking and shopping by 4–5 percentage points. Additionally, they discovered that expressing concern about cybercrime has roughly double the amount of negative impact on online activity as actually becoming a victim of cybercrime. People who have not heard anything about cybercrime from their coworkers or from news reports are more likely to be willing to use Internet banking than people who have heard information about cybercrime.

Data interception, data alteration, data theft, network crime, and access crime are the forms of cybercrime that Das and Nayak (2013) identified in their classification of the phenomenon known as cybercrime. In addition, the authors have made an effort to comprehend the influence that cybercrime has on modern society. In essence, the authors have made an effort to evaluate the influence that cybercrime has on adolescents and the impact it has on the private sector, consumer behaviour, business, and on young people. In addition to that, the study made an attempt to forecast potential developments in cybercrime.

In order to gain a better understanding of the effects that cybercrime has on the financial industry, Lagazio (2014) proposed a multilevel model that was founded on the system dynamics methodology. The findings, which are in line with more recent research, demonstrate that substantial dynamic interactions exist between tangible and intangible elements, which influence the cost of cybercrime and take place at various levels of society and the value network. To be more specific, modifications in the strategic priorities of financial firms, with the protection of client trust and loyalty as a primary objective, together with considerations connected to market positioning in relation to competitors, are important variables in determining the cost of cybercrime. The majority of these expenses are not determined by the amount of cybercrime occurrences that financial organizations face; rather, they are determined by the methods that financial companies choose to utilize in order to safeguard their business interests and market positioning in the face of cybercrime. The strategic behaviour of financial organizations as a response to cybercrime, particularly with regard to excessive spending on defence measures and chronic under-reporting, has also an important consequence at the whole sector and societal levels, potentially increasing the cost of cybercrime even higher. It is possible for unintended consequences, such as ineffective police and international frameworks for combating cyberattacks, as well as an increase in the jurisdictional arbitrage options available to cybercriminals, to drive up the cost of cybercrime while simultaneously impeding the implementation of comprehensive and efficient solutions to the problem.

Yu (2014) identified the following as the three primary predictors of a fear of cybercrime: previous experience being a victim of cybercrime, the perceived risk of being a victim of cybercrime, and the perceived seriousness of cybercrime. The impact of these elements on cybercrime was investigated, and the study also investigated the links between these parameters and the fear of cybercrime. It simultaneously discussed four different types of cybercrime and handled the relationship between the fear of cybercrime and the three primary predictors of its occurrence. The results related to the fact that fear of cybercrime does not typically share the same predictors, and the usage of the Internet plays an essential part in the fear of cybercrime as well.

Wekundah (2015) concentrated their research on the many forms of cybercrime that target small and medium-sized businesses. In this particular study, both quantitative and qualitative research methodologies were utilized to collect information regarding cybercrime assaults from a variety of small and medium-sized businesses. The findings demonstrated that the majority of small and medium-sized businesses do not concentrate or allocate sufficient resources on the issue of cybercrime attacks, despite the fact that they are frequently the targets of such assaults. Because they lack the skills and resources necessary to combat cybercrime, small and medium-sized businesses heavily rely on the information provided by the Internet or by friends in the event of a cyberattack.

Gañán et al. (2017) conducted research to determine the extent of financial damage caused by cybercrime. The authors employed a methodology that combined top-down and bottom-up approaches, and they offered a theoretical framework to systematically determine the short-term and long-term effects of cybercrime at both the agent level and the society level. The purpose of this paradigm was to provide the basis for assessing the economic repercussions of cybercrime beyond the monetary costs, with a particular emphasis on the effect that cybercrime has on economic growth.

Chatterjee et al. (2019) found the characteristics that influence the population of India to prevent crimes committed online. The authors constructed a conceptual model to determine the elements that prevent cybercrimes from occurring. The total number of participants in the study was 315, and the data were analysed by employing structural equation modelling with software packages SPSS and AMOS. According to the findings of the study, "awareness of cybercrimes" is a crucial factor that determines the actual utilization of technology to prevent cybercrimes in India's smart cities. It was also said that government initiatives (GI) and legal awareness are not as influential in the process of disseminating awareness of cybercrimes (AOC) to the residents of the projected smart cities in the world.

Approach and Method

The research is purely descriptive in nature, and only secondary sources of information were used in its compilation. The investigation incorporated all of the sources from published literature, which primarily consists of books, research papers, and journal articles. A concerted effort was made to incorporate extremely recent research, and as a result, only papers written and published within the past 10 years were considered for this study and its subsequent analysis. In order to compile scholarly publications for this investigation, researchers made use of a number of different search engines, including Google Scholar, Scopus, and Web of Science.

Results and Discussions

Cybercrime's victimization effects imply that these effects might be severe and could be similar to those of traditional crime (Holt & Bossler, 2008). The majority of the time, it seems as though victims of cybercrime appear to suffer financial and psychological consequences (Leukfeldt et al., 2018). Because of the persistent nature of many cybercrimes, victimization can either continue for a longer period of time or occur more frequently. The victims of cybercrimes are frequently held responsible for their own victimization, despite the fact that the evidence presented above demonstrates that cybercrimes can have a significant influence on the people who are victimized by them. It is quite common for the social environments and legal systems of victims of cybercrime to "blame the victim". This may be supported by the fact that many victims of cybercrime actively assist in the commission of the crime by performing certain acts, such as supplying login information, which are required for the crime to be carried out. The psychological impacts of victimization, such as feelings of loneliness, embarrassment, and insecurity, can be made worse when other people react negatively or in a manner that is unsupportive. As a result, assigning blame to victims of cybercrime has the potential to amplify the impact of victimization, which is already very considerable.

In the same way, as it is essential to describe the various types of cybercrime, it is also necessary to identify the consequences that these crimes have on their victims. Previous research has thoroughly divided the effects of victimization into four main categories: physical, financial/material, psychological, and social/behavioural. The phenomenon of the effect categories being interconnected is one that is frequently seen in practice. The purpose of this research is to determine whether there is a connection between the monetary and psychological costs of committing a crime, with a particular emphasis on the possible gravity of the psychological repercussions. This research tries to investigate whether the psychological effects are more prominent in situations when the financial cost of a crime outweighs its psychological impact by examining examples in which the financial cost of a crime outweighs its psychological impact. This inquiry will add to the existing body of knowledge regarding the multidimensional nature of crime and the implications it has for the well-being of individuals. It is not uncommon for there to be a convergence of impacts on both the physical and emotional aspects of a person's life. It is possible for a person to develop wounds as a result of direct physical impact that occurs during a physical assault. This is a plausible scenario.

In today's climate of cybercrime, there is a striking absence of immediate physical implications. This is a contemporary phenomenon. The purpose of this study was to investigate whether or not there is a correlation between being a victim of cybercrime and experiencing indirect bodily impacts. In particular, the purpose of this study was to determine whether persons who have been victims of cybercrime are more likely to suffer from a variety of health problems, such as skin disorders, sleep disruptions, headaches, and weight loss. This study makes a contribution to the current body of research on the multidimensional impact that cybercrime can have on the well-being of individuals by investigating the indirect physical consequences of cybercrime. The above-mentioned phenomenon is frequently seen as a direct consequence of illegal activities, and it can be considered an essential component of the psychological implications that these activities have. The ramifications of the most fundamental physical impact have not been taken into consideration in this investigation. Because the dataset that is being used for this research does not include any other types of material impacts save financial ones, the purpose of the current study was to analyse the impact that various factors have on a company's finances. Non-financial impacts will not be investigated. As a direct result of this, we restrict our attention entirely to the monetary effects. Examining the impact on participants' mental health is the major reason for conducting this research. The fact that the social and behavioural influence was not taken into account can be explained by the fact that it was not included in the dataset. Additionally, it is essential to recognize that social or behavioural repercussions frequently follow in the wake of financial or psychological repercussions. This is an essential fact that cannot be ignored.

Conclusion

Cybercrime, as opposed to traditional crimes, which are often committed in a single geographical location, is committed online and is frequently not clearly linked to any one geographical location. This is in contrast to traditional crimes, which are typically committed in a single geographical location. In order to effectively combat the problem of cybercrime, it is necessary to make a consolidated and coordinated effort on a global basis. This is mostly due to the fact that there are many different problems, each of which constitutes a barrier that inhibits an effective reduction in the quantity of cybercrime that occurs. Some of the most serious problems are a direct result of the gaps that now exist in the applicable legislation, technologies, and cyber criminology. These gaps have led to a number of other problems as well.

There are a number of different criminological viewpoints, the majority of which define crime based on the social, cultural, and material components, and they regard crimes to take place in a specific geographical region. These perspectives also differ in the ways in which they examine the nature of criminal activity. Because of this definition of criminal conduct, it is now possible to classify criminal behaviour, which, in turn, has made it possible to tailor approaches to crime prevention, mapping, and assessment to the particular audience that is being addressed. The setting in which cybercrime is committed, on the other hand, cannot be nailed down to a single geographical place or to a specified set of social or cultural groups. Cybercrime can happen anywhere, at any time, in any culture. Because of this, it is impossible for this classification to be applied to the problem of cybercrime.

According to Bendle (2019), cybercrime is a problem produced by the irresponsible behaviours of computer and Internet users. These users take advantage of the weaknesses connected with computer networks and the Internet medium to do criminal acts. Crimes committed online are frequently carried out by well-organized gangs that have the capability of causing enormous amounts of financial damage. Because the Internet is accessible to everyone and provides no barriers to entry, it has become a breeding ground for criminal activity online. Additionally, anonymity on the Internet masks the intents of cybercriminals (Laudon & Traver, 2016), which makes it more difficult to combat actions related to cybercrime. If appropriate safety precautions are not taken, conducting business through the Internet poses a major danger or threat to both the company's customers and its suppliers. If these precautions are not taken, the risk may even become catastrophic (Patel & colleagues, 2017). Customers and retailers alike are impacted when legitimate online transactions result in financial losses owing to fraudulent activity. In point of fact, Boateng et al. (2011) implied that actions related to cybercrime have the potential to hinder growth in nations that are not as developed as others.

Fraudulent online sales, electronic fund transfers, identity theft and related crimes, advance fee schemes, and fraudulent investments are some of the most common types of online-related criminal activity, according to Clough (2010). Because of the acts of cybercriminals, many people are concerned about the dangers that are involved in conducting business via online platforms like e-commerce. According to Apau et al. (2019), in order for businesses to conduct successful transactions over the Internet, it is necessary to implement safeguards that protect the privacy and safety of both the customers and the businesses themselves. Many nations that are considered to be less developed have made substantial progress towards the implementation of e-commerce technologies. However, notorious computers users continue to commit crimes against other users by taking advantage of the vulnerabilities associated with the Internet medium and computer networks (Warner, 2011). According to Patel et al. (2017), those who commit cybercrime look for loopholes and security flaws in e-commerce platforms, and then use a variety of techniques to take advantage of their victims and profit from the vulnerabilities they have found.

Policy Recommendations

The number of the economic, social, and political repercussions of online attacks and cybercrimes has been difficult to arrive at since it has been difficult to obtain numbers that are accurate enough to be considered meaningful. One school of thought contends that the extent of the damage is sometimes grossly overestimated as a result of the fact that many cyberattacks are never brought to light. The counterargument claims that there may be financial motivations for security businesses to exaggerate estimates of the prevalence of Internet criminal behaviour in order to generate more business for themselves. After triangulating the data obtained from a wide range of sources, the researchers came to the conclusion that cyberattacks lead to significant economic losses.

The effects of cybercrime on society are difficult to dissect in their entirety due to the complexity of the topic. There is a large body of knowledge pertaining to real-world criminal activity, but due to the fact that criminal activity has shifted online, a portion of that knowledge may now be obsolete, necessitating more research in order to reconstruct the body of knowledge. The flexible and dynamic nature of the phenomenon, in addition to unanticipated developments such as the growing liberalization of piracy and the spontaneous production of CAM by minors, makes it abundantly clear that there are significant obstacles involved in studying cybercrime and any societal impact associated with it. According to Aiken et al. (2019), in the not-too-distant future, it may be possible to remark that a crime may be labelled as a "cybercrime" if it ever even marginally utilizes cyber technology.

There are many different strategies available for preventing fraud committed online. People can protect themselves by being cautious about the information they disclose online, by making use of robust passwords, and by remaining informed on the most recent schemes involving online fraud. Investing in security measures like firewalls and antivirus software is one way for businesses to guard themselves against potential threats. Investing in cybersecurity infrastructure and collaborating with law enforcement to investigate and prosecute cyber criminals are two ways for governments to protect themselves from potential threats posed by hackers.

References

Aiken, M., Mc Mahon, C., Haughton, C., O'Neill, L., & O'Carroll, E. (2019). A consideration of the social impact of cybercrime: Examples from hacking, piracy, and child abuse material online. In *Crime and society* (pp. 91–109). Routledge.

Allam, Z. (2020). The forceful reevaluation of cash-based transactions by COVID-19 and its opportunities to transition to cashless systems in digital urban networks. *Surveying the COVID-19 Pandemic and Its Implications, 107.*

Allam, Z., & Jones, D. S. (2021). Future (post-COVID) digital, smart and sustainable cities in the wake of 6G: Digital twins, immersive realities and new urban economies. *Land Use Policy, 101*, 105201.

Apau, R., Nti, F., & Adu, S. (2019). Cyber-crime and its effects on e-commerce technologies. *Journal of Information, 5*(1), 39–59.

Balabantaray, S. R., Mishra, M., & Pani, U. (2023). A sociological study of cybercrimes against women in India: Deciphering the causes and evaluating the impact on the victims. *International Journal of Asia-Pacific Studies, 19*(1).

Balasubramanian, P. (2023). Automation in data science, software, and information services. In *Springer handbook of automation* (pp. 989–1014). Springer International Publishing.

Bendle, M. N. (2019). Cyber crimes: A challenge to e-commerce. *Our Heritage, 68*(9), 358–364.

Bernik, I. (2014). Cybercrime. *Cybercrime and Cyberwarfare*, 1–56. https://doi.org/10.1002/9781118898604.ch1

Boateng, R., Molla, A., Heeks, R., & Hinson, R. (2011). Advancing e-commerce beyond readiness in a developing economy: Experiences of Ghanaian firms. *Journal of Electronic Commerce in Organizations, 9*(1), 1–16.

Böhme, R., & Moore, T. (2012, October). How do consumers react to cybercrime? In *2012 eCrime researchers summit* (pp. 1–12). IEEE.

Buteau, S. (2021). Roadmap for digital technology to foster India's MSME ecosystem – Opportunities and challenges. *CSI Transactions on ICT, 9*(4), 233–244.

Chatterjee, S., Kar, A. K., Dwivedi, Y. K., & Kizgin, H. (2019). Prevention of cybercrimes in smart cities of India: From a citizen's perspective. *Information Technology & People, 32*(5), 1153–1183.

Clough, J. (2010). *Principles of cybercrime.* Cambridge University Press.

Das, S., & Nayak, T. (2013). Impact of cyber crime: Issues and challenges. *International Journal of Engineering Sciences & Emerging Technologies, 6*(2), 142–153.

Deora, R. S., & Chudasama, D. (2021). Brief study of cybercrime on an internet. *Journal of Communication Engineering & Systems, 11*(1), 1–6.

Gañán, C. H., Ciere, M., & van Eeten, M. (2017, October). Beyond the pretty penny: The economic impact of cybercrime. In *Proceedings of the 2017 new security paradigms workshop* (pp. 35–45). ACM Digital Library. https://doi.org/10.1145/3171533.3171535

Holt, T. J., & Bossler, A. M. (2008). Examining the applicability of lifestyle-routine activities theory for cybercrime victimization. *Deviant Behavior, 30*(1), 1–25.

Holt, T. J., & Bossler, A. M. (2014). An assessment of the current state of cybercrime scholarship. *Deviant Behavior, 35*(1), 20–40.

Kovalchuk, O., Shynkaryk, M., & Masonkova, M. (2021, September). Econometric models for estimating the financial effect of cybercrimes. In *2021 11th international conference on advanced computer information technologies (ACIT)* (pp. 381–384). IEEE.

Lagazio, M., Sherif, N., & Cushman, M. (2014). A multi-level approach to understanding the impact of cyber crime on the financial sector. *Computers & Security, 45*, 58–74.

Lallie, H. S., Shepherd, L. A., Nurse, J. R. C., Erola, A., Epiphaniou, G., Maple, C., & Bellekens, X. (2021). Cyber security in the age of COVID-19: A timeline and analysis of cyber-crime and cyber-attacks during the pandemic. *Computers & Security, 105*, 102248. https://doi.org/10.1016/j.cose.2021.102248

Laudon, K. C., & Traver, C. G. (2016). *E-commerce: Business, technology, society* (12th ed.). Pearson Education.

Leukfeldt, E. R., Notté, R. J., & Malsch, M. (2018). *Slachtofferschap van online criminaliteit: Een onderzoek naar behoeften, gevolgen en verantwoordelijkheden na slachtofferschap van cybercrime en gedigitaliseerde criminaliteit [Victims of online crime: A study on the needs, consequences and responsibilities following the victimization of cybercrime and digitized crime].* WODC.

Notté, R., Leukfeldt, E. R., & Malsch, M. (2021). Double, triple or quadruple hits? Exploring the impact of cybercrime on victims in the Netherlands. *International Review of Victimology*, *27*(3), 272–294.

Patel, P., Patel, R., Patel, V., & Pathrabe, T. (2017). Survey of privacy and security issues in spice world e-commerce website. *International Journal for Innovative Research in Science & Technology*, 19–23.

Pazarbasioglu, C., Mora, A. G., Uttamchandani, M., Natarajan, H., Feyen, E., & Saal, M. (2020). *Digital financial services* (p. 54). World Bank.

Phillips, K., Davidson, J. C., Farr, R. R., Burkhardt, C., Caneppele, S., & Aiken, M. P. (2022). Conceptualizing cybercrime: Definitions, typologies and taxonomies. *Forensic Sciences*, *2*(2), 379–398. https://doi.org/10.3390/forensicsci2020028

Sterle, L., & Bhunia, S. (2021, October). On SolarWinds Orion platform security breach. In *2021 IEEE smart world, ubiquitous intelligence & computing, advanced & trusted computing, scalable computing & communications, internet of people and smart city innovation (SmartWorld/SCALCOM/UIC/ATC/IOP/SCI)* (pp. 636–641). IEEE.

Tiwari, S., Rai, S. K., & Sisodia, V. (2023). Rising cybercrime on social media during covid pandemic and its impact on digital marketing. *Academy of Marketing Studies Journal*, *27*(S4).

Vermesan, O., & Bacquet, J. (Eds.). (2017). *Cognitive hyperconnected digital transformation: Internet of things intelligence evolution.* River Publishers.

Warner, J. (2011). Understanding cyber-crime in Ghana: A view from below. *International Journal of Cyber Criminology*, *5*(1), 736–749.

Wekundah, R. N. (2015). *The effects of cyber-crime on e-commerce; a model for SMEs in Kenya* [Doctoral dissertation, University of Nairobi].

Yang, H., Kumara, S., Bukkapatnam, S. T., & Tsung, F. (2019). The internet of things for smart manufacturing: A review. *IISE Transactions*, *51*(11), 1190–1216.

Yu, S. (2014). Fear of cyber crime among college students in the United States: An exploratory study. *International Journal of Cyber Criminology*, *8*(1), 36.

4 Perception of Investment Behaviour in the Light of Corporate Frauds with Special Reference to India

A. Lakshmana Rao, G. Ramakrishnan, and Nikhil Kulshrestha

Introduction

Fraud can be defined as an intentional deception made for personal gain or to damage another person/entity. Fraud can be of civil or criminal nature, and it is one of the major sources for loss of anybody's financial strength, and its presence is increasing throughout the globe. It can happen to an individual, an organization, or a group of stakeholders. The risk of fraud is increasing considerably in corporate bodies at an alarming rate. As per some surveys, organizations are losing 7% of their annual turnover due to fraud, and the world economy is losing approximately $1.5 trillion each year. The historical genesis of fraud relates to the genesis of corporate bodies itself. One of the important theories of corporate governance, the "agency theory" failed due to its fundamental error of "the so-called agents, who represent corporate body cannot be reliable, as their master has no control over them". Fundamentally, the agents use the money and property, which belongs to the principal (company), who is also under the control of agents (the directors). The same led to many scandals in corporate bodies, and consequently, two sets of theories named stewardship theory and stakeholder theory emerged. These theoretical bases are intended to reduce the complexity of governing the affairs of corporate bodies in the best possible way. However, in today's scenario, the corporate world is not free from fraudulent environment, and the magnitude of fraud is increasing in different spears. The scenario can be better understood by considering the involvement of fraud in various corporate bodies.

Objectives of the Study

The study is intended to see

a) how effectively investors manage "fraud risk" in managing their portfolios and
b) to assess the impact of fraud on the efficiency and effectiveness of banking and financial institutions.

DOI: 10.4324/9781003517290-6

Review of Literature

According to the Reserve Bank of India (RBI 2014 circular), fraud can be broadly classified into three categories: deposit-related, loan-related, and customer service-related.

A survey made by the Association of Certified Fraud Examiners (ACFE) estimated that a firm loses 5% of its income annually to fraud. Furthermore, it also revealed that the cumulative global annual loss to fraud during 2011 exceeded US$3.5 trillion. The average loss due to fraud ranges from as low as $700,000 recorded in India to as high as $2.0 million recorded in the Americas (ACFE, 2012). As per the KPMG 2011 survey, the Asia-Pacific countries recorded an average loss due to fraud of $1.4 million; Australia and New Zealand recorded fraud of $1.1 million, Europe $1.9 million, and Middle East and North Africa (MENA) $900,000 (KPMG, 2011). It is also reported that global fraud cases continue to increase every year.

As per a 2014 KPMG survey, Fraud cases in the United Kingdom increased from 314 cases in 2010 to 354 cases in 2014. In Australia and New Zealand, the average number of fraud cases increased from 530 in 2008 to 813 in 2010. In Nigeria, as per an ACFE (2016) report, fraud cases have been on the increase from 21 fraud cases in 2010 to 70 cases in 2016. In Singapore, it was reported that fraud incidence increased from 47% in 2011 to 58% in 2014, and it was reported by KPMG that it increased quite significantly in 2013 in Malaysia as well, with the value of fraud above RM1 million increasing from 9% in 2009 to 10%. Earlier literature talked about an effective fraud risk management approach that encompasses controls and measures, and these can be grouped into three broad dimensions: preventives, detectives, and deterrent measures (ACFE, 2015; Alavi, 2016; Albrecht et al., 2012; Boateng et al., 2014; KPMG, 2016; Zhang, 2012). The impact of fraud is more severe in the financial industry than in other sectors of the economy. In the banking sector, fraud may cause a loss of reputation and lead to loss of potential customers (Vousinas, 2016).

There is a vast literature that estimates the impact of fraud revelation on investor behaviour. Gurun and Yonker (2015) visualized the collapse of the multibillion-dollar Ponzi scheme orchestrated by Bernard Madoff and found that residents of communities that were more exposed to the fraud subsequently withdrew assets from investment advisers and increased deposits at banks. Similarly, Giannetti and Wang (2016) found evidence that a one-standard-deviation increase in fraud revelation intensity in a state during a year leads to a 0.4 percentage point decrease in the households' equity holdings, with a huge impact on firms' cost of capital.

In light of the above literature review, researchers were interested in understanding the investment behaviour of select individuals, and in that context, they considered variables such as investment based on age, gender, financial literacy, and disposable income. The select individuals were exposed to various investment options available at their disposal and evaluated their investment interests.

In a research paper by Kieffer and Mottola (2016), it was discussed that 10% of investors will be victimized by investment fraud in the lifespan of the individuals, especially those more prone to retirement.

A research paper by Johannes Hagen and Amedus Malisa (2022) examined the effects of financial frauds in Sweden on individual investor behaviour and how investors diverted their funds, especially the pensioners once it came to their notice of the alleged financial fraud "Allra".

An article by Grant Thornton India LLP (2016) mentioned that as per the ACFE Report to the Nations 2016, India ranked second in terms of victim organizations reporting fraud cases; furthermore, the study showed the urgency of regulators and other bodies to assess the risks of frauds emerging in business.

It was discussed in a research paper by Efstathios Kirkos et al. (2007) about the effectiveness of data mining (DM) classification techniques in detecting firms that issue fraudulent financial statements and deals with the identification of factors associated with fraud, commonly referred to as fraudulent financial statements (FFS).

Carolyn Strand Norman et al. (2010) conducted an experiment involving 172 experienced internal auditors, and an added survey in the study indicated that internal auditors perceive more personal threats when they report high levels of risk directly to the audit committee, relative to management. Perceived threats lead internal auditors to reduce assessed levels of fraud risk when reporting to the audit committee relative to when reporting to management.

A research study carried out by Alexander Dyck et al. (2010) to identify the most effective mechanisms for detecting corporate fraud reported the fraud cases in large US companies between 1996 and 2004. It was found that fraud detection does not rely on standard corporate governance actors (investors, SEC, and auditors) but rather takes a village, including several non-traditional players (employees, media, and industry regulators). Differences in access to information, as well as monetary and reputational incentives, help explain this pattern.

In a survey conducted by Madan Lal Bhasin (2015), it was discussed that banks are not fully proof of fraud risk; it was opined that internal audit professionals play a predominant role in mitigating fraud risk.

In a study conducted by Carr et al. (1995), a prolonged period of stability was noticed prior to the introduction of deposit insurance in 1967. Furthermore, it was argued that the Canadian banking system was stable because the absence of deposit insurance provided incentives for both prudence on the part of management and monitoring by depositors and regulators, and also the absence of unit banking and other regulatory barriers to competition facilitated efficient mergers, which produced a relatively small number of well-managed banks.

Methodology of the Study

The present study was conducted using both primary and secondary sources of data. The secondary sources mainly consisted of reports, journal articles, handouts, unpublished thesis, and other published sources. Primary data were obtained through face-to-face interviews of select individuals on attitudes concerning their investment behaviour in varying conditions. The researchers conducted a random survey in India, with a total of 100 males and 100 females, and obtained inputs on certain aspects of their investment preferences. The results revealed, quite interestingly, that the majority of the selected respondents barring a few were not interested in investing in shares. The major reason cited for their attitude towards investment in shares is the element of fraud involved in the process, and they opined they can be deceived by various scrupulous persons. Furthermore, quite remarkably regarding their firm attitude towards risk-free and low-return aspects of term deposits, according to them, the loss of revenues in investments in banking and financial institutions was not very significant in comparison to the unknown loss or risk caused by stock market (see Appendix 2).

The research methodology used to achieve the objective is as follows:

Table 4.1 Research methodology for objective 1

Objective	*i. How effectively investors manage "fraud risk" in managing their portfolios*
Research design	Descriptive research study
Questionnaire design	**i.** Variable identification through literature review (various facets of corporate fraud) **ii.** Questionnaire preparation **iii.** Pilot testing questionnaire **iv.** Administering the questionnaire to the selected sample
Sampling design	Convenience sampling – the samples were conveniently selected as some of the parameters used to elicit data are complex
Data analysis	Descriptive statistics

Table 4.2 Research methodology for objective 2

Objective	*ii. To assess the impact of fraud on the efficiency and effectiveness of banking and financial institutions*
Research design	Descriptive research study
Face-to-face interview Design	**i.** Variable identification through literature review (various facets of corporate fraud) **ii.** Preparation of structured interview **iii.** Pilot testing **iv.** Administering the structured interview to the selected sample
Sampling design	Convenience sampling – The samples were conveniently selected as some of the parameters used to elicit data are complex
Data analysis	Descriptive statistics

Problem Statement

The review of various research works elicited a common business problem, that is "fraud". Fraud has a very dangerous negative impact on business growth and prosperity. It was further observed, in the case of banking and finance firms, that to a maximum extent an organization's image is determined by its name and fame, rather than its published reports. So if a news item of fraud is published on any firm, the matter has a serious impact on various stakeholders. Therefore, fraud directly affects the business performance. It is in a fact a common problem to all organizations.

Sample Size

Various yardsticks were considered for arriving at the sample size. Osborne and Costello (2004) suggest that the sample size should be 1:5; the rule of 200 is advised by Guilford and Fruchter (1978) who said that a sample size of 200 is enough to conduct a study. MacCallum et al. (1999, p. 84) and Arrindell and van der Ende (1985, p. 166) suggested that the sample size should be at least 200. Considering the above, a sample size of 200 is considered for the study.

The size of the sample for the study was 100 members for each question, under various clusters. Thus for 10 different questions, a total number of 1000 persons were surveyed. The convenience sampling method was adopted with face-to-face interviews based on a structured questionnaire (see Appendix 1), which was used (without supplying hard or soft copies of the questionnaire to respondents) to elicit the data, and the sample population was picked from various geographical locations/parts of India. The sample population was selected conveniently as some of the parameters used to elicit data are complex. The sample selected represents the actual population, and hence, the results were free of sampling errors.

A total of 1000 respondents were selected from the following categories to pick the data with maximum permutations and combinations to avoid researcher bias:

1. Income >15 lakhs, gender male, age > 40 years
2. Income >15 lakhs, gender female, age > 40 years
3. Income < 15 lakhs, gender male, age < 40 years
4. Income < 15 lakhs, gender female, age < 40 years
5. Have financial literacy, gender male, age < 40 years (no income criterion)
6. Have financial literacy, gender (female), age < 40 years (no income criterion)
7. Have no financial literacy, gender (male), age > 40 years (no income criterion)
8. Have no financial literacy, gender (female), age > 40 years (no income criterion)
9. From rural areas, all age groups, without any bar on gender, income, and financial literacy
10. From urban areas, all age groups, without any bar on gender, income, and financial literacy

The motive behind selection of a sample from various localities of India as sample for the survey is as follows:

The researchers undertook their survey in India because of a big scandal that took place in the country. Furthermore, a company named AgriGold started a scheme in which it instigated investors by promising to give higher returns for their investments and also announced another scheme for extra commission for those who join the firm with investments. The attractive interests and dividends attracted many poor, middle-income groups including the literate and illiterate to invest in this company. Subsequently, the company announced its bankruptcy. The scam spread across many states, involving 3.2 million people across India. The company appointed agents to develop its business, grabbed huge amounts of investments, and looted the pockets of many investors. The Andhra Pradesh government took the issue and tried to protect the investors by granting a relief of INR 264 crore as the first instalment against the company's collection of INR 7,000 crores. This issue triggered the researchers to survey the investing patterns of investors on various portfolios, and the same is used as a basis for the present research study.

Results

The results of the study under each category were as follows:

Result 4.1 Income >15 lakhs, gender male, age > 40 years:

The group was selected through known connections across the region with above 15 lakhs revenue, and information was gathered based on the following parameters:

1. Living standards of the individual and family
2. Possession of property in the form of land, building, car, and other things of important value
3. Holding of pink ration card (white ration card is issued to those below the poverty line)
4. Frequent trips abroad
5. Occupation: job, profession, or business

The individuals were asked about their investment priorities on their savings using pre-formulated questions. The respondents were given options about various investment portfolios/criteria, and responses were elicited as follows (see Figure 4.1).

The respondents were asked to rank their priorities on the following investment patterns:

1. Gold
2. Land
3. Housing
4. Shares

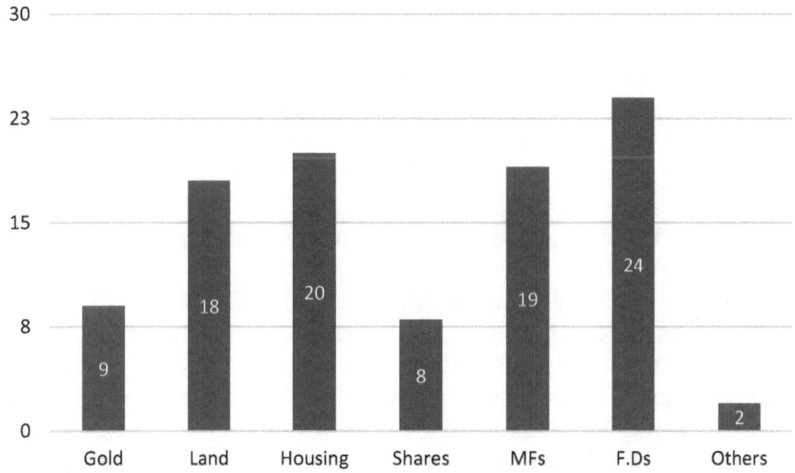

Figure 4.1 Investment criterion of 100 male members above 40 years of age

Source: Survey Results

5. Mutual funds (MFs)
6. Fixed deposits (FDs)/term deposits
7. Other forms like chits, gold equity funds, insurance products, etc.

Out of 100 male respondents, 24 showed their interest in FDs, and it was also noticed that many of these investors seemed to be conservative on their investment, and there was a sharp low trend concerning investment in stock market, although MFs were the only exception.

Result 4.2: Income >15 lakhs, gender female, age > 40 years

Similar to the information used in Result 1, in Result 2, the only change that was made was concerning gender; in this case, 100 female respondents were used.

Investment criterion of women with income above 15 lakhs and aged 40 years

Survey Results:

Out of 100 female respondents, 21 showed interest towards FDs, and it was also noticed that much of these investors seemed to be conservative in their investment, and there was a sharp high trend concerning investment in housing and gold.

Result 4.3: Income < 15 lakhs, gender male, age < 40 years

Without changing the other conditions, the only change that was considered was reducing the income criterion to below 15 lakhs; the 100 male respondents' investment priorities were depicted.

Survey Results:

Out of 100 male respondents, 19 showed their interest towards FDs, and it was also noticed that much of these investors seemed to be aggressive in their investment, and there was a sharp high trend concerning investment in MFs, stock markets, housing, and land.

Result 4.4: Income < 15 lakhs, gender female, age < 40 years

Out of 100 female respondents, 66 were conservative concerning their interest in housing, FDs, gold, and land. In all, 36 female members were interested in MFs and stock market. A large number of this category were risking adverse type.

Result 4.5: Have financial literacy, gender male, age < 40 years (no income criterion)

In the survey conducted among 100 male members who have financial literacy, the results under this criterion looked drastically different from previous results as these were backed majorly by three investment criteria, viz., MFs, housing, and land. Furthermore, they were distributed almost evenly on the securities market, FDs, and other patterns of investment.

Result 4.6: Have financial literacy, gender female, age < 40 years (no income criterion)

In the survey conducted among 100 female members who have financial literacy, the results under this criterion looked more or less similar to those of the male counterparts concerning their investment patterns as these were backed majorly by three investment criteria, viz., MFs, housing, FDs, land, and gold.

Result 4.7: Have no financial literacy, gender male, age > 40 years (no income criterion)

In the survey conducted among 100 male members who have no financial literacy, the results under this criterion looked drastically different from earlier combinations as these were majorly backed by three investment criteria, viz., land, housing, and FDs.

Result 4.8: Have no financial literacy, gender female, age > 40 years (no income criterion)

In the survey conducted among 100 female members who have no financial literacy, the results under this criterion looked similar to those of their male counterparts with no financial literacy, and these were majorly backed by three investment criteria, viz., FDs, housing, land, and gold. Furthermore, one of the important observations was that these were completely dark about the securities market.

Result 4.9: From rural areas, all age groups, without any bar on gender, income, and financial literacy

In the survey conducted among 100 members without any bar on age, gender, financial literacy, and income, with the only exception that these were from the rural region, these members were majorly backed by investment in land followed by other investment criteria, viz., housing and FDs. Quite interestingly, at least 11 members invested in MFs and 5 in the securities market.

Result 4.10: From urban areas, all age groups, without any bar on gender, income, and financial literacy

In the survey conducted among 100 members without any bar on age, gender, financial literacy, and income, with the only exception that these were from urban areas, these members were majorly backed by housing followed by MFs, and other patterns were noticed in land, FDs, and the securities market.

Discussions

Recent Corporate Frauds

Table 4.3 shows that there are economic and other means of loss to varied stakeholders. Therefore, it is necessary to curb this problem to get magnifying returns and provide a congenial environment for economic sustainability of any nation.

Table 4.3 Some examples of corporate fraud

S. No.	*Company*	*Nature of fraud*
1	Himachal Futuristic Communications	Massive price rigging
2	Lupin Laboratories	Massive price rigging
3	Zee Telefilms	Massive price rigging
4	Padmini Polymers	Massive price rigging
5	Enron	Accounting and price rigging
6	WorldCom	Overstating of EBITDA
7	Tyco International	Tax evasion
8	Global Crossing	Accounting fraud
9	Adelphia Communications	Non-disclosure of loans to promoters
10	Computer Associates	Inflated revenue
11	Lucent Technologies	Revision of revenues
12	AOL Time Warner	Accounting scandal
13	Bristol Myers	Inflated sales and revenues
14	Elan	Disclosure failures
15	Halliburton	Fraudulent employment offers
16	ImClone Systems	CEO guilty of criminal cases
17	MicroStrategy	Administrative reporting charges
18	Network Associates	Overstating of revenue
19	PNC Financial	Concealing fraudulent transfers
20	Qwest	Accounting fraud
21	Reliant Resources	Commodities manipulation
22	Rite Aid	Accounting scandal
23	Vivendi Universal	Securities fraud
24	Xcel Energy	Illegal representations
25	Xerox	Accounting fraud
26	Satyam	Accounting scandal
27	Kingfisher	Loan fraud case
28	Punjab National Bank	Largest Indian fraud case in banks
29	Sahara India Pariwar	Investor fraud case
30	ICICI	Related party transactions

Source: Authors

Scenario of Frauds in Banking and Financial Institutions

Among various frauds, "frauds in banking and financial institutions" occupy a major role. This is because these institutions deal with money, the centre of attraction for fraud. Due to the greedy nature of human beings and the tempting phenomenon of money, the rate of fraud in banking and financial institutions is higher than in other types of institutions. Let us have a look at various types of frauds that can happen in banking and financial institutions.

The major types of bank frauds can be listed as follows:

1. Fraudulent loans
2. Ponzi schemes
3. Fraudulent investments
4. Identity frauds
5. Phishing
6. Card fraud
7. Skimming
8. Fund transfer scams

The above types of frauds are commonly prevalent in most banking institutions across the world apart from other crimes such as robbery, theft, and embezzlement. Every day there is a huge amount of financial loss, to either individuals or institutions who are suffering from this kind of fraud. The only remedy to counter this kind of fraud is "prevention", which can be done again at an institutional level or an individual level.

Are banking and financial institutions safeguarded and secured against this kind of fraud? To answer this question, it is worthwhile to see the existing literature on this issue.

Scenario of Control of Fraudulent Practices Banking and Financial Organizations

Although an effective fraud detection system may not give 100% security from and guarantee on the occurrence of fraud, on a lighter note fraudulent practices can be controlled through three-phase steps. They are

- Prevention
- Detection
- Deterrence

The above three phases are adopted by the majority of the organizations.

Concerning prevention, organizations nowadays are relying on technological sources and policy frameworks such as the establishment of good corporate governance systems in their organizations. The technological aspects can range from the application of Internet of things (IoT) to artificial intelligence (AI), and the policy framework of corporate governance acts as a watchdog on legal and ethical aspects on the part of various stakeholders, especially on "internal management" of the organization. Some of the organizations adopt good ethical codes to "whistle-blower" policies as well in preventing fraudulent practices in their organizations. Much of the fraudulent practices are visible only after their occurrence; therefore, organizations are adopting filing of charge sheets to take civil and criminal actions against the persons who are in default of such practices.

At this juncture, it is worthwhile to comment on the legal environment of various countries. In some of the countries, the punishment for economic crimes is very low in comparison to that for civil crimes, and the prevailing system of corruption is also acting as a major aid for escaping even after committing such frauds. Therefore, deterrence is not acting as a force in controlling such practices in such countries.

Findings and Observations

1. From all the 10 result areas, one of the key observations was that FDs ranked among the top 3 investment criteria except in the last combination, which shows how strong this criterion (FDs) is for the public to rely on and invest in.
2. The majority of the people's investment behaviour was towards risk-free and high-return criteria, and they diversified their portfolio to mitigate risk.
3. Securities market was to the maximum extent ignored by low-income groups, those aged above 40, female population, people from rural areas, and those with no financial literacy.
4. An important observation was the shifting of investment from securities markets to MFs by the majority as a good investment option due to the high volatility of the stock market.
5. People's interest towards housing (own) was phenomenally visible in all result areas.
6. Investment in gold as a liquid asset to substitute cash was also found in almost all result areas.
7. Fear of fraud in the securities market and inclination towards more secure and risk-free investments were widely found in the region.
8. Non-reliance on high-return portfolios due to deception by concerns and by fraudulent persons was also expressed by respondents, especially by the non-financial literate group.

The most important observation of the research work was "the mounting raise of bank deposits are majorly due to the lucrative interest rates and because of the risky investment options available at the desk of the people and accordingly they preferred FDs as their preferred choice for yielding returns with assurance, though yield is very less."

Another important observation was that banks' performance is majorly dependent on their lending patterns, and lending happens only when they have adequate deposits. Therefore, banks' performance is accredited majorly to external forces rather than their internal efficiencies.

Banks that are operationally running economically and efficiently can hike interest on deposits, in comparison with other banks, and they can show better results than the ones offering low-interest rates.

The protection mechanism by the Deposit Insurance and Credit Guarantee Corporation (DICGC) available to FDs through counter-guarantees as per a RBI mandate also can impact banks' efficiency and effectiveness in getting more FDs.

Acceptance of future value of money for lesser value by people through FDs is a good sign for banks but not for investors. Due to the increase in fraud in various forms and fashions, endangering the principal amount of investors, people were in one way forced to switch to the option of bank deposits because of many risk factors associated with each investment. Despite this advantage to many nationalized banks, their performance is not up to the mark due to the mounting increase in non-performing assets (NPAs), which is the best indicator of their non-performance.

The other observation was liquidity needs. Investors tend to invest in bank deposits in the form of FDs, which also contributes to the increase in FDs.

The low interest rates of banks on FDs as low as below 7% also became lucrative for these investors because of their inability to judge the right investment option.

Scope for Future Research through Current Research Work

The current research work provides scope for future research in the following directions:

1. Introduction of algorithms to calculate the rate of yield through all forms of investments by incorporating various types of risks associated with each investment
2. Growth rate of securities market if there is a shift in investment from the traditional form to securities market
3. Incorporation of right to investor education for improving the economic wealth of individuals
4. Incorporation of insurance and other riders for investment in securities market
5. Establishing the competitive environment between various product portfolios
6. Effectiveness and efficiency of various regulatory bodies in controlling fraud
7. Introduction of technologies such as AI and ML to assess and mitigate fraud vis-à-vis cybersecurity
8. Cross-country analysis
9. New policy formulations by responsible governments
10. Robust behavioural studies

11. The growth of Fintech has provided a dearth of research areas for exploration under financial technology
12. There is an enormous scope under "governance framework" for basic to in-depth studies on financial performance and financial scams

Suggestions for Control of Fraudulent Practices

Fraud is one of the common elements found in the society. The major reason for this element is "greediness" on the part of subjects in the society. Therefore, elimination of fraud from the grass-root level is a complex aspect. This can be done through social reforms and attitudinal changes in society. Yet some of the suggestions from this work are as follows:

1. Adoption of true "corporate governance" framework in the concerns
2. Adoption of ethical and spiritual work culture
3. Surveillance with the help of existing technological sources, which can range from simple security checks to the use of IoT and AI
4. Rewards for good ethical behaviour
5. Stringent internal audit control system
6. Monitoring by stringent regulatory bodies

The above has already been adopted by many organizations, yet the number of corporate scandals is quite surprisingly increasing in the corporate world, and there could be a greater number of unreported scandals.

Limitations of the Present Research Work

The present research work was based on certain presumptions. They may limit the true results of the study and are as follows:

1. The research is purely an academic work and hence cannot impose any binding norm on anyone; however, it gives an insight into the prospective organizations to look forward.
2. The researchers were not able to give a true and complete answer on selecting age groups above and below 40 years; however, they considered the total Indian population age group, which comes majorly around 40 years, and, on that basis, the researchers considered 40 years as the criterion for undertaking the present research.
3. For certain confidential questions about income and investment, the researchers cannot assure a full guarantee of correct responses from the respondents, as some of the respondents can hide their actual and real investment behaviours.
4. Fixing the threshold of above and below INR 15 lakhs for four clusters is another important quantitative value in determining the behaviours, but the question may not be answered in its true sense of investment behaviours,

as the researchers selected INR 15 lakhs as a baseline because it gives some solid answers concerning portfolio investment.

In spite of the above limitations, the study and survey were carried out with a lot of time and money constraints, and obtaining information on investment behaviour under the influence of fraudulent practices of financial institutions is not an easier affair. The researchers succeeded with the help of their network in completing this crucial research.

Conclusions

1. If the element of fraud is controlled, it acts as a good economic booster to the economy of any country. Huge amount of public money is blocked in the form of "debt capital" by investments, especially in ornamental gold and short-term bank deposits. If this can be diverted to investment in the corporate sector either for the establishment of entities or for investment in the stock market, many of the economic problems of any country can be mitigated.
2. The efficacy and effectiveness of banking and financial institutions are not majorly due to their performance, but due to the deception and prevalence of fraud in other investment patterns and financial institutions and other entities. The move of investors' investment in banking and financial institutions cannot be completely accredited to effective performance of banks and other financial institutions.
3. Quite interestingly, conclusion 4.2 could be a serious and unexpected indirect result of the current research and supported some of the previous research as quoted in the review of literature and also supplemented by current research work.

To sum up, financial institutions with prudent fraud detecting mechanisms and also assurance of risk-free return are capable of attracting more inflows into their organization and sometimes due to the failure of other institutions, as some organizations tap that benefit, and the same is also depicted in the current research work.

Appendix 1
Questionnaire

The researchers have close association with some of the respondents, who have assisted through their network in administering questionnaires and getting responses through face-to-face interviews. No hard copies were used; responses were elicited only through chit-chat with these structured questions in mind. Disclosing financial information is sensitive; hence, the respondents were selective.

1. What is your view on investment of your surplus earnings?
2. Where you will invest your surplus earnings?
3. Can you give ranking on the given investment opportunities to you?
4. Why are you more interested in investing in banks?
5. Can you change your investment from most secured to unsecured investment opportunities?
6. Out of the investment options like gold, land, housing, shares, FDs, and MFs, which one is interesting to you most?
7. Do you have any investment options other than gold, land, housing, shares, FDs, and MFs?

Appendix 2

Complete Analysis of Investors' Attitude

Investment criterion/ portfolio	*Income >15 lakhs, gender, age > 40 years*				*Income <15 lakhs, gender, age < 40 years*				*Have financial literacy, gender, age < 40 years*				*Have no financial literacy, gender, age > 40 years*				*From rural area*				*From urban area*			
	M	*R*	*F*	*R*	*M*	*R*	*F*	*R*	*M*	*R*	*F*	*R*	*M*	*R*	*F*	*R*	*M*	*R*	*F*	*R*	*M*	*R*	*F*	*R*
Gold	9	5	17	3	6	6	14	4	8	5	13	3	11	5	21	4	13	5	20	3	8	5	13	5
Land	18	4	14	4	15	4	11	5	14	3	15	2	25	1	23	3	32	1	29	1	18	3	14	4
Housing	20	2	24	1	17	3	21	1	16	2	19	1	23	2	26	1	17	3	18	4	24	1	27	1
Shares	8	6	4	6	14	5	8	6	13	4	10	4	3	7	0	–	5	6	1	7	13	6	7	6
MFs	19	3	14	4	23	1	18	3	22	1	19	1	12	4	3	5	11	4	5	5	21	2	17	3
FDs	24	1	21	2	19	2	20	2	13	4	15	2	22	3	25	2	21	2	25	2	14	4	19	2
Others	2	7	6	5	6	6	8	6	14	3	9	5	4	6	2	6	1	7	2	6	3	7	3	7
Total (N)	100		100		100		100		100		100		100		100		100		100		100		100	

Glossary: M, male; R, rank; F, female.
Source: Authors

References

ACFE (2012). *Report to the Nations on Occupational Fraud and Abuse: 2012 Global Fraud Study*. Association of Certified Fraud Examiners, Inc. World Headquarters. The Gregor Building 716 West Ave. Austin, TX 78701-2727. USA. URL: https://www.acfe.com/-/media/files/acfe/pdfs/rttn/2012/2012-report-to-nations.pdf (Retrieved on July 2024).

ACFE. (2015). *Fraud risk management: Overview the United States of America* (p. 3). ACFE. https://doi.org/10.1002/9781119203889.ch8

ACFE. (2016). *Report to the nations: On occupational fraud and abuse*. The Global Fraud Study, ACFE.

Alavi, H. (2016). Mitigating the risk of fraud in documentary letters of credit. *Baltic Journal of European Studies*, *6*(1(20)), 139–156.

Albrecht, S. W., Albrecht, C. O., Albrecht, C. C., & Zimbelman, M. F. (2012). *Fraud examination* (4th ed.). South-Western Cengage Learning.

Arrindell, W. A., & van der Ende. J. (1985). An empirical test of the utility of the observations-to-variables ratio in factor and components analysis. *Applied Psychological Measurement*, *9*, 165–178

Bhasin, M. L. (2015). Menace of frauds in the Indian banking industry: An empirical study (October 20, 2015). *Australian Journal of Business and Management Research*, *4*(12).

Boateng, A. A., Boateng, G. O., & Acquah, H. A., (2014). Literature review of fraud risk management in microfinance institutions in Ghana. *Research Journal of Finance and Accounting*, *5*(11), 42–52.

Carr, J., Mathewson, F., & Quigley, N., (1995). Stability in the absence of deposit insurance: The Canadian banking system, 1890–1966. *Journal of Money, Credit and Banking*, *27*(4), 1137–1158.

Dyck, A., Adair, M., & Luigi, Z., (2010). Who blows the whistle on corporate fraud. *Journal of Finance*, *65*, 2213–2253.

Giannetti, M., & Wang, T. Y. (2016). Corporate scandals and household stock market participation. *Journal of Finance*, *71*(6), 2591–2636.

Grant Thornton India LLP. (2016). Financial and Corporate Frauds. Assocham India. https://www.grantthornton.in/globalassets/1.-member-firms/india/assets/pdfs/financial-and-corporate-frauds.pdf

Guilford, J. P., & Fruchter, B. (1978). *Fundamental statistics in psychology and education* (6th ed.). New York: McGraw-Hill.

Gurun, S., & Yonker. (2015). *Trust busting: The effect of fraud on investor behavior*. https://pdfs.semanticscholar.org/1a5e/185a9b138e6a8706b2d095cc3a1307e1a974.pdf

Hagen, J., & A. Malisa (2022). Financial fraud and investment behavior. *Journal of Economic Behavior & Organization 203*, 593–626.

Kieffer, C. N., & Mottola, G. R., (2016). *Understanding and combating investment fraud* (Wharton Pension Research Council Working Papers 59). Wharton Pension Research Council.

Kirkos, E., Spathis, C., & Manolopoulos, Y. (2007). Data Mining techniques for the detection of fraudulent financial statements. *Expert Systems with Applications*, *32*(4), 995–1003. https://doi.org/10.1016/j.eswa.2006.02.016

KPMG. (2011). *KPMG analysis of global patterns of fraud, who is the typical fraudster?* KPMG.

Norman, C. S., Rose, A. M., & Rose, J. M. (2010). Internal audit reporting lines, fraud risk decomposition, and assessments of fraud risk. *Accounting, Organization and Society (Elsevier)*, 546–557.

Osborne, J. W., & Costello, A. B. (2004). Sample size and subject to item ratio in principal components analysis. *Practical Assessment, Research & Evaluation*, *9*.

Vousinas, G. L. (2016). The critical role of internal auditing in addressing bank fraud: A conceptual framework. *Journal of Economics Literature, M4, 25*(3), 67–81.
Zhang, Y. (2012). Documentary letter of credit fraud risk management. *Journal of Financial Crime, 19*(4), 343–354.

Websites

1. https://www.thehindubusinessline.com/news/national/agri-gold-scam-andhra-pradesh-releases-264-crore-as-compensation-for-victims-in-the-first-phase/article29755955.ece
2. https://ucfs.nek.uu.se/digitalAssets/796/c_796916-l_1-k_phd-workshop-ucfs-a-pascal-malisa.pdf
3. https://www.grantthornton.in/globalassets/1.-member-firms/india/assets/pdfs/financial-and-corporate-frauds.pdf

5 Legal Framework of Cybercrimes against E-Banking in India

Reena Roy and Anil Kumar Dixit

Introduction

Over the past few years, the banking business has seen a significant amount of upheaval. Information technology (IT) techniques have been utilized by the majority of banks in India to provide financial services to their customers. Conventional banking has been eradicated from the Indian financial scene as a result of the transformation of banks from ritual banking to core banking, which was made possible by the advent of electronic banking. However, the same technology that made it simpler for banks and their clients to conduct business transactions also made it possible for worldwide organized crime networks to take advantage of the opportunities it presented. The proliferation of data and communication technology has resulted in the turning of the world into a global village; yet, it has also resulted in the emergence of "cybercrimes", which pose a significant risk to both established and newly founded financial institutions. Data technology (IT) was responsible for the invention of cyberspace, which made it possible for everyone to have access to information and to store data. As a result of the rise in the number of people using the Internet, the misuse of technology has emerged as a significant factor in the commission of cybercrimes on a global scale. Any illegal behaviour that is carried out utilizing a computer, another electronic device, or the Internet as the medium and is sanctioned by local law is referred to as a "cybercrime". Cybercrime can also refer to any activity that is carried out remotely. One of the challenges faced by countries when attempting to combat cybercrime is the fact that engineering is a global industry. Internal solutions are unsatisfactory because the majority of computer desktops are accessible from various locations across the world, and the Internet does not have any physical or other barriers. Over the past few years, there has been a huge rise in the amount of cybercrime that has occurred in India. This trend is spreading across the globe as well. Thus, this research study seeks to look into the effects of regulatory measures in combating cybercrimes targeting e-banking in India, as the number of such events continues to rise. The cyberlaws of nations are established to regulate and oversee cases of cybercrimes targeting e-banking. If the cyberlaws of a country are sufficiently competent and efficient in monitoring and regulating cybercrimes, then there will be no significant increase or well-managed growth in cybercrimes.

DOI: 10.4324/9781003517290-7

Research Problem/Gap

In recent years, the Indian banking system has seen substantial transformations, transitioning from conventional banking to electronic banking. Consequently, the proliferation of cybercrimes has emerged, encompassing criminal activities that have the potential to impact any nation around the globe. To tackle this problem, the Indian government has implemented the E-Commerce Act of 1998 and the Information Technology Act of 2000, which was approved on October 17, 2000. The primary objective of the IT Act 2000 was to penalize a wide range of cybercrimes and provide stringent penalties. Nevertheless, the IT Act 2000 has several constraints, such as its inability to encompass the entirety of the Negotiable Instrument Act, which primarily deals with negotiable instruments. In 2002, the Negotiable Instrument Act was modified to specifically cover electronic checks in electronic format and abbreviated cheques. The IT Act 2000 lacks effectiveness in addressing cybercrimes due to its numerous inconsistencies in handling copyright, trademark, and patent issues related to electronic information and data.

Despite the implementation of the IT Act 2000, IT Amendment Act 2008, and other revised traditional laws such as IPC, CrPC, CPC, banking laws, IEA Act, RBI Act, and Indian Evidence Act, the Indian banking industry continues to grapple with the issue of increasing cybercrime incidences. The researchers' objective was to identify the deficiencies in the IT Act 2000 and ITAA 2008, as well as other national banking laws, to understand why these legislations are ineffective in regulating cybercrimes targeting e-banking.

The increasing dependence on IT exposes critical infrastructure to greater susceptibility to attacks, especially those aimed at networked systems connected by computer and communication networks. Terrorist attacks refer to illegal acts and intimidations aimed at computers, networks, and the data they contain. These assaults are intended to manipulate governments or their citizens to achieve political or social goals. Additional forms of terrorist activities encompass cyber money laundering, terrorism financing, hacking, Trojan horse deployment, dissemination of viruses and worms, and denial of services. Although the IT Act 2000 and the IT Amendment Act of 2008, along with other revised laws, were implemented to regulate cybercrimes, the Indian banking sector still encounters challenges with incidences of cyberterrorism. The researchers' objective was to assess the efficacy of various legislations, such as the IT Act 2000 and the IT Act 2008, in addressing cyber terrorism targeting e-banking in India.

Data theft is a substantial concern in the banking sector, as it enables unauthorized access to computer systems and networks at any location and time. This issue is not exclusive to any particular statute but rather arises in multiple existing statutes including contract law, banking law, criminal law, evidence law, and intellectual property law. The IT Act 2000 does not specifically tackle the issue of "data theft". However, the Indian banking industry continues to experience cybercrime occurrences despite the implementation of many laws to combat such instances.

The Indian banking industry encounters difficulties in implementing jurisdiction beyond its territory as stipulated by the IT Act 2000 and in ascertaining the location where the offence took place. The researchers' objective was to identify the legal recourse options provided by cyberlaw and other laws for dealing with criminals who are outside the jurisdiction and to facilitate their extradition.

The emergence of IT has resulted in the worldwide integration of the Internet and computers, transforming the world into a global community. To address cybercrime, some nations have enacted domestic legislation. This study examines and contrasts the current cyber legislation of different nations to address cybercrime occurrences specifically targeting e-banking.

Obstacles arise when attempting to pursue legal action against entities that operate across borders. These obstacles include determining jurisdiction, resolving conflicts of law, addressing practical issues related to gathering evidence, extraditing offenders, and getting international mutual assistance from the participating countries. The OECD and G20, both international organizations, have jointly proposed a precise plan for cooperation to address the menace of cybercrime. Nevertheless, the majority of the countries are unable to address their internal problems, resulting in the lack of repatriation of cybercriminals.

The proliferation of computers has posed challenges for legislators and law enforcement authorities. Legislative regulations mandate the maintenance of diverse types of records, including physical records, records with signatures, and authentic documents. With the increasing prevalence of electronic transactions, it is crucial to have accessible proof of these transactions to demonstrate the legal rights that arise from them. The Indian banking industry encounters challenges in substantiating evidence in the court of law when presented in digital and electronic formats.

Thus, this study aims to examine the legal measures in place to combat cybercrime targeting e-banking in India. It will assess the impact of cybercrime on e-banking and analyse the effectiveness and efficiency of the IT Act 2000, Information Technology Amendment Act 2008, and other relevant national laws in addressing recent developments in cybercrimes against e-banking in India.

Research Objective

The primary objective of this research was to conduct a thorough analysis of the legal measures in place to combat cybercrimes targeting e-banking in India. The aim was to acquire fresh perspectives and a comprehensive understanding of this topic.

- Study of the history of the Indian banking industry
- Analysing the advancement and execution of banking reforms through the IT Act 2000 and 2008.
- Examining present advancements and potential future situations in the banking industry
- Comprehending the concept and mechanisms of e-banking in India

- Researching cybercrimes associated with e-banking in India
- Conducting investigations into cybercrimes in India
- Assessing the importance of domestic legislation about e-banking in India
- Identifying deficiencies in current national legislation
- Analysing RBI regulations to regulate cybercriminal activities
- Proposing effective strategies to regulate cybercrimes targeting e-banking in India

This study demonstrates that the current legal frameworks in India are still insufficient in regulating cybercrimes and offering redress for both clients and banking institutions. Furthermore, it indicates that comprehensive and fool-proof revisions in legal regulations are necessary to enable effective legal oversight of cybercrimes targeting e-banking activities in India.

Review of Literature

The foundation of any economy is a robust and effective financial system. Thanks to technology, banks can now provide the convenience of anytime and anywhere banking. Banks are currently reengineering how their services might be offered to their clients by giving their distribution channels more flexibility (Asifulla, 2016).

Shah (2009) discussed the legal aspect of facilities on the Internet and extended the area of e-banking to all big banks around the globe. The focus of e-banking orientations revolves around addressing issues related to individuals, functional aspects, management, and strategic organizational challenges in the field of e-banking.

Kamath (2000) commented on how the Internet is progressively becoming a source of income and a place where both legal and illegal businesses are conducted.

Mehta and Mehta (2009) expressed their views about different card kinds, smart cards, and card attributes as well as on money and plastic money. They also discussed the card cycle and the ways to detect fraud and credit card fraud. They explained the investigation process for credit card theft. The connection between credit cards, criminal law, and bank and cardholder liability was also covered by the authors.

Jatana and Uppal (2007) explored the conveyance of banking facilities and goods through electronic modes, like phone, Internet, etc., which are the collective term of e-banking.

Kaptan (2003) explored the challenges posed by cutting-edge concepts and the influence of the Internet and IT on the Indian banking sector.

Poonia (2014) stressed that cybercrime has huge potential and thus has a high impact when it is done. It has become challenging and risky for the criminal justice system and those who fight crime due to its simplicity of commission and requirement of no physical presence.

Haq and Khan (2013) talked about how banking sectors would be capable of decreasing traffic at banks and operational costs as a result. Banks are currently making significant investments in IT, but the government needs to fund infrastructure like the Internet and energy. Since e-banking benefits both customers and banks, it will revolutionize traditional banking in the next years.

Kalpana and Mahalakshmi (2020) highlighted the benefits of i-banking in India for both customers and bankers in their article and offered some strategies with potential solutions, such as increasing i-banking awareness.

Vijayalakshmi et al. (2021) examined the many types of cybercrimes associated with e-banking and their effects on the banking sector in their article.

Research Methodology

The current study is based on doctrinal analysis. We have reviewed several books and articles to have a huge understanding of the topic. The next step was to develop a concluding viewpoint. In addition to gathering, classifying, and systematizing legal arguments, examining case law and investigating legal institutions using legal justification were also components of the doctrinal analysis.

Results and Discussion

Concept of E-Banking

The electronic banking, known as "e-banking", provides each customer with affordable services online. By using an Internet browser and a personal computer, a customer can access his bank's website and do some basic banking operations. The bank's centralized database is web-enabled and is part of the Internet banking system. The menu on the bank's website lists all the services it offers. There won't be any manual branch identification once a bank's branch offices are linked together by satellite and tellurian links. A limitless entity, it would permit banking at any time, any place, and in any way.

Definition of E-Banking

Online financial services are given to a client by an electronic bank, or "e-bank". With the aid of a computer and a browser, any customer can use e-banking to log onto his bank's website and carry out any online transactions. The bank has a main database that is web-enabled for its online banking system. There is a list of all the online services the bank provides on the menu. As soon as a bank's branch offices are connected by terrestrial or satellite networks, each office will lose its unique physical identity. Electronic, interactive channels are used to automatically deliver both cutting-edge and traditional banking products and services to customers. A series of systems collectively known as "e-banking" allow financial institutions, customers, consumers, individuals, and businesses to transact business, access accounts, or gather data about financial products and services over a network, including the Internet. When a customer does financial transactions electronically, this is known as "e-banking", and they do not need to go somewhere in person. Phone banking, Internet banking, virtual banking, online banking, home banking, remote electronic banking, and personal computer (PC) banking are just a few of the words that are used to describe various forms of electronic banking. The most often used terms in this context are PC banking and Internet or online banking. It is crucial to remember that the terminology used to describe the various forms of e-banking is frequently used interchangeably.

E-banking, as defined by Oxford Reference Online, is "a method of banking in which the user conducts financial transactions electronically over the Internet".

History of E-Banking in India

The Rangarajan Committee developed a tier-based bank computerization plan in the 1980s that indicated different degrees of bank computerization. Placement of automated teller machines (ATMs) in strategic areas like airports, train stations, healthcare centres, etc., was among the second Rangarajan committee's primary suggestions. Other proposals included computerizing branches and communicating between branches. The HSBC bank established an ATM in Mumbai in 1987, and in 1989, the Bank of India, one of the nation's first nationalized banks, did the same in its Mahalaxmi branch in Mumbai. The first Internet banking service was introduced by ICICI Bank in India. Following suit were City Bank and HDFC Bank. The methodical implementation of core banking solutions (CBS) was another important innovation in India's history of CBS. As the first public sector bank, the Syndicate Bank introduced CBS in Bangalore, India, in 2001. The creation of NEFT and RTGS eased interstate financial transactions and contributed to the growth of India's e-banking sector. The Institute for the Development and Research in Banking Technology (IDRBT), founded in Hyderabad in the middle of the 1990s, significantly contributed to the development of e-banking technology.

Development of E-Banking

Following the start of the liberalization and globalization processes in 1991, the development of e-banking has had an impact on the financial industry, notably the banking sector. The advancement has considerably transformed how the banking industry operates. Banks are offering a variety of services, from cash deposits to cash withdrawals, utilizing electronic means; thus, we can conclude that the number of electronic transactions is expanding. As a result, the globe will soon be a cyber-world where everyone will be connected via the Internet. Economic interconnection is one of the hallmarks of the emerging global market. With the interrelated impact of technology, information flows, and international investor mobility, national frontiers have become less significant. With the increase in technology over the previous 30 years, banks' operating efficiency has grown, and as a result, the time they need to execute various transactions has decreased. To boost their revenue, banks are interested in attracting more and more clients, and they utilize a range of technical instruments to achieve this. To provide financial services around the clock, banks increasingly offer e-banking. Nowadays, customers rarely visit banks; instead, they complete all of their transactions online, which enables banks to operate more cheaply.

Overview of E-Banking in India

Internet banking is the practice of receiving financial services remotely using the Internet, such as opening a deposit account or transferring funds between accounts. The development of online banking is ongoing. For both traditional and online banks, some characteristics are essential, such as promptness, dependability, and accessibility. A bank must first create a web page, which is the basis of Internet banking, to offer information about its goods and services. Higher-level elements of this include providing access to other financial services like investing and insurance, as well as services like account access, money transfers, and integrated sales of other processes. Clients can use online share trading, electronic bill payment systems, rail reservations, money transfers from one customer's account to another, loan applications, and other services through Internet banking. Internet banking has three functional layers: informational, communicative, and transactional. It has been determined that banks have promotional materials for their services and goods on different servers, depending on the degree of information. Online banking's level of communication makes it possible for some clients and banking systems to participate. Bank customers can electronically transfer money to and from their accounts, pay bills, and engage in other financial transactions online, thanks to transactional-level Internet banking.

Concept of Cybercrime

One of the most challenging problems the legal system will face in the present and the future, and one that poses a very real threat to both, is cybercrime. Instead of being driven by violence, the majority of cybercrimes are driven by perversity, vanity, avarice, and lack of moral character of the criminal. Because the Internet can be a dangerous network of lies and is accessible from anywhere in the world, it is challenging to identify the offender. Cybercrime is therefore referred to as "white-collar crime". The list of crimes that have an impact on society, either directly or indirectly, has recently been expanded to include cybercrime. Due to rising Internet usage and the computerization of many daily activities, cybercrime has recently grown at an astounding rate. A "cybercrime" is an illegal act that involves the use of the Internet, a computer, or another electronic device as a medium, and is punishable by law if proven. The use of digital technologies to perpetrate more conventional crimes, like the theft of personally identifiable information and other kinds of private data or property, is known as cybercrime. Due to the growth of the Internet, businesses are increasingly more exposed to the dangers of harmful conduct and cybercrimes. Computers and other contemporary technologies are used by cybercriminals to carry out their heinous crimes. There is no haven from cybercrime as long as people are the weakest link, whether they are employees or unidentified intruders engaged in activities such as hacking, cracking, phishing, or phreaking, which refers to the unauthorized use of or attempt to get around the security measures of an information system or network. IT permeates every part of life in this era of incredible advancement. Today, man cannot live without a phone or computer because of the profound influence of technology.

Cybercrime

The IT Act of 2000, the IT Amendment Act of 2008, or any other piece of Indian legislation in no way defines cybercrime. The Indian Penal Code, 1860, and other laws, which define particular offences and related penalties, offences, and crimes, have been meticulously addressed. No statute or law contains a definition of "cybercrime". You can find the definitions listed below, though.

The Oxford Reference Online defines cybercrime as "a crime performed online".

Cybercrime is defined by the *Encyclopaedia Britannica* "as any crime that is committed with the aid of specialized knowledge or the skilful application of computer technology".

Cybercrime is defined by the CBI Manual as "crimes, including traditional crimes, perpetrated by using computers as a method (Computers are the target of some crimes)".

Of course, the fact that certain conduct by this definition could be legal in one country but prohibited in another complicates these criteria. There are some examples.

1. Unauthorized access
2. Destroying computer data or programs
3. Computer sabotage, unauthorized communication interception
4. Computer espionage in more instances

These definitions serve as an excellent place to start when figuring out the exact meaning of the phrase "cybercrime".

Cybercrime in the E-Banking Sector

A computer, transmission invention, or computer reseau can be used to perform or encourage any unlawful act, according to the definition of cybercrime in general. Cyber fraud is increasingly a common occurrence in banks, costing customers a sizable sum of money annually. Cybercrime is the term used to describe any criminal action carried out via computers and the Internet.

This can involve everything from unauthorized file downloads to the theft of numerous rupees from online bank accounts. Non-financial violations like making and propagating viruses on other computers and circulating non-public company details online are also considered forms of cybercrime. Today, the Internet is accessible to more than 50% of the population, and everyone can readily utilize it for daily tasks like banking, entertainment, education, and other things. Smartphone use and accessibility have made a huge contribution to the Internet's astonishing expansion. The demand for online services has made it impossible to guarantee reliability to users due to the surge in cybercrimes, which pose a severe threat to economic institutions and banks. Internet banking scams and card-related duplicity, like ATM cards, are various types of cybercrime. There have been substantial swaps in the banking business as a result of new technologies and the IT revolution. However, when it comes to financial cybercrimes that are perpetrated online, the following types predominate.

Hacking

It is a means for acquiring an unauthorized approach to a computer system or network for theft, manipulating, or seeing data unlawfully.

Strategies for prevention:

1. The fastest and most efficient way to combat malware is to keep your security software and operating system up to date. Make certain a new programme has an established track record before introducing it. You should avoid illegally downloading software at all costs.
2. Make certain that every device and account is secured with a rigorous PIN or passcode. Never divulge your password or PIN to anyone.
3. Firewalls and antivirus software should be installed, enabled, and updated on computers and laptops.
4. Never download or instal pirated software, programs, or other content on your desktop, laptop, or mobile device.
5. Always check out extraneous devices for viruses while linking to the computer.
6. Use common Wi-Fi networks with caution and refrain from logging into your personal and business accounts.

Phishing

An online conference participant can only access personal information, such as user names and payment card details, by posing as a genuine participant.

Strategies for prevention:

1. Make certain that each appliance and account is protected with a rigorous PIN or password. Never reveal your PIN or password to others.

2. If the request appears to be coming from your bank or credit union, never give out your OTP, phone banking pin, or CVV number. If something goes wrong, notify your bank immediately.

Vishing

Access to another person's personal or financial information through the use of phone-based social engineering techniques has been outlawed under federal law.

Strategies for prevention:

1. Don't forget that the card number/CVV number/OTP will never be asked by the bank.
2. Don't give your ATM card number, CVV number, OTP, or any other secret banking details over the phone, by SMS, or via WhatsApp to anyone.

Spamming

Spammers regularly bombard their victims' email inboxes with spam – a problem that necessitates that we make certain changes to our service to fix it.

Strategies for prevention:

1. Never divulge or publish your email address online.
2. Ponder before opening your email and avoid unsolicited emails.
3. Be aware when downloading clearing applications and antivirus software for spam.
4. Steer clear of utilizing your personal or business email IDs.

Denial of Service

To stop genuine users from using the service, an attacker can flood networks with traffic, disconnect two workstations, or prevent a single user from accessing the service at all.

Strategies for prevention:

1. Purchase high bandwidth
2. Build redundancy into the infrastructure

ATM Skimming and Point-of-Sale Crimes

It is possible to compromise point-of-sale (POS) systems or ATMs by attaching a skimming device to the card reader or an ATM keypad to make it appear as though it is a real keypad or a crucial component of the device. Malware thefts can acquire credit card information straight from these devices and can infect them. Skimmers operate by taking card numbers and personal recognition numbers (PIN) from ATMs, which are later copied to carry out fraudulent transactions.

Strategies for prevention:

Regularly review your bank and credit card statements.

- Before using an ATM, scan the area for skimmers or people watching the PIN.
- Be sure to hide the PIN when entering it.
- Check the keypad visually to make sure there are no overlay devices there.
- No one should be behind or next to you when using an ATM, debit card, or credit card.
- Refrain from using a PIN that is easy to figure out. Repeatedly change the PIN.
- Ensure that you get a confirmation or receipt via SMS for the transaction.
- Inspect the ATM's parts to see if any part is loose or open.

Worms, Trojan Horses, and Viruses

A program known as a computer virus is made to infiltrate a computer, corrupt or modify the files, and then replicate the alterations. Worms are harmful computer programs that repeatedly replicate themselves on local drives, network shares, etc. Trojan horses are not viruses. It's a malicious program that pretends to be a trustworthy application. Despite not replicating as viruses do, Trojan horses can still be extremely dangerous. Trojans provide backdoor access to your computer that allows unauthorized users and programs to enter and steal sensitive data.

Strategies for prevention:

1. Spend money on a reputable antivirus program
2. Use email attachments with caution
3. Avoid downloading from unofficial sources
4. Install a Domain Name System (DNS) server as well as a hardware-based firewall

Impersonation and Identity Theft

The use of another person's electronic impression, passcode, or some other distinctive recognition feature without that individual's consent or knowledge constitutes impersonation and identity theft.

Strategies for prevention:

1. Avoid giving strangers information regarding or copies of identifying documents or address verification.
2. When visiting websites that seem dubious, use identity documents with caution.
3. Refrain from sharing personal information on public forums, such as your date of birth, place of birth, kinship information, address, and phone number.

4. Always mark the identity proof photocopy with a cross and write the purpose of the document in its place. Reusing the photocopy is made difficult by this.
5. Never throw away your electronic banking card receipts in a place where people can see them, like a bank, an ATM, or a place of business.

Fraud Involving a Link or QR Code from Google Pay, PhonePe, or Paytm Requesting Money

To deposit money into their bank accounts using Google Pay, PhonePe, or Paytm, cybercriminals send their victims debit links or QR codes via email. The money is taken out of the victim's account rather than being received because scammers convey a message for funds via a QR code or link.

Strategies for prevention:

1. Don't accept or click on links from questionable websites because they might send you one that is altered, and never scan QR codes.
2. It is not necessary to have an MPIN or a UPI PIN to receive money.

Effects of E-Banking

The cost of e-banking transactions is significantly lower than that of traditional banking. Many new trends in banking are being introduced as an outcome of the setup cost of e-banking being somewhat lower than that of banks. Traditional banking systems might have difficulties raising additional funds or making stock market investments, in contrast to the banking system, which seems to find it relatively easy to connect with investments. E-banking is now a critical element of the global financial market because it can be tailored to meet the needs of different financial markets and organizations. As a result, e-banking has a significant impact on both national and international economies, and it is becoming more and more popular as Internet usage increases globally. Financial institutions and customers both benefit from e-banking in various ways. Below is a list of a few of them.

From the Viewpoint of a Financial Institution

1. Brings down the cost of providing services
2. Gives banks a competitive advantage over rival banks
3. Banks could make some extra cash by running advertisements for promotions on their website
4. Cashless deals
5. A rise in investments because customers can apply for loans online and avoid going to the bank

From the Viewpoint of the Client

1. 24/7 accessibility to banking services
2. Access to account activity is quick and simple

3. Loan, ATM, and other applications
4. Online payment for purchases, home-based money transfers, etc.

Electronic Banking Issues

Electronic banking has just recently been made available to Indian financial organizations. We can't influence most of these actions. It is now possible for a wider spectrum of consumers to benefit from financial services because of financial liberalization and cutting-edge technological advances. Customers must be satisfied with computerized banking services.

Security Risk

The risk of security is one of the major problems facing banks today. Many customers turn down e-banking options because of uncertainties and safety concerns. Based on a 2006 report by the Internet and Mobile Association of India (IAMAI), 43% of Indian Internet users choose not to utilize Internet banking due to concerns regarding security. Due to its ability to alleviate consumers' safety worries, it presents a substantial opportunity for marketers and has the potential to incentivize a larger number of individuals to utilize online banking.

The Issue of Trust

For the majority of customers, a lack of trust is the biggest deterrent to using Internet banking. Clients prefer traditional banking because they don't trust the security of online transactions. They contend that fraud can occur because online transactions can be risky. Two things are on the minds of online banking customers. Is there any evidence that the transaction was completed? Counting the number of times, I press the "Transfer" key gives me an idea of how frequently I make use of the service. Online sales increase when customers have faith in a brand. Two things are on the minds of online banking customers. Is there any evidence that the transaction was completed?

Customer Awareness

In India, there is still a lack of broad customer awareness of e-banking services and procedures. The advantages, applications, and features of Internet banking are not adequately explained by banks. The general lack of understanding of new technology and its advantages is one of the main obstacles to the expansion of e-banking.

Privacy Risk

One of the main reasons customers decide against using Internet banking services is the danger of disclosing personal information and the concern over identity theft. The majority of consumers believe that using online banking services increases their risk of experiencing identity theft. Customer data are routinely misused for purposes other than those for which they were intended by banks and financial institutions.

Strengthening Public Support

A combination of private and public sector companies is sometimes required in the implementation of e-finance in underdeveloped nations. If public sector organizations are unable to undertake these obligations, private partnerships like the World Bank may be necessary.

Personnel Services Are Easily Accessible

There is a great deal of trepidation among existing banks about the impending computerization and mechanization of bank operations. As a result, financial institutions have to cope with customers who have exaggerated notions of their capabilities. To put it another way, they are a product-selling firm.

Adoption of Global Technology

Poor countries must first invest in their physical infrastructure and human resources to benefit from global technology. In many developing nations, electronic payments are challenging to deploy due to the lack of confidence and infrastructure.

Non-Performing Assets

Non-performing assets (NPAs) are also a problem for banks. NPAs for retail bank portfolios increased as interest rates rose, collection methods improved, and property prices increased (50%). Every bank has a deadline for loan payback.

Competition

Commercial banks, nationalized banks, and new private sector banks all compete with one another. Banks have several issues, including cross-selling and product positioning. This programme aims to save expenses by reducing the number of bank workers necessary to perform regular operations. It is essential to hire competent and specialized labour, and it is anticipated that result-focused employees will be appointed.

Handling Technology

When it comes to keeping expenses low and long-term profitability for shareholders, a lot of issues must be taken into consideration. If new technology is made available to organizations, they may be able to compete more effectively in the market. As a result of recent technical improvements, banks in India face a big hurdle.

Reserve Bank of India's Guidelines on Internet Banking in India

On October 17, 2000, the Ministry of Information Technology published a notification using the power granted to them under Section 1(3) of the IT Act 2000. On June 14, 2001, the Reserve Bank of India (RBI) responded by issuing a notification and forming a working group under the leadership of S.R. Mittal. The RBI formed this working group intending to analyse various i-banking-related issues and suggested technological, security, procedural, and statutory standards while taking into consideration the very best international practices. Experts in business banking, law, technology, banking regulation, and banking supervision were represented in this group. The working committee recommended regulations for Internet banking in India in its report titled "Internet Banking Guidelines 2001". The report and recommendations concentrated on three key issues.

Technology and Security Issues

The group believed that banks should hire a network and database administrator with well-defined job responsibilities. A security policy for banks had to be duly approved by the board of directors. The security officer's duties and those of the IT department, which implements the computer systems, ought to be distinct from one another. Furthermore, banks must adopt and put into operation updated security inspection guidelines and inform customers about developing e-banking technologies.

Legal Concerns

Banks are required to keep accurate manual and electronic records of their customers at all times. When a consumer opens an account online, they must obtain all required identification documents and perform a physical verification. Legally, signatures must be recognized as a valid replacement for the security procedures that banks use to confirm users. Customers' requests to stop paying must adhere to strict rules, and banks must be upfront and truthful about the consequences of granting those requests.

Regulatory and Supervisory Issues

Indian citizens can only use Internet banking through banks that have a physical presence in India and are approved and regulated there. Only account holders should have access to the bank's products or services, not account holders from beyond the bank's territorial authority. Internet access is necessary for Indian overseas banks. A supervising authority must be chosen to aid in thwarting any illegal transactions.

In conformity with these requirements, all scheduled commercial banks must apply for RBI authorization in advance before providing Internet banking services. After analysing each of the aforementioned regulations and suggesting that only those provisions continue to apply to e-banking, the RBI issued another notification in 2005. However, to offer e-banking, previous RBI permission is no longer required.

Security Guidelines from the RBI

- Public and private keys, which are two different kinds of keys, are both used in digital signatures. Before RBI's suggestion that public key infrastructure (PKI) transactions be used to safeguard transactions, security socket layer (SSL) was instead employed because there were no PKIs that had been approved for deployment. SSL is very safe and complies with all international regulations. For secure transactions, the RBI advises the use of 128-bit SSL.
- Following the RBI's suggestions, the board of directors of each financial institution shall formally approve its security policy. According to the regulations, each institute must appoint a security officer to oversee compliance with IT-related laws and deal exclusively with information systems.
- New ideas were presented, such as those relating to user identity and passwords. Banks were required to provide logical access controls for data, systems, applications, phone connections, etc. User identification, passwords, smart cards, and other biometric technologies are frequently used in logical access control.
- Banks must implement security measures to avoid a direct link between the Internet and the banking system. High degrees of control and monitoring were made possible by this action. At the absolute least, banks should have a firewall that mimics a proxy server. It was strongly advised to instal a firewall that could carefully review the data in the bank's delicate systems.
- To prevent further proxy servers from gaining access to the network, each machine linked to the modem needs to be separated.
- All idling services should be disabled. As much as possible, keep these services separate from the server.
- Any security breach must be notified right away, and any necessary corrective measures must be taken into account when formulating new rules. The equipment required to keep an eye on the system and protect it from threats must be purchased by banks. Such technologies should be used frequently to ensure security and prevent security breaches. The banks should continue instructing both their security professionals and end customers in addition to the aforementioned things.
- To back up banking data, banks must provide a dependable infrastructure and adhere to reasonable schedules. The guidelines advised regularly

checking the backed-up data to ensure that it could be accessed quickly and without causing any data loss.

- Banks are required by law to retain a functional infrastructure for record-keeping. Both encrypted and unencrypted versions of its chats and transactions must be recorded.
- Security infrastructure needs to be thoroughly evaluated before regular Internet banking activities can resume. Regular updates are required for the system application for banking systems to correct faults and upgrade to a newer version that would offer better service and security.

Legal Framework of E-Banking in India

In addition to the laws governing electronic records and systems, the Reserve Bank of India Act of 1934 and the Banking Regulation Act of 1949 also play a significant regulatory role in Indian banking. In 2008, changes were made to the IT Act 2000 to take these changes into account. Internet banking, which is the act of conducting business online, is one of the many services that banks provide. In India, there are many laws and regulations governing Internet banking. The Indian Contract Act of 1872, the Banking Regulation Act of 1949, and the IT Act 2000 are a few examples of these legislation. Let us look more closely at each of these important financial principles.

The Information Technology Act, 2000

The Information Technology Act, 2000 is the main law in India that regulates online commerce and cybercrimes. One may argue that doing so is essential because the IT Statute 2000 directly affects how Internet banking functions in India. The IT Act 2000 is essential for Internet banking, as shown by the following details.

Document Analysis

The extensive paperwork needed for any banking transaction may now be examined and saved online, thanks to Internet banking. Only the IT Act provides legal status for these electronic documents.

Electronic Transaction

The IT Act's rules apply to any transaction made electronically. No Internet banking transaction may be challenged in court without also complying with the requirements of Section 10A of the IT Act, which makes electronic transactions legal and enforceable.

Authentication

Before these electronic records can be used for e-banking following the requirements of this act, authentication is necessary.

Digital Signature

Only the rules outlined in this act apply to documents that have been digitally or electronically signed. This would fulfil the requirement to sign a document for Internet banking.

Privacy

The online banking industry might not have survived without privacy and security. It is essential since anonymity is a factor in online banking.

Identity Theft

As per the IT Act, several offences involving the theft of data from computer systems are considered crimes under Section 66. Examples of these behaviours include hacking, the introduction and spread of viruses across computer networks, and other similar behaviours.

An analysis of the aforementioned issues reveals that the IT Act 2000 has created the fundamental legal framework necessary for Indian Internet banking. To maintain uniformity and harmony between the requirements of the IT Act and the RBI's directives, a detailed strategy must be followed.

Some Other Key Provisions of the IT Act

Section 3(2): It only permits the use of the crypto function and the hash function as suitable methods for electronic record authentication. This strategy has been kept technology-neutral by several nations.

Section 4: In this section of the article, the legality of all electronic agreements and transactions is established.

Section 72: This is regarding the effects of violating someone else's privacy.

Section 79: This provision safeguards network service providers against any illegal activity that occurs on their network.

The G Gopalakrishna Working Group was founded by the RBI in January 2011 to consider the safety of e-banking in India. In April 2011, the committee declared a few changes to the current regulatory criteria.

Indian Penal Code, 1860

The Indian Penal Code (IPC) imposes punishments for several Internet banking infractions. Several IPC laws prohibit using online banking to commit theft, fraud, and other felonies. It is not surprising that there are parts of the IPC and the IT Act 2000 that are similar. Following are some information on a few of these clauses.

Data Theft

Unauthorized data collection from the Internet or other sources is considered data theft under Section 378 of the IPC. Several techniques, such as hacking, the spread of viruses, computer system failure, and denying access to authorized users, can be used to steal online banking information. Data security is crucial as a result. The IPC also forbids such conduct to safeguard the interests of persons who use Internet banking. Data theft is prohibited by Section 424 of the IPC, and anyone who aids or conceals the theft faces consequences.

Receipt of a Stolen Property

Following Section 411 of the IPC, anyone found in possession of a stolen item through an online banking transaction is guilty and subject to a maximum sentence of 3 months in jail, a fine, or both. The violation covered by this provision of the IPC is the same as that addressed by Section 66B of the IT Act, which lays out the consequences of dishonestly receiving stolen computer assets or communication devices.

Cheating by Personation

Under IPC Section 411 (dishonestly accepting stolen property), any conduct involving cheating by personation is illegal. Section 66C of the IT Act forbids the same. One who violates the law by using a computer to cheat is referred to as "cheating through personation".

Mischief

Anyone who intentionally introduces viruses into a computer system to harm it or prevents someone who has permission to use it from accessing it is guilty of mischief, which is punishable by up to three months in jail, a fine, or both under Section 425 of the IPC.

Forgery

When engaging in Internet banking activities, fraud may be committed by presenting falsified electronic documents or other records. There are several other criminal activities that the IPC doesn't punish but are punishable under the IT Act. A few of them are as follows:

1. Anyone who tampers with or manipulates a computer system or computer network to charge the services they provide to someone else's account is not subject to penalties under the IPC. Such action is prohibited by Section 43(h) of the IT Act.
2. Making changes to a computer-generated source document. Even though Section 409 of the IPC imposes fines, it doesn't go into great detail about these consequences. Section 65 of the IT Act is relevant as a result.
3. The IT Act's Section 66E forbids interfering with Internet security or privacy. When checking in, entering a password, and making purchases online, privacy is essential.

4. Preservation by intermediaries: Section 67 requires that "intermediaries" keep any necessary information on file. In this case, banks have access to that information. This clause was challenged in court in the *Shreya Singhal v. UOI* case, and the judge upheld the section's validity.

Some additional Legislation

Income Tax Act, 1961

As per Section 40A (3), only the account holder has access to this feature when sending money via check or online banking. This component ensures that all bank transactions over INR 20,000 are tracked to prevent tax avoidance.

Negotiable Instrument Act, 1881

The terms "shorter check" and "electronic check" were first introduced in Section 6 of this act. These inspections are provided as electronic trading instruments. This pertains to online banking. It is made sure that all of these tools comply with the minimum-security requirements by using digital signatures (which could include biometrics).

Prevention of Money Laundering Act, 2002

As per Section 11, every economic institute and intermediary must comply with this law's requirement to maintain a history of each transaction. It applies to all banks, whether they deliver services offline or online. With the aid of this clause, online banking money laundering is prevented.

Consumer Protection Act, 1986

This was passed to cover the interests of clients. This holds for banking facilities. The presented law safeguards the confidentiality of client accounts as well as the rights and obligations of both banks and clients.

Conclusion and Suggestions

The Indian banking industry cannot escape e-banking transactions in the current context; however, since cybercrime is a more serious transgression than traditional crimes, the following recommendations can be helpful.

- Users of online banking should set up safe passwords and distinctive user names for each of their accounts and websites.
- Law enforcement should be highly tough and updated continuously to maintain track of such infractions.
- Fast-track mobile courts should be developed to settle these issues, address public grievances, and increase public confidence.

- The government should monitor how the operating networks are used by using massive data banks.
- Consistently applying penalties and punishments is necessary to lessen the effects of these problems and punish the offenders.

References

Ahmed, M. S., Mr, A., & Gopinathan, D. N. (2021). *Cyber law vis-à-vis net banking in Indian sector*. Available at SSRN 3849586. https://papers.ssrn.com/sol3/papers.cfm?abstract_id=3849586

Asifulla, A. (2016). *Introduction to electronic banking*. FSP Media Publications.

Chaimaa, B., Najib, E., & Rachid, H. (2021). E-banking overview: Concepts, challenges and solutions. *Wireless Personal Communications*, *117*, 1059–1078.

Chakraborty, D. (2015). E-banking: Challenges and development in India. *Asian Journal of Management*, *6*(1), 53–60.

Devi, S. (2019). Cyber security in the national security discourse. *World Affairs: The Journal of International Issues*, *23*(2), 146–159.

Dheenadhayalan, V. (2010). Automation of the banking sector in India. *Yojana*, 32–40.

Dixit, A. K. (2006). *Press laws and media ethics*. Reference Press.

Douglas, T., Thomas, D., & Loader, B. (Eds.). (2000). *Cybercrime: Law enforcement, security and surveillance in the information age*. Routledge.

Goel, S. (2016). Cybercrime: A growing threat to the Indian banking sector. *International Journal of Science Technology and Management*, *5*(12), 552–559.

Haq, S., & Khan, M. (2013). E-banking challenges and opportunities in the Indian banking sector. *Innovative Journal of Business and Management*, *2*(4), 56–59.

Jain, R. (2021). Legal framework of internet banking in India. *International Journal of Law Management & Humanities*, *4*(1), 699.

Jatana, R., & Uppal, R. K. (2007). *E-banking in India: Challenges and opportunities*. New Century Publications.

Kalpana, S., & Mahalakshmi, M. (2020). Cyber crime : A growing threat to Indian E-banking sector. *Journal of Emerging Technologies and Innovative Research (JETIR)*, *7*(12), 964–969.

Kamath, N. (2000). *Law relating to computers, internet, and e-commerce: A guide to cyber laws and the Information Technology Act, 2000, with rules and notifications*. Universal Law Publishing Co Ltd.

Kaptan, S. (2003). *Indian banking in the electronic era*. Sarup & Sons.

Khan, H. R. (2014). *Digital India: Emerging challenges & opportunities for the banking sector* (pp. 1–22). Indian Bank Association.

Kolekar, Y. (2015). E-banking in India. *International Journal of Multifaceted and Multilingual Studies*, *2*(3), 6.

Kshetri, N. (2010). Diffusion and effects of cyber-crime in developing economies. *Third World Quarterly*, *31*(7), 1057–1079.

Lal, R., & Saluja, R. (2012). E-banking: The Indian scenario. *Asia Pacific Journal of Marketing & Management Review*, *1*(4), 16–25.

Makhija, P., & Chacko, E. (2021). Efficiency and advancement of artificial intelligence in service sector with special reference to banking industry. *Fourth Industrial Revolution and Business Dynamics: Issues and Implications*, 21–35.

Mehta, R., & Mehta, R. (2009). *Credit cards: A legal guide, with special reference to credit card frauds*. Universal Law Publishing Company.

Nagarajan, V., & Selvan, S. C. B. S. (2019). *Indian scenario of e-banking* (p. 8). https://www.researchgate.net/publication/351224566_Indian_Scenario_of_E-_Banking

Nainta, R. P. (2005). *Banking system, frauds and legal control: Evolution, RBI, bank frauds, legal control, security measures, recent trends*. Deep and Deep Publications.

Neeta, & Bakshi, V. K. (2019). Cyber crimes in banking sector. *Aayushi International Interdisciplinary Research Journal (AIIRJ)*, *VI*(V), 25–31. http://www.aiirjournal.com/uploads/Articles/2019/05/3799_08.Ms.Neeta & Dr. V.K.Bakshi.pdf

Poonia, A. S. (2014). Cybercrime: Challenges and its classification. *International Journal of Emerging Trends & Technology in Computer Science (IJETTCS)*, *3*(6), 119–121.

Rao, H. S. (2019). Cybercrime in banking sector. *International Journal of Research-Granthaalayah*, *7*(1), 148–161.

Rawandale, C. J., Deshpande, M. M., & Rajadhyaksha, V. P. (2018, February). Banking on online banking. In *2018 international conference on advances in communication and computing technology (ICACCT)* (pp. 240–244). IEEE.

Roy, N. C., & Basu, S. (2021). Bank's battle against insider frauds ignitors and mitigators: An emerging nation experience. *Journal of Facilities Management*, *19*(4), 437–457.

Shah, M., & Clarke, S. (Eds.). (2009). *E-banking management: Issues, solutions, and strategies*. IGI Global.

Singh, D. J., & Davidson, J. (2015). *Introduction to internet scams and Fraud-Credit card theft, work-at-home scams and lottery scams*. Mendon Cottage Books.

Singh, N. (2023). Impact of e-banking: Prior and after effects on banking activities. *Journal of Pharmaceutical Negative Results*, 310–317.

Singh, N. P. (2007). Online frauds in Banks with phishing. *Journal of Internet Banking & Commerce*, *12*(2).

Sravani, K., & Sekhar, K. G. (2021). E-banking issues & challenges concerning cybercrime. *Indian Journal of Law and Legal Research*, *2*, 1.

Vijayalakshmi, P., Priyadarshini, V., & Umamaheswari, K. (2021). Impacts of cybercrime on Internet banking. *International Journal of Engineering Technology and Management Sciences*, *5*(2).

Wall, D. S. (Ed.). (2001). *Cybercrimes and the Internet* (pp. 1–17). Routledge.

6 Economic Impact of Perceptible Benefits and Adverse Sides of Blockchain in Bancassurance along with Cybersecurity*

Diksha Verma, Pooja Kansra, and Sushanta Kumar Mahapatra

Introduction

An innovative technology that has captured the attention of the banking sector in India is blockchain technology along with the rise in the research efforts of academicians and researchers (Dashkevich et al., 2020). In recent times, the banking sector has been actively investigating different avenues to utilize blockchain technology. Participants within the industry perceive the potential to apply blockchain to their offerings and create collaborative solutions. These initiatives aim to address existing challenges in the industry by enhancing transparency and promoting better practices. Ben Dhaou and Rohman et al. highlighted a significant perspective that associates interest in blockchain technology and the recognition that traditional financial tools are becoming limited in their effectiveness and showing signs of becoming outdated (Ducas & Wilner, 2017; Dhaou & Rohman, 2018; Oberoi & Kansra, 2021).

The inherent benefits of blockchain technology such as tamper-resistant, consensus-based, and safe recording of online transactions can be handled by several applicants. Bankers are in search for these opportunities to avail benefits from the same. The Bank for International Settlement (BIS) asserts that the implementation of distributed ledger technology (DLT) in the banking sector has the potential to fundamentally transform various aspects, including the storage and maintenance of assets, fulfilment of obligations, enforcement of contracts, and management of risks (Benos et al., 2017). When considering a hypothetical payment, clearing, and settlement (PCS) system that is based on blockchain technology and operated by a central bank, experts forecast that such a system has the potential to deliver value by enhancing efficiency through the modernization of the underlying technology used in financial market infrastructures (Bhatia & Singh, 2019).

* The contributors of this chapter used ChatGPT for the purposes of language improvement and idea exploration. After using this tool, contributors reviewed and edited the contents to ensure scholarly rigor was maintained. The contributors take full responsibility for the originality, validity and integrity of their submission.

DOI: 10.4324/9781003517290-8

Bancassurance, like many other industries, is not immune to the need for digital transformation in response to evolving customer demands. The global pandemic and subsequent lockdowns have accelerated the adoption of technology in people's daily lives. As a result, there is a significant opportunity for banks and insurers to seize this moment and embrace digital models by leveraging technological advancements and innovations. In a digitally headed area, dynamic demands of customers can be met with advancements and innovations (Bhardwaj, 2021). Bancassurance is experiencing a revival within the financial services sector, primarily driven by the changing expectations of consumers and the increasing integration of digital banking ecosystems with other industries. The shift towards customer-centric design thinking and the convergence of boundaries between different industry sectors have propelled the resurgence of bancassurance, but this time with a range of new digital capabilities and enhanced experiences (Sean, 2021). India's insurance penetration stands at a mere 3.7% of GDP, significantly lower than the global average of 6.31%. Even if the middle-class population of India is more than 250 million, then also the penetration level is comparatively low. Bancassurance, on the other side is coming as a promising opportunity for insurance companies to advertise and market their products with the help of banks which ultimately will help the insurance companies to fetch the customers from every nook and corner of India.

As per a survey report by McKinsey, online bancassurance channels have contributed to 19 percent for non-life insurance sales and wo percent for life insurance sales in more than 100 banks all over the world. Adoption of digitalization by insurance companies helps in reducing cost by 15-20 percent especially for life insurance. Several advantages have been offered to customers by digitalization in insurance companies likewise improved convenience, quick processing time, enhanced safety protocols for offering insurance services. Customized tailored products are offered by companies to their customers resulting in minimizing risks of online fraud, hacking or theft of data etc. It has become easy for customers to trace the details of their clients by tracking their address details, their medical history etc. (Ninova, 2018).

Bancassurance is a collaborative model between banking and insurance companies that offers customers the same range of services. This model is widely regarded as highly promising and poised for growth. Extensive literature suggests that banks are increasingly investing in bancassurance due to reasons such as effective organizational management, expertise in investment, and wealth competence (Relan, 2020).

The insurance industry is undergoing significant changes, driven by evolving customer demands for personalized attention. In this context, the partnership between insurance and banking companies for insurance sales proves to be fruitful. Concurrently, the banking sector is embracing various omnichannel strategies, leveraging digitization to provide optimal services to customers. Recent surveys have revealed that several Indian banks have signed memoranda of understanding and established partnerships with numerous life insurance companies. These banks are particularly focusing on implementing omnichannel approaches and encouraging customers to utilize diverse platforms for their insurance services with a single click.

Customers want flexibility in their services like easy accessibility, customer-oriented services etc. (Piotrowicz & Cuthbertson, 2014; Verhoef et al., 2015). Earlier, insurance companies used to depend on the physical services for their customers (Abhishek et al., 2017). However, the entry of omnichannel in banking industry has transformed the pattern of insurance sales (Deloitte, 2015; Efma & Backbase Report, 2015; Verhoef et al., 2015; McKinsey & Company Report, 2017). The introduction and collaboration of bancassurance with blockchain technology helps in improving security, transparency, automated contracts, claims processing, safeguarding data integrity and privacy, saving of cost and other alternative opportunities etc. Providing these advantages to bancassurance companies help in transformation of operations like prioritizing security, providing efficiency and satisfaction of customers. Although, recognizing and tackling the negative aspects associated with implementation of blockchain technology involves addressing scalability, solving data privacy challenges etc. By actively tackling the challenges, the banking industry help in harnessing the full potential of blockchain technology in banking industries.

Literature Background on Digitization of Bancassurance

Based on research conducted by IMARC Group, the global banking and insurance market reached a value of $1,191 billion in the year 2020. It is projected to grow at a compound annual growth rate (CAGR) of approximately 6% from the year 2021 to 2026, reaching an estimated value of $1,696 billion. The primary regions driving the global banking and insurance market include Europe, North America, and Africa. Among these regions, European nations take the lead, with countries like France, Portugal, Italy, and Austria making significant contributions to industry growth. Additionally, Luxembourg, Russia, and Slovenia are identified as potential markets for banking insurance within Europe (Stoyanova, 2022). The boom in digitization and good mobile and Internet connectivity in remote areas of the world have made it convenient for insurance distributors to fetch customers (Ahmed, 2021).

Bancassurance provides reciprocal advantages to banks and their insurance partners. Numerous bancassurance agreements concentrate on selling insurance through the physical branches of banks. However, the bank's extensive branch network is now less advantageous as customer preferences shift towards digital channels, and the banks themselves are reducing their network to manage expenses (Tijoe, 2019). Presently, the banking sector is undergoing rapid and extensive transformations due to technological advancements that align with customers' preferences for banking facilities and tailored and unified banking experiences. Alongside this progress, an omnichannel approach is becoming an inherent characteristic of the banking sector. Nevertheless, its role in this specific context has not yet been fully comprehended (Komulainen & Makkonen, 2018). There has been a complete departure from the previous banking system that was prevalent before nationalization in 1969, and the current system follows a "purpose-oriented lending" approach (Hamouda, 2019).

At present, bank customers are transitioning into becoming "customers of the banking system". Customers have started trusting modern methods of advertisements, which include advertisements through digital marketing (Hamouda, 2019). Customers in the banking sector are now highly engaged with digital experiences provided by innovative financial products and services. This trend is facilitated by the widespread availability of the Internet, the proliferation of smartphones, and the growth of telecommunication networks, among other factors. As a result, digital banking has emerged as a means for customers to save time, reduce costs, and eliminate spatial constraints (Rafiq, 2019).

Digitalization of various channels of distribution of banking services led to the creation of various alternatives for the customers and challenges for the organizing sector, that is bankers. An information system is a way out of this that has helped in dealing with different multi- and omnichannel scenarios (Pavlovski, 2013). Due to digitalization, customers have shifted their perception from being stationery and foreseeable to self-driven and adjustable. Customers expect improved communication and collaboration as well as real customer experience when interacting with banks, and banks also need to adopt a support system for the development and improvement of appropriate internal structures and processes (Schmidt et al., 2016).

To stay competitive, banks need to continuously enhance and introduce innovative, customized packages and services. The success of bancassurance relies heavily on banks' ability to establish and maintain strong customer relationships, which can be facilitated through technological advancements. The integration of industrial modernizations and progressions is dominant to the process of digitization, which is poised to play a pivotal role in the significant success of the digital bancassurance model (Bhardwaj, 2021). This study aimed to examine the gap in the field of blockchain, a promising technology that has attracted the interest of central banks and is considered highly disruptive. The analysis involves mapping this gap by exploring the trends in peer-reviewed research papers, which are categorized thematically to focus on the use cases of DLT for various services, operations, and functions carried out by central banks (Judmayer et al., 2017; Verma & Kansra, 2022).

Material and Methods

The primary objective of this study was to examine the significance of blockchain technology within the realm of bancassurance, focusing on its benefits and potential drawbacks for the industry. This study primarily relied on a theoretical approach to analysing the advantages and potential drawbacks of utilizing blockchain technology in the context of bancassurance, which involves selling insurance through banking channels. The analysis was grounded on secondary sources of information obtained from a variety of published sources.

Findings

The findings have been presented in two distinct sections: one focusing on the evident advantages and the other addressing the negative aspects of utilizing blockchain technology in the field of bancassurance. Due to the current market dynamics of the banking sector and high level of competition, optimum cost allocation for banks is required, and an effective way for this optimum allocation of cost is not only to transfer operations from the traditional branch network to remote channels (Internet banking, website, call centres, etc.) but also to implement competent management omnichannel for banking and insurance services, especially bancassurance. A large number of products and processes needed to be organized and automated during the application of the omnichannel approach, for both banking companies and insurance companies. Significant capital expenditure for the development and maintenance of software and the purchase of equipment is required (Vasiliev & Serov, 2019).

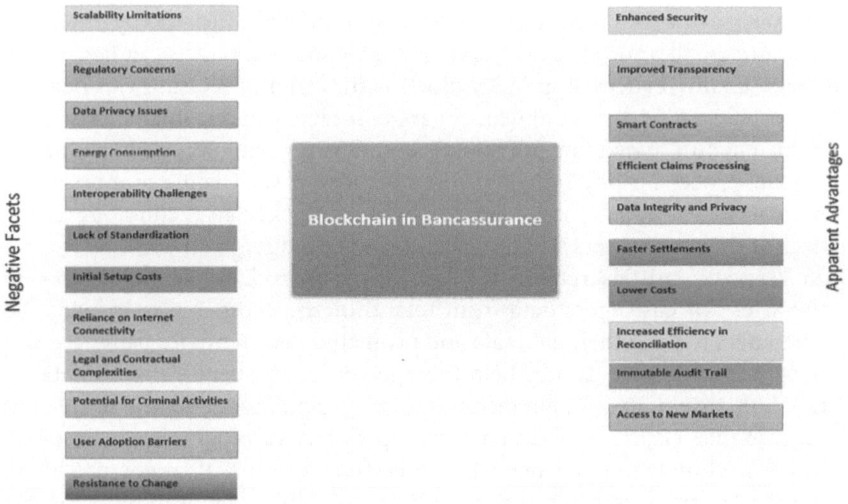

Figure 6.1 Apparent advantages and negative facets of blockchain in bancassurance

Source: Author's compiled model based on literature review

Perceptible Benefits of Blockchain in Bancassurance

Blockchain technology has the potential to revolutionize the bancassurance industry by offering various advantages that can enhance efficiency, security, and transparency. Here are ten key advantages of blockchain technology in bancassurance:

Enhanced Security: Blockchain provides a decentralized and immutable ledger that ensures transparency and reduces the risk of fraud or unauthorized alterations of data. This heightened security can protect sensitive customer information and prevent fraudulent activities. The transactions related to bancassurance can be secured using blockchain technology as detailed data are shared by the clients to banks, and it becomes imperative for the bankers to safeguard the data of customers.

Improved Transparency: The distributed nature of blockchain allows all participants in the bancassurance ecosystem to have access to the same transparent and verified information. This transparency can enhance trust among customers, insurers, and banks by providing a clear audit trail of transactions. With the help of blockchain technology, customers will be able fetch the details regarding insurance policies through digital platforms with a single click, and blockchain will help in securitizing the data of customers at the same time.

Smart Contracts: Blockchain enables the implementation of self-executing smart contracts. These programmable contracts automatically execute when predefined conditions are met, streamlining and automating the process of insurance underwriting, claims settlement, and policy administration. The software can help bankers fetch the details of potential customers by observing their preferences automatically, and ultimately smart contracts can be created.

Efficient Claim Processing: With blockchain, claim processing can become more efficient and streamlined. Smart contracts can automatically trigger claim payouts based on predefined conditions, eliminating the need for manual processing and reducing administrative costs. Claim reimbursement by banks can become easy with the help of blockchain technology as the data of their customers will be available in the ledgers transparently.

Data Veracity and Discretion: The benefits of blockchain technology ensure the safety of customers data from unauthorized accessibility. It helps the customers to keep their data safe and protected and therefore banks are also benefited with same as they help them in protecting bank's client's data.

Quick Solutions: Block chain technology can help in reducing the settlement of insurance claims. The decentralized property of blockchain technology helps in eliminating the need for intermediaries and also aids providing quick solutions in settling the claims process. Also, it helps in reducing the time for settlement of claims and queries in a decentralized structure.

Reduced Expenses: With the help of block chain technology, there is reduced paper work, automation in processing, elimination of brokers and hence it ultimately reduces the cost of bancassurance. These reduced expenses will be beneficial for banks as well as insurance companies in reducing cost and expenses.

Helpful in reconciliation of ledgers: With the help of blockchain technology, banks and insurance companies can reduce their time and efforts for reconciliation of their bancassurance documents and data can be managed effortlessly.

Unassailable Audit Stream: Blockchain technology has an immersible feature of maintaining and keeping records which help the banking institutions to keep their records ready for audit and an unassailable audit stream is maintained. The regulatory standards can be maintained with the help of compliance checks, audits or fraud investigations.

Access to potential markets: Blockchain technology amalgamated with bancassurance services provided with banks help in removing barriers like geographical barriers, decentralized networks etc. through which banks and insurance companies can reach to the potential markets and fetch the customers.

Adverse Sides of Blockchain in Bancassurance

Although blockchain technology as positive and prospective sides along with bancassurance industry, still it is obvious that adverse sides of blockchain with bancassurance should be considered.

Problem of scalability with blockchain and bancassurance: When number of participants increase and scalability increase then blockchain technology with bancassurance may face challenges.

Regulatory Concerns: The regulatory landscape for blockchain technology is still evolving. Compliance with existing regulations and the adaptation of new regulatory frameworks can be complex and time-consuming. Regulators may have concerns regarding data protection, consumer rights, and the potential for money laundering or fraud within blockchain-based bancassurance systems.

Data Privacy Issues: Blockchain's transparent nature poses challenges regarding data privacy. While blockchain ensures the security and integrity of data, it can be difficult to implement privacy controls that comply with stringent data protection regulations, such as the General Data Protection Regulation (GDPR).

Lack of Standardization: The absence of universally adopted standards in the blockchain technology sector creates obstacles to interoperability and results in fragmentation. The lack of standardized protocols and frameworks can give rise to compatibility challenges, thereby restricting the seamless integration of diverse blockchain-based solutions within the bancassurance ecosystem.

Initial Setup Costs: Incorporating blockchain technology entails substantial initial expenses, such as infrastructure establishment, network participation, and ongoing maintenance. These costs can act as a deterrent for smaller players in the bancassurance industry or organizations with limited financial resources.

Reliance on Internet Connectivity: Blockchain systems rely heavily on uninterrupted internet connectivity. Any disruption or downtime in internet access can hinder the availability and accessibility of blockchain-based services, affecting bancassurance operations and customer experience. Blockchain systems heavily depend on consistent internet connectivity.

Legal and Contractual Complexities: The application of blockchain technology in bancassurance can introduce legal and contractual complexities. Smart contracts, while efficient, may require legal expertise to ensure compliance with applicable laws and regulations. Additionally, determining liability and dispute resolution mechanisms in blockchain-based transactions can be challenging.

Potential for Criminal Activities: Blockchain's pseudonymous nature can attract illicit activities, such as money laundering or illegal transactions. The perception of blockchain's association with criminal activities may create regulatory hurdles and affect the reputation of the bancassurance industry.

User Adoption Barriers: Blockchain technology may require users, including customers and employees, to adopt new tools, interfaces, and processes. Resistance to change and the need for education and training can be barriers to the widespread adoption and utilization of blockchain-based bancassurance systems.

Resistance to Change: The adoption of blockchain technology requires a shift in organizational mindset and processes. Resistance to change from stakeholders within the bancassurance industry, including employees, customers, and traditional intermediaries, may hinder the implementation and acceptance of blockchain-based solutions.

Discussion

The advantages of blockchain technology in bancassurance include Enhanced Security, Improved Transparency, Smart Contracts, Efficient Claims Processing, Data Veracity and Discretion, Quick Solutions, Reduced Expenses, Helpful in reconciliation of ledgers, Unassailable Audit Stream and Access to potential markets. By adopting these advantages, banking companies can transform their operations and can provide better, safe, efficient and more customer specific insurance services to their customers. Although blockchain technology with bancassurance provides immense potential and benefits to banks, insurance companies and customers still there are numerous negative facets that all the three parties have to face such as Problem of scalability with blockchain and bancassurance, Regulatory Concerns, Data Privacy Issues, Lack of Standardization, Initial Setup Costs, Reliance on Internet Connectivity, Legal and Contractual Complexities, Potential for Criminal Activities, User Adoption Barriers, Resistance to Change.

Managerial Implications

For successful implementation of blockchain technology with bancassurance need management to focus on improving safety and security, providing trust, discovering contracts, streamlining and handling claims and processes, prioritizing data privacy, getting quicker solutions, reducing cost and expenses etc. Managers of the banking companies, have to face several challenges as well like management of data, evaluating cost and expenses, ensuring internet connectivity, addressing legal complexities, mitigating criminal activities, and managing user adoption, they can successfully harness the benefits of blockchain technology and drive its integration in the industry. Providing bancassurance services to customers with the ais of blockchain technology can be a fruitful avenue for the banking institutions and can help the banks, insurance companies, customers and government as well for giving them a win-win position.

Conclusion

The adoption of blockchain technology in bancassurance by banking institutions have given a great boost to efficiency and effectiveness of their operations. Various benefits which are provided by banking companies to their customers through bancassurance and taking blockchain along with the services help in reaching to maximum customer strength, maintaining ledgers, data safety, data security, data safety etc. However, if implementing new technology, transformation demands few challenges which should be overcome to adopt blockchain in the industry successfully. The blockchain technology in bancassurance field has come so far with lot many successes but still has many more journeys to cover and help in cyber security.

References

Abhishek, V., Geng, D., Li, B., & Zhou, M. (2017). *When the bank comes to you: Branch network and customer omni-channel banking behavior*. SSRN.

Ahmed, K. (2021). Digital revolution and insurance industry: Some important issues for India. *International Journal of Law Management and Humanities*, *4*(3), 4194.

Benos, E., Garratt, R., & Gurrola-Perez, P. (2017). *The economics of distributed ledger technology for securities settlement*. Available at SSRN 3023779. https://ledger.pitt.edu/ojs/ledger/article/download/144/159/927

Bhardwaj, G. (2021, November). Analysis of digitization, IoT and blockchain in Bancassurance. In *2021 International conference on technological advancements and innovations (ICTAI)* (pp. 506–509). IEEE.

Bhatia, S., & Singh, A. K. (2019). Developments in artificial intelligence: A global perspective. *Delhi Business Review, 20*(1), 1–15.

Deloitte. (2015). *Omni-channel-2015: A Deloitte point of view*. https://www2.deloitte.com/content/dam/Deloitte/se/Documents/technology/Omnichannel2015.pdf

Dhaou, S. I., & Rohman, I. K. (2018). Everything and it's opposite: Socio-economic implications of Blockchain technology: Case of monetary policy. *Proceedings of the 11th International Conference on Theory and Practice of Electronic Governance*, 631–639. https://doi.org/10.1145/3209415.3209502

Ducas, E., & Wilner, A. (2017). The security and financial implications of blockchain technologies: Regulating emerging technologies in Canada. *International Journal, 72*(4), 538–562.

Efma & Backbase Report. (2015). *Omni-channel-banking: The digital transformation roadmap (Colloquium of the Belgian financial forum in cooperation with SUERF)*. Efma & Backbase Report.

Hamouda, M. (2019). Omni-channel banking integration quality and perceived value as drivers of consumers' satisfaction and loyalty. *Journal of Enterprise Information Management, 32*(4), 608–625.

Judmayer, N., Stifter, K. K., & Weippl, E. (2017). Blocks and chains: Introduction to bitcoin, cryptocurrencies, and their consensus mechanisms. *Synthesis Lectures on Information Security, Privacy, and Trust, 9*(1), 1–123.

Komulainen, H., & Makkonen, H. (2018). Customer experience in omni-channel banking services. *Journal of Financial Services Marketing, 23*(3), 190–199.

McKinsey & Company Report. (2017). *The winning formula for omni-channel banking in North America*. McKinsey & Company Report.

Ninova, V. (2018). Bancassurance-application and advantages for the insurance market in Bulgaria. *Journal of Innovations and Sustainability, 4*(2), 9–21.

Oberoi, S., & Kansra, P. (2021). Motivating antecedents and consequences of blockchain technology in the insurance industry. In *Blockchain technology and applications for digital marketing* (pp. 276–285). IGI Global.

Pavlovski, C. (2013). A multi-channel system architecture for banking. *International Journal of Computer Science, Engineering and Applications, 3*(5), 1–12.

Piotrowicz, W., & Cuthbertson, R. (2014). Introduction to the special issue information technology in retail: Toward omnichannel retailing. *International Journal of Electronic Commerce, 18*(4), 5–16. https://doi.org/10.2753/JEC1086- 4415180400

Rafiq, M. (2019). Digital banking is an important ingredient for the future of banking. *Journal of Digital Banking, 4*(2), 144–151.

Relan, M. (2020). Digitalization in the bancassurance model of distribution – opportunities and challenges. *Bimaquest, 20*(3). http://bimaquest.niapune.org.in/index.php/bimaquest/article/view/79

Schmidt, J., Drews, P., & Schirmer, I. (2016). *End-users' perspective on digitalization: A study on work order processing in the German banking industry*. Presented in AMCIS, San Diego.

Sean, R. (2021). With digital advances, bancassurance leaps forward. *Journal of Digital Banking, 6*(2), 161–171.

Stoyanova, G. R. (2022). *Banking insurance and future sustainable insurance literacy*. https://jei.uni-rus0e.bg/Issue-2021/9.JEI-article-2021.pdf

Tijoe, L. H. (2019). *Bringing bancassurance into the digital era*. https://www.linkedin.com/pulse/bringing-bancassurance-digital-era-lee-han-tjioe/

Vasiliev, S. A., & Serov, E. R. (2019). Omnichannel banking economy. *Risks, 7*(4). https://doi.org/10.3390/risks7040115

Verhoef, P. C., Kannan, P. K., & Inman, J. J. (2015). From multi-channel retailing to omni-channel retailing. *Journal of Retailing, 91*(2), 174–181. https://doi.org/10.1016/j.jretai.2015.02.005

Verma, D., & Kansra, P. (2022). Blockchain technology in digitizing bancassurance: A theoretical perspective of prospects and confronts in India. In *Applications, challenges, and opportunities of blockchain technology in banking and insurance* (pp. 193–203). IGI Global.

Part 3

Cybercrime, Law, and Technology

7 Quashing Cybercrime and Putting Up Consumer Confidence in E-Commerce

Anshima, Bhawana Bhardwaj, and Dipanker Sharma

Introduction

Modern technology has completely changed every element of human existence (Bhardwaj et al., 2023a). The unveiling of innovation brings with it both boons and banes in equal measure. Cybercrime is a darker side of innovations happening in the stream of online technological advancement. It affects every element of life, from banking to travel, from shopping to classes, from paying rent to eating, and more. Understanding both the advantages and disadvantages of technology is crucial for adjusting to the shift brought about by the technological environment (Bhardwaj et al., 2023b). Although humans have benefited from such a high degree of interconnectedness, computer-assisted crimes have also surged at the same time. The definition of "cybercrime" is broad, and it can refer to a variety of illegal actions. It ranges from online bullying on social media to personal identity theft, financial fraud, spamming, phishing, malware, and more. Cyberattacks can affect governments, organizations, and any other Internet service users in one way or another. India saw a rise in cybercrimes from 26,931 in 2018 to 49,708 in 2020, according to the National Crime Record Bureau. Just in the past 2 years, India's crime rate has nearly doubled. There is evidence that, since COVID-19, there has been a noticeable global increase in cybercrimes: 907,000 spam messages, 737 instances of malware, and 48,000 malicious URLs were discovered between January and April 24, 2020, and they were all linked to COVID-19 (Interpol, 2020). The user is unable to fully utilize new technologies due to security concerns (Anshima & Bhardwaj, 2023).

The history of IC3 reveals as many as 880,418 complaints filed against cybercrime in 2023 (FBI, 2023). Users are exposed to the Internet with minimal security, and attackers utilize every possible opportunity to harm them. Once the perception of cyber fraud is developed among consumers, it affects the online business negatively. If consumers are afraid of financial fraud, they will resort to traditional means of business instead of bearing the risk of financial loss. Thus, this chapter intends to address the following research questions: 1) What effect does cybercrime have on e-commerce? 2) What can be done to

DOI: 10.4324/9781003517290-10

mitigate the unfavourable consequences? The study examines how cybercrime affects online business and the role of consumer confidence in technology in increasing or decreasing e-commerce fashion. Additionally, what measures can be taken to strengthen e-transaction security and boost online businesses? Online business has the potential to sell products globally. Cybercrime, however, restricts the online market to make its growth. There is a need to secure the e-commerce network and build the confidence of the consumers in online vendors. Understanding the consumer aspect of cybercrime aids in developing strategies for offering consumers a safe online environment and advancing digital commerce. To reduce the threat from cyberspace, it is important to be aware of these activities. It is also beneficial to constantly update programs and devices.

Cybercrime and E-Commerce: A Review

We have come so far along with technology that imagining oneself without gadgets and the Internet is somewhat difficult. Penetration of the Internet has pulled down all the boundaries amidst different nations with the sizable increase in online transactions through e-commerce. Additionally, terms like phishing, identity theft, and malware are receiving highlights. To boost online business and digital transactions, cyberattacks must be controlled.

Cybercrimes in E-Commerce

The world has been entering the digital age. Small to big enterprises are navigating their businesses to the digital platform (Anshima et al., 2024; Sharma et al., 2024). In addition, cybercrimes are growing alongside. It is not only the case with developed nations, but developing nations are also equally under the grip of cyberattackers. E-commerce facilitates both consumers and sellers, but cyber threats associated with online trade are a big issue. Many a time cybercrimes go unreported by enterprises to prevent the reputation among consumers (Alghamdi, 2020). Consumers are also reluctant to report crimes when there is reputational damage attached to such action. The trust of consumers in online transactions has considerable importance in elevating e-commerce purchases (Apau et al., 2019). The most popular way of committing cybercrimes is identity theft, which elevates the emotion of fear of identity theft (FOIT) among consumers (Hille et al., 2015). People do not feel secure adopting any technology that is associated with any degree of financial loss (Kumar & Debnath, 2018). Cybercrimes are proliferating because of their cost-effectiveness and minimal risk of getting caught (Jang-Jaccard & Nepal, 2014).

Measures to Strengthen Transaction Security

Technology has dissolved human life in such a way that both are inseparable now. Therefore, we are forced to find ways to zero down on the effects of cybercrimes. Awareness among the users of the Internet is the one and foremost cure to limit cybercriminal activities. Governments are also required to take a firm stand to strengthen the laws and their enforcement against such acts. Along with the advancement of technology, cybercriminal activities have advanced. Users have to be smart enough to be protected while downloading files, using websites, or entering an online environment where the security status is unknown (Martin & Rice, 2011).

The organization needs to be more cautious about retaining important data only. Data that are no longer required to fulfil the organization's goals should not be saved in archives. This will somewhat control unauthorized access to sensitive information. Access to the network should be restricted or timely terminated for the third party that is not required to have the same. Awareness about the latest means of breaching security should be up to date, so that the security measures are strengthened (Bendovschi, 2015). Prior research has focused on maturity models that managers can use to manage security and mitigate online risks, including the capability maturity model (CMM), information security evaluation model (ISEM), cybersecurity capability maturity model (C2M2), and community cybersecurity maturity model. Existing models lack quantitative measurements and, therefore, do not access overall security (Le & Hoang, 2016). However, blockchain offers strong security measures in terms of cryptographic verifiability and multi-signature protection. Additionally, it does not allow third parties to see the information of the user. Blockchain is at the infant stage as of now. Governments should grant funds for the development of the blockchain mechanism, and private enterprises should also encourage the R&D project in the same direction. The use of blockchain security has a bright future, and it can prove a nightmare for those who enjoy posing threats using the Internet (Kshetri, 2017).

Significance of Consumer Trust in Online Shopping

The trust of consumers is critical for a boost in online sales. Consumers feel insecure shopping through a medium in which legitimacy is limited. Therefore, it is significant that online vendors have the overall trust of the consumer. Consumer trust is based on three dimensions: *competence, integrity,* and *benevolence.* Competence is the ability of the firm to keep its promises, integrity is the honesty and reputation of an online vendor, and benevolence is the supremacy of the consumer's interest over the vendor's own. An important role is played by consumer characteristics, firm characteristics, website infrastructure, and interaction between the consumer and the firm (Chen & Dhillon, 2003). Another important element that moderates the effect of a vendor's integrity or other antecedents of trust is the consumer's propensity to trust. Trust propensity moderates the effects of trustworthiness issues on consumer action to purchase (Lee & Turban, 2001). Consumer trust plays an important role in mitigating risk perception. Vendors need to stress the security of the transaction and their reputation to positively impact the online buying decisions of consumers. However, perceived size and multichannel integration have the least impact on e-commerce (Teo & Liu, 2007). Additionally, cultural aspects also have an impact on trustworthiness. It is not essential that all aspects in terms of Hofstede's model equally contribute to the trustworthiness (Hallikainen & Laukkanen, 2018).

Jamming the Digital Traffic

Consumers will make more online purchases if they are ensured by organizations about security measures. Authorization and authentication are major concerns in this respect. Sign-on security systems help prevent unauthorized activities, and encryption of data also makes the network secure. Additionally, consumers should use antivirus software, a safe browsing platform, and use strong passwords. Before going ahead with online shopping, consumers should verify the credibility of the store (Vos et al., 2014). Elevating e-commerce consumer perception holds a significant contribution. Perceived utility and ease of being used encourage e-businesses to extend their market, while the number of e-transactions is decreased by perceived risk related to products, services, and online transactions (Park et al., 2004). Privacy and security concerns of consumers have a great impact on perceived risk. However, brand familiarity and product understanding can lessen perceived risk according to previous research. Product knowledge has comparatively more impact; therefore, organizations should initiate plans that fulfil the aim. Those online stores that are successful in building a security image are also successful in elevating the number of e-transactions (Nepomuceno et al., 2014). With lenient return policies, consumers do not invest much of their time in purchase decisions, and it simultaneously increases the rating of the quality of products (Wood, 2001). Digital sellers should adopt a dual payment system (pay-for-order and pay-on-delivery). This approach suits consumers and the seller. Many a time online orders are not placed because of the time gap between payment and receipt of delivery; in such cases, pay-on-delivery facilitates the consumer. To keep the reliability of the product, pay-for-order plays an important role (Xu et al., 2017).

Methodology

Our research's objectives are to comprehend how cybercrime affects e-commerce and identify countermeasures. The research is descriptive, and secondary sources are used to gather data. Secondary data sources included India Brand Equity Foundation (IBEF), the Federal Bureau of Investigation, INTERPOL, and the National Crime Record Bureau.

Results

Cybercrime and E-Commerce: An Upshot

Online businesses have multiplied as Internet usage and accessibility have expanded. In the first week of seasonal shopping in October 2020 (October 15–21), e-commerce companies in India reported a 55% increase in sales across platforms, totalling US$ 4.1 billion (29,000 crores), driven by a higher demand for smartphones and a boost in demand from Tier 2 cities. Amazon's India unit revealed plans to establish ten new warehouses in the nation in July 2020. Flipkart purchased a 140-acre plot of land in Manesar, Gurgaon, for INR 432 crore in October 2020 to scale its fulfilment infrastructure to meet increased demand post-COVID-19. The massive investment that the e-commerce sector is garnering demonstrates the huge potential of the Internet market (IBEF, 2021).

The number of individuals using the Internet was 560 million in 2018; this increased to 718.74 million in 2019, and it was anticipated that there will be 835 million people worldwide by 2023 (IBEF, 2020). The numbers clearly show that the number of Internet users in India is rising quickly.

- **Cybercrime reported in India:** According to the National Crime Record Bureau, the number of cybercrimes reported in India has increased over time from 27,248 (2018), to 44,735 (2019), to 50,035 (2020).

Furthermore, cybercrimes are gaining momentum along with the usage of the Internet. The total number of cybercrimes reported in 2018 was 27,248,

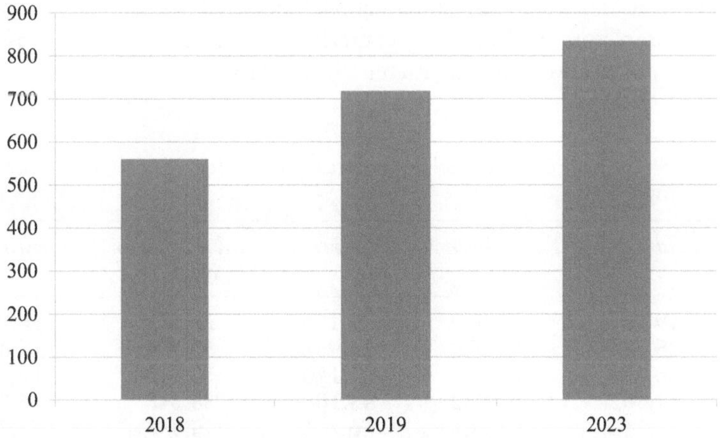

Figure 7.1 Internet users in India (in millions)

Source: Compiled by authors from India Brand Equity Foundation (2020)

which increased by 64% within a year and reached up to 50,035 complaints by 2020. Technology has successfully revolutionized the lifestyle of people all over the world. Similarly, it has changed the medium of crimes.

Phishing is one type of cybercrime in which an attacker attempts to steal some important information like passwords, credit card numbers, and other information impersonating authenticated organizations or officials. Table 7.1 reveals that phishing has increased over the years massively. The number of complaints registered in 8 years shot up many folds. In online business, there are cases of non-delivery of goods, and sometimes goods are delivered but not paid. Such cases were 81,029 in 2016 and 1,08,869 in 2020. However, the number slowed down to 50,523 by 2023; nevertheless, it still exists. Such cases affect online businesses and cause damage to consumers and organizations. Another big trouble faced by organizations is extortion in which online business operations of the target organization are disabled by attackers, and a large amount is demanded against confidential data. The number of such cases is increasing consistently in the United States. Personal data breaches result in illegal destruction, unintended loss, and unauthorized dissemination. Identity theft is another form of cybercrime where the personal information of an individual is stolen to commit fraud. Financial frauds with customers take place through this medium, and it causes loss of customers to organizations.

IC3 complaint statistics of 8 years: FBI (2020, 2023) records the pieces of evidence of a constant rise in complaints against cybercrime and losses occurring to online businesses.

In 2016, complaints filed against cybercrimes were 2,98,728, and losses to online businesses were approximately $1.5 billion.*
In 2017, complaints filed against cybercrimes were 3,01,580, and losses to online businesses were approximately $1.5 billion.*
In 2018, complaints filed against cybercrimes were 3,51,937, and losses to online businesses were approximately $2.7 billion.*

Table 7.1 IC3 (Internet crime complaint centre) complaint statistics (top 5 crime type comparisons)

Year	*Phishing*	*Non-delivery/ non-payment*	*Extortion*	*Breach of user information*	*Identity theft*
2016	19,465	81,029	17,146	27,573	16,878
2017	25,344	84,079	14,938	30,904	17,636
2018	26,379	65,116	51,146	50,642	16,128
2019	1,14,702	61,832	43,101	38,218	16,053
2020	2,41,342	1,08,869	76,741	45,330	43,330
2021	323,972	82,478	39,360	51,829	N/A
2022	300,497	51,679	39,416	58,859	N/A
2023	298,878	50,523	48,223	55,851	N/A

Source: Compiled by authors from Federal Bureau of Investigation (2020, 2023)

In 2019, complaints filed against cybercrimes were 4,67,361, and losses to online businesses were approximately $3.5 billion.*
In 2020, complaints filed against cybercrimes were 7,91,790, and losses to online businesses were approximately $4.2 billion.*
In 2021, complaints filed against cybercrimes were 847,376, and losses to online businesses were approximately $6.9 billion.
In 2022, complaints filed against cybercrimes were 800,944, and losses to online businesses were approximately $10.3 billion.
In 2023, complaints filed against cybercrimes were 880,418, and losses to online businesses were approximately $12.5 billion.

It has been observed that a constant increase in losses occurs with the increase in the number of complaints. Over the years, cybercrimes have been causing damage to online businesses. The ability of e-commerce to increase the GDP is threatened by these illicit activities.

Consumer Reactions after Experiencing a Security Breach

It is observed that after experiencing cyberattacks, 77% of consumers take steps to identify and use online services that promise an increased level of security, change their antivirus or security software, create new e-mail accounts, and delete existing ones, and 55% of consumers restrict their e-shopping and other online activities. Also, 34% of them close their shopping accounts and stop dealing with websites; 18% of victims of cybercrimes communicate the incidents in their social circle to warn them; 10% take legal action; and only 9% of consumers choose to take no action. It is perceptible from the consumer reactions that cybercrimes negatively change the consumer behaviour of online vendors (Deloitte, 2015).

Guidelines to Mitigate Cyberattacks

How to mitigate and prevent cybercrimes has always been a matter of concern for consumers and policymakers. Dedicated agencies to strengthen cybersecurity identify a few strategies to prevent cybercrimes.

- **National Cyber Security Centre (Ncsc.gov.uk)**

4.3.1 **Risk management approach**: Considering the risk that an organization is willing to take to achieve its objectives will help in managing the risk of cybersecurity.
4.3.2 **Participation and instruction**: People working in the organization should be trained to work online securely. An effort should be made to establish a cybersecurity culture.
4.3.3 **Asset monitoring**: You can lessen the risk of operating susceptible assets by properly planning for updates and replacements when you are aware when your systems will no longer be supported.

4.3.4 **Configuration and architecture**: Considering the security issues right from designing, building, maintaining, and managing devices and services rendered online.

4.3.5 **Risk administration**: Attackers take advantage of vulnerabilities as soon as they are disclosed. Thus, the organization should keep updating security systems to stay protected from cyberattacks.

4.3.6 **Access and identity management**: Companies must be cautious about whom to allow access to their systems and data.

4.3.7 **Data protection**: It comprises ensuring data security while it is in use, when it is at rest, and when it is no longer necessary (essentially destroying or sanitizing the storage medium after use).

4.3.8 **Recording and surveillance**: Systems should be designed in such a manner that they can detect and investigate suspicious acts or incidents.

4.3.9 **Issue resolution**: When an organization experiences cybercrime, it has to bear a huge loss in terms of finance, reputation, and cost.

4.3.10 **Distribution network protection**: Organizations do not produce the whole of the product themselves. To meet their objectives, they rely on suppliers. Cyberattacks on suppliers are equally damaging to dependent organizations. Involving partners and suppliers in *cyberattack response* exercises should be considered by organizations.

- **Cybersecurity and Infrastructure Security Agency (Cisa.gov)**

4.3.11 **Multifactor confirmation**: Some important accounts such as email accounts, online banking, and accounts with stored payment details and social media should be activated with multifactor authentication (MFA). MFA makes it difficult for cybercriminals to successfully commit cybercrime.

4.3.12 **Update your programme:** Keep updating laptops, mobiles, desktops, apps, programs, and smart devices to avoid cyber threats. Attackers take advantage of known weaknesses, and an updated version is free from any such weaknesses. Protect your account with MFA.

4.3.13 **Consider your option before clicking**: If any link appears familiar to the user, but at the same time the user is a little suspicious because it asks the user to change the password and share personal details for verification, the user needs to be alert in such situations because they become victims through such tactics.

4.3.14 **Use strong security code**: Names or dates as passwords are easy to crack; thus, passwords should consist of random numbers, characters, and signs to make them unique and lengthy.

- **Australian Cyber Security Centre (Cyber.gov.au)**

4.3.15 **Update your device to protect important information:** The use of updated software, updated applications, and advanced technology prevents the users from cybercriminals as the updated version is more secure and strengthened compared to the older version.

4.3.16 Protect your accounts with MFA: It is difficult to breach passcode using MFA.

4.3.17 Backup data regularly to the cloud or external hard drive: Cybercriminals often steal important data from the user's device and ask ransom amount to release data. Online and offline backup of data plays an important role against such crimes. Set secure passphrases: a passphrase is a string of words used to gain online access to accounts. In the case of non-availability of MFA, passphrase is the only solution. It picks some random words as passwords and then changes them into passphrases to make them lengthy, unpredictable, and unique. This process makes cybercrime more difficult.

- **Watch out for scams**: Cybercriminals use calls, messages, and emails to cause damage.

Pay attention to the following to mitigate scams:

- **Authority:** Does the message appear to be sent by an official?
- **Urgency**: Is the user time-bound to respond?
- **Emotion**: Is the message you received making you feel scared or anxious?
- **Scarcity**: Is the message making some tempting offers in a limited time?
- **Current events**: Is this message related to current news like the pandemic, COVID-19?

Discussion

The objective of this study was to build an insight into how cybercrime affects e-commerce and the possible measures to mitigate its negative consequences. After a thorough examination of the secondary data included in the study, it is clear that rising Internet usage has resulted in expanded e-commerce potential. Additionally, cybercrime is rapidly increasing due to weaknesses in online systems and services. The penetration of Internet services is faster than that of secure digital platforms. Cyberattacks on consumers and businesses are on the rise due to a lack of safe digital platforms. Following the analysis of the data, it is obvious that following a security breach, consumers' responses result in fewer online activities and increased trust difficulties, affecting online business. To counteract the cyber danger, secure infrastructure and online services must be developed. Additionally, raising awareness about cybercrime and taking steps to avoid becoming a victim can make a major difference. In the absence of cybercrime, e-commerce has enormous potential for significant expansion.

Conclusion and Policy Implication

Online shopping has a great deal of potential to boost the global economy and spread economic activity. However, rising cybercrime activity has a detrimental impact on customer trust in online shopping, which has an impact on digital commerce. We performed a descriptive analysis using data from credible agencies to confirm this association. Results confirmed that cybercrime has a detrimental impact on e-commerce. Policymakers are advised to implement awareness campaigns to increase user knowledge of online criminal activity so that users may recognize inappropriate Internet use. Additionally, manufacturers are urged to provide technology with the least amount of vulnerability to cyber threats. It is also advised to often upgrade the software being used.

References

Alghamdi, M. I. (2020). A descriptive study on the impact of cybercrime and possible measures to curtail its spread worldwide. *International Journal of Engineering Research Technology (IJERT)*, *09*(06).

Anshima, & Bhardwaj, B. (2023). Leveraging AI for the reinforcement of GHRM. In *AI and emotional intelligence for modern business management* (pp. 64–76). IGI Global.

Anshima, Bhardwaj, B., & Sharma, D. (2024). Artificial intelligence: Shifting the landscape of the human resources ecosystem. In *Leveraging AI and emotional intelligence in contemporary business organizations* (pp. 371–381). IGI Global.

Apau, R., Koranteng, F. N., & Gyamfi, S. A. (2019). Cyber-Crime and its effects on E-Commerce technologies. *Journal of Information*, *5*(1), 39–59. https://doi.org/10.18488/journal.104.2019.51.39.59

Bendovschi, A. (2015). Cyber-Attacks – Trends, patterns and security countermeasures. *Procedia Economics and Finance*, *28*, 24–31. https://doi.org/10.1016/s2212-5671(15)01077-1

Bhardwaj, B., Sharma, D., & Dhiman, M. C. (2023a). Artificial intelligence vs emotional intelligence: Unraveling the companionship and paradoxes. In *AI and emotional intelligence for modern business management* (pp. 1–13). IGI Global.

Bhardwaj, B., Sharma, D., & Dhiman, M. C. (2023b). *AI and emotional intelligence for modern business management*. IGI Global.

Chen, S. C., & Dhillon, G. S. (2003). Interpreting dimensions of consumer trust in E-commerce. *Information Technology and Management*, *4*(2), 303–318.

CISA. (2022, May 21). *Cybersecurity*. https://www.cisa.gov/4-things-you-can-do-keep-yourself-cyber-safe

Deloitte. (2015). *Consumer data under attack: The growing threat of cybercrime*. The Deloitte–UK–Consumer Review. Retrieved March 17, 2022, from https://www2.deloitte.com/content/dam/Deloitte/uk/Documents/consumer-business/deloitte-uk-consumer-review-nov-2015.pdf

FBI. (2020). *Internet crime report*. Retrieved March 30, 2022, from https://www.fbi.gov/news/press-releases/press-releases/fbi-releases-the-internet-crime-complaint-center-2020-internet-crime-report-including-covid-19-scam-statistics

FBI. (2023). *Internet crime report*. Retrieved March 19, 2024, from chrome-extension://bocbaocobfecmglnmeaeppambideimao/pdf/viewer.html?file=https%3A%2F%2Fwww.ic3.gov%2FMedia%2FPDF%2FAnnualReport%2F2023_IC3Report.pdf

Hallikainen, H., & Laukkanen, T. (2018). National culture and consumer trust in e-commerce. *International Journal of Information Management*, *38*(1), 97–106. https://doi.org/10.1016/j.ijinfomgt.2017.07.002

Hille, P., Walsh, G., & Cleveland, M. (2015). Consumer fear of online identity theft: Scale development and validation. *Journal of Interactive Marketing*, *30*, 1–19. https://doi.org/10.1016/j.intmar.2014.10.001

IBEF. (2020). *E-commerce*. Retrieved May 10, 2022, from https://www.ibef.org

IBEF. (2021). *E-commerce*. Retrieved May 10, 2022, from https://www.ibef.org

Interpol. (2020). *Cybercrime: COVID-19 impact*. Retrieved May 11, 2022, from https://www.google.com/search?q=july+2020+interpol+cybercrime+report&oq=july+2020+interpol+cybercrime+&aqs=chrome.1.69i57j33i160l4.16748j0j4&sourceid=chrome&ie=UTF-8

Jang-Jaccard, J., & Nepal, S. (2014). A survey of emerging threats in cybersecurity. *Journal of Computer and System Sciences*, *80*(5), 973–993. https://doi.org/10.1016/j.jcss.2014.02.005

Kshetri, N. (2017). Blockchain's roles in strengthening cybersecurity and protecting privacy. *Telecommunications Policy*, *41*(10), 1027–1038. https://doi.org/10.1016/j.telpol.2017.09.003

Kumar, A., & Debnath, N. (2018). Factors affecting mobile banking adoption behavior in northeastern states of India. *International Journal of Mechanical Engineering and Technology*, *9*(4), 479–483.

Le, N. T., & Hoang, D. B. (2016). Can maturity models support cyber security? *2016 IEEE 35th International Performance Computing and Communications Conference (IPCCC)*, 1–7. https://doi.org/10.1109/PCCC.2016.7820663

Lee, M. K., & Turban, E. (2001). A trust model for consumer Internet shopping. *International Journal of Electronic Commerce*, *6*(1), 75–91. https://doi.org/10.1080/10864415.2001.11044227

Martin, N., & Rice, J. (2011). Cybercrime: Understanding and addressing the concerns of stakeholders. *Computers and Security*, *30*(8), 803–814. https://doi.org/10.1016/j.cose.2011.07.003

NCRB. (2021). *Cyber-crimes*. https://ncrb.gov.in/en/cyber-crimes-statesuts

Nepomuceno, M. V., Laroche, M., & Richard, M. O. (2014). How to reduce perceived risk when buying online: The interactions between intangibility, product knowledge, brand familiarity, privacy and security concerns. *Journal of Retailing and Consumer Services*, *21*(4), 619–629. https://doi.org/10.1016/j.jretconser.2013.11.006

Park, J., Lee, D., & Ahn, J. (2004). Risk-focused e-commerce adoption model: A cross-country study. *Journal of Global Information Technology Management*, *7*(2), 6–30. https://doi.org/10.1080/1097198X.2004.10856370

Sharma, D., Bhardwaj, B., & Dhiman, M. C. (2024). *Leveraging AI and emotional intelligence in contemporary business organizations*. IGI Global. 10.4018/979-8-3693–1902–4

Teo, T. S., & Liu, J. (2007). Consumer trust in e-commerce in the United States, Singapore and China. *Omega*, *35*(1), 22–38. https://doi.org/10.1016/j.omega.2005.02.001

Vos, A., Marinagi, C., Trivellas, P., Eberhagen, N., Skourlas, C., & Giannakopoulos, G. (2014). Risk reduction strategies in online shopping: E-Trust perspective. *Procedia – Social and Behavioral Sciences*, *147*, 418–423. https://doi.org/10.1016/j.sbspro.2014.07.122

Wood, S. L. (2001). Remote purchase environments: The influence of return policy leniency on two-stage decision processes. *Journal of Marketing Research*, *38*(2), 157–169. https://doi.org/10.1509/jmkr.38.2.157.18847

Xu, N., Bai, S. Z., & Wan, X. (2017). Adding pay-on-delivery to pay-to-order: The value of two payment schemes to online sellers. *Electronic Commerce Research and Applications*, *21*, 27–37. https://doi.org/10.1016/j.elerap.2016.12.001

8 Application of Activity Theory in Technology Law

Manuj Darbari, Naseem Ahmed, and Abhishek Kumar Singh

Introduction

New technology with the use and support of artificial intelligence (AI) has grown tremendously. AI encompasses a collection of related techniques and decision-making, which includes machine learning (ML) applications in various Internet-trending activities. There are various marked and unmarked activities and domains in which AI tools are being used. Moreover, their classification is divided into two parts: weak AI and strong AI. Weak AI can perform only a specific task, while strong AI has human-level intelligence and can work in the autonomic mode. Most AI systems currently in use are limited to specific tasks and only possess intelligence in those areas. However, as technology advances, there is a growing interest in a new concept called "Artificial General Intelligence" (AGI), which aims to develop intelligence that can be applied across multiple fields. There are various debates on whether to provide artificial intelligence personhood or not. Till now only corporates are granted personhood. The research focuses on the utilization of such a model to enumerate the information compromise caused by whom and whose information was compromised. By combining aspects of privacy econometrics with the legal domain, the activity theory (AT) model helps fortify the connection between social context and technological application.

AI Categorization in Current Scurvies

Big data supports the porosity of AI to the next level of information processing, and both data and AI are intermingled. Artificial intelligence (AI) is commonly employed to analyze data for government e-governance initiatives, such as the processing of Aadhaar data. Additionally, AI is used to handle the vast amounts of data generated by the Internet of Things (IoT) in various sectors, including online shopping, public health systems, and online public platforms. AI algorithms are capable of automatically filtering out private information to ensure privacy. AI is closely associated with machine learning, which is a computer science application (Grodzinsky, 2011; Grodzinsky et al.,

DOI: 10.4324/9781003517290-11

2011; Koops, 2007; Ubena, 2008). There are several companies and financial institutions that are exclusively using customer data to predict their future customer purchases, thereby challenging the issue of privacy. Deep learning is a subpart of ML that exploits neural networks, that is, using multi-large architecture, which works as a Black Box. It is an extremely powerful tool that can interconnect complex databases to provide necessary inferences. The faster and multiple-layer processing has been extensively used for predicting future behaviour and prospective clientage by companies. Even Alexa and Google Home take commands based on what we say to them for searches. The above-mentioned emerging technologies extensively use human interface, which means there are chances of misuse of technology. The absence of legislation, specifically the (I.T. Act-2000), for this technology is still in a state of uncertainty. There is a need for a well-defined implementation of legal rules and regulatory systems that align with the existing legal framework legal system.

AI Characterization in Terms of Law

The general characterization of AI is Tort, where various types of liabilities are classified as vicarious and strict liability, but the AI generally cannot be held liable as it is not a legal person. There could be a situation in which AI could be held for breach of duty where AI application accidentally shares highly confidential information of some set of customers to a public domain. The owner of the dataset will be held to strict liability for the damage caused due to the loss of information. Artificial Intelligence (AI) is currently regarded as a significant concept in today's context, particularly with the presence of advanced electric vehicles equipped with cutting-edge technology and smart interfaces. This progress is leading to the development of humanoid robots, which will pose challenges in terms of legal regulations.

Literature Review of Technology Law, Usage, and Policy Implication

In his initial work, Vincent (2017) extensively debated about the issue of citizenship to robots. The authors are motivated by the work of Kemp (2018) which highlights the legal aspect of AI usage. Vincent also broadly classified the information privacy law which circumvents The Personal Data Protection Act of 2014 discusses the Organization for Economic Cooperation and Development's regulations and approaches on the protection of privacy and the transfer of data across borders (Brownsword, 2011; Burk, 2002; Koops, 2006). OECD guidelines (2024) are way exhaustive relating to privacy legislation around the world. The UK Information Commissioner Office (ICO) manual on big data, AI, ML, and data protection also sets various guidelines on data breaches.

Proposed Dustman Model of Impact of AI in the Law Domain

The study proposes the amalgamation of AI technologies and law. The cognitive side of AI is analysed in this study along with the concept of AT.

Artificial intelligence (AI) has significantly benefited both individuals and corporations by boosting their commercial value. However, it is important to acknowledge that AI also carries several inherent hazards. To associate the risk of AI and law, we used the concept of AT as the main domain to analyse the real problem and ways to overcome it.

Concept of AT

AT identifies the concept model elements and relates them together. Basically, it maps the relationship among each element of a human activity model.

It consists of the following submissions:

- **Subject:** It is the individual subgroups selected for the study.
- **Tools:** These are the methods used.
- **Community:** It refers to individual subgroups with the same synergy.
- **Divisions of Labour:** Task segregation based on individual groups formed.
- **Rules:** The guidelines for interaction among subjects, object, and tools.
- **Object:** The medium on which the activity is being performed.

Basic Structure of AT Framework

The basic structure of the AT model consists of the following main components: tools, subject, and object. An activity is composed of a subject and an object connected by a tool, and the basic meditational triangle from cultural-historical psychological tools are both physical/technical tools and

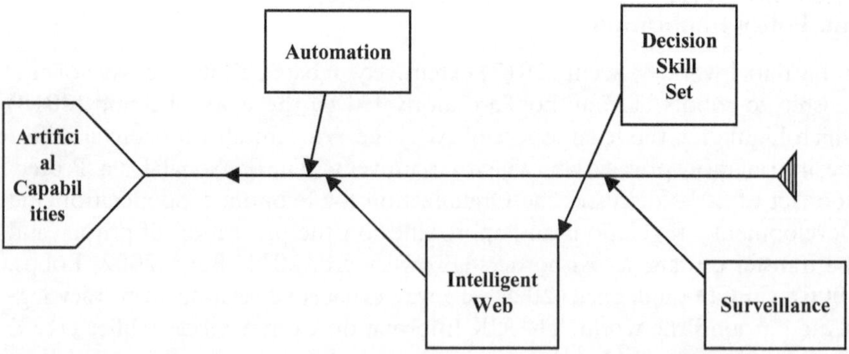

Figure 8.1 AI capabilities

Source: Author

psychological/mental tools as described by Vygotsky. The model, as proposed by Leontiev, a sociologist who studied human dynamics, combines fundamental components.

Engestrom developed an improved model that aimed to achieve a perfect correlation between different artifacts. We have analysed this model for a problem domain of AI tools and law by commentary the as shown in Table 8.1.

Table 8.1 shows the link between various artifacts of AT notations and the legal terminology, which is suitable when we are deriving the relationship between AI and law. The primary challenge lies in identifying the precise area where we are deficient, and the utilization of AI has been given preference over the personal lives of users. In order to determine the underlying factors that contribute to the change in information utilization resulting from the employment of Artificial Intelligence as a tool, we utilize a base connection Notational Diagram (fig 2). This diagram provides a clear depiction of how the information is processed and identifies any necessary corrective measures.

From the above figure, we analyse that there exists a direct relationship between the activity (usage) of AI technology and other factors in the Engstrom triangle.

Based on the vulnerability level, existing law needs to be the main force: the higher the latest technology and ease of use, the higher the lack of awareness of the user to safeguard it, leading to a breach. A conflict resolution of breach of data or collection of personal information by tools/community achieved by the Division of Labour to remodify the object in the problem space is achieved by rules (existing laws). Finally, a vulnerability model is created using the OECD guidelines.

Let: LC = Level of conflict/total of information gathered using AI

DI = Number of dissenting issues/total number of issues

DI is supposed to be in proportional relationship to LC if the conflict strength (CS) is a region in which two sets of numerical variables $LC = [LC_1, LC_2, ... LC_n]$ and $DI = \{DI = \{DI_1, DI_2, ... DI_n]$.

Table 8.1 Conversion of activity theory into legal terminology

S. No.	*AT notation*	*Developed terminology*
1.	Subject	Plaintiff/defendant
2.	Community	Organization utilizing AI
3.	Tools	AI-based systems
4.	Object	AI capability
5.	Rules	Law as defined
6.	Division of labour	Decomposition
7.	Outcome	Technology-based crime

Source: Author own Compilation

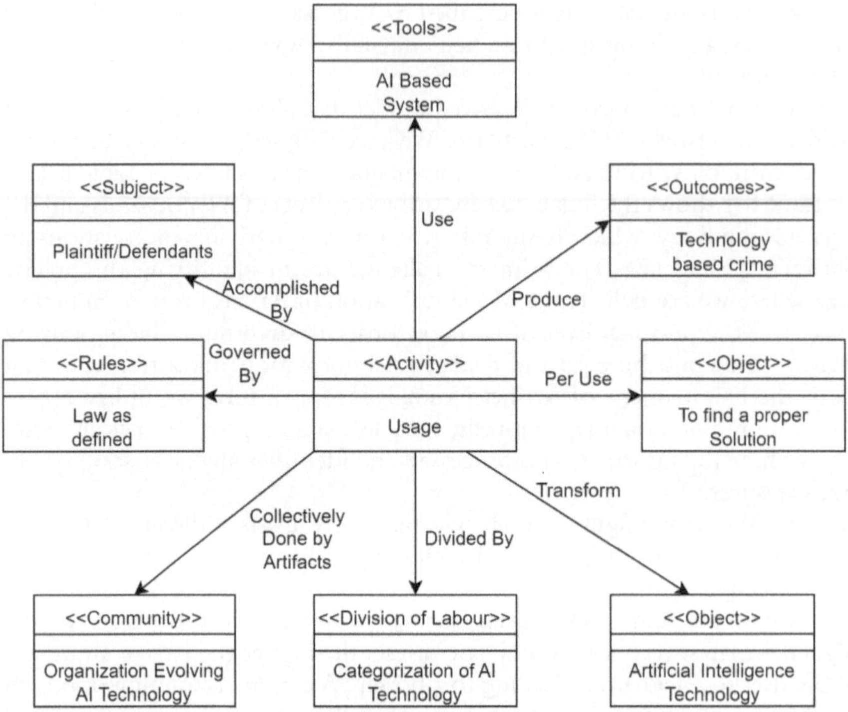

Figure 8.2 Conversion of AT principles in crimes possible through AI usage
Source: Adopted from Author

The total conflicts of the information gathered and dissenting issues relating to law enforcement are given as:

$$\textbf{Conflict Strength} = \mu\ (\textbf{LC} + \textbf{DI}),$$

where is the probability of occurrence of events LC and DI.

Finally, we get the dissenting issues, which has a subset developed earlier as a function AT domain, which is given as

$$\mathbf{f\,(DI)} = \left\{ \begin{array}{l} \textbf{Tools, Subject, Rule, community,} \\ \textbf{Division of Labor, Object} \end{array} \right\}$$

The above relation can be significantly confirmed by enforcement genies and then by mitigating the risk of information breach using high-end technologies.

Conclusion

We are living in a digital world where technology has certainly made our life easier, but at the same time it has changed the face of information privacy. With more and more advancement in technologies, we must think of various means to regulate them. A few mediation models need to be developed that will finally answer the privacy questions raised using high-end technologies. The study highlights the use of such a model to enumerate the compromise of information by whom and whose information is compromised. The AT model strengthens the social setting and technology usage linkage by developing some privacy econometrics with the legal domain. In the current social setting, the government must play a very social role in developing confidence among the end-user and service provider for a safe and fair environment.

The words from AT are converted into legal taxonomy using Engestrom's triangle, which assists in determining the precise characterization of the employment of technology and its interaction in a social situation. Based on the information presented above, a model has been constructed that illustrates the perfect correlation between trust, which can be broken using advanced technologies, and the law that is tied to it, as well as the power of law to break that law. The correlation matrix between AI and the efficiency of law enforcement is established by this research.

Based on the vulnerability level, the existing law needs to be the major force. The more advanced the technology and the simpler it is to operate, the greater the likelihood that the user will not be aware of how to protect it, which can result in a breach. A conflict resolution of breach of data or collecting of personal information by tools/community achieved by the division of labour to alter the object in a problem space is achieved by rules (existing laws), and finally a vulnerability model is created using the OECD guidelines. The study establishes the relationship between dissenting issues, as a subset developed of tools, subject, rule, community, division of labour, and object.

References

Brownsword, R. (2011). Lost in translation: Legality, regulatory margins, and technological management. *Berkeley Technology Law Journal*, *26*, 1321.

Burk, D. L. (2002). Lex genetica: The law and ethics of programming biological code. *Ethics and Information Technology*, *4*(2), 109–121.

Grodzinsky, A. J. (2011). *Fields, forces, and flows in biological systems* (1st ed.). Garland Science. https://doi.org/10.1201/9780429258749

Grodzinsky, F. S., Miller, K. W., & Wolf, M. J. (2011). Developing artificial agents worthy of trust: "Would you buy a used car from this artificial agent?". *Ethics and information Technology*, *13*(1), 17–27.

Hon'ble Dr. Justice A. R. Lakshmanan Chairman, Law Commission of India (2009, August). *Reforms in Indic any – Some suggestions.* Law Commission of India (Report No. 230).

I.T. Act. (2000). Retrieved November 23, 2021, from https://www.indiacode.nic.in/bitstream/123456789/13116/1/it_act_2000_updated.pdf

Kemp, R. (2018). *Legal aspects of artificial intelligence* (v2. 0). Published in Kemp IT Law.

Koops, B. J. (2006). Should ICT regulation be technology-neutral? In B.-J. Koops, M. Lips, C. Prins, & M. Schellekens (Eds.), *Starting points for ICT regulation. Deconstructing prevalent policy one-liners, it & law series* (Vol. 9, pp. 77–108). TMC Asser Press.

Koops, B. J. (2007). *Criteria for normative technology: An essay on the acceptability of 'Code as Law' in light of democratic and constitutional values.* Tilburg University Legal Studies (No. 007, p. 2007). Working Paper.

OECD guidelines. (2024). *Recommendation of the Council on Digital Security Risk Management.* Retrieved June 16, 2024, from https://legalinstruments.oecd.org/en/instruments/OECD-LEGAL-0479

Ubena, J. (2008). Legislative techniques and ICT: In the wake of law keeping pace with technology. *National Research Institute of Legal Policy Research Communications, 105*, 171.

Vincent, J. (2017). Giving robots 'Personhood' is about making corporations accountable. *The Verge.*

9 Reporting Cybercrime

A Bird's Eye View of the Procedural Framework

Sandeep Mishra, Pradeep Kumar Singh, and Jai Shankar Ojha

Introduction

The world has been progressing since its inception. The 21st century witnessed development on the technological front. The Internet was born in 1983, and the 21st century is facing its implications (*A Brief History of the Internet*, n.d.). Implications of the Internet are good and evil in terms of usage. The Internet can be used to connect with an estranged loved one and also to bully a person. The Internet has solved various problems but has also introduced new ones. Cybercrime is one such problem. Talking about the good implications of the digital era, social media is one thing that has shrunk the world to computer screens. You can connect with anyone through your machine and the Internet. As everything good has some bad, social media also has it. Social media contributes to spreading false news, luring users into clickbait, cyber-bullying, manufacturing consent through ads, and tracking user behaviour along with other physical and mental issues such as addiction, fear of missing out (FOMO), increased screen time, and self-image issues. The Internet era can be called "*globalization after globalization*" because it has opened the possibility to travel virtually, trade virtually, and much more. But the exposure to the Internet has also put our not-so-tech-educated population at greater risk of cyberspace crimes. Cyberspace crimes are the crimes committed through the combined use of the Internet and computer or mobile, e.g. phishing, spamming, spoofing, cyber-bullying, pornography, breach of privacy, identity theft, cyberterrorism, cyber-extortion, online gambling, cyberstalking, hacking, abusing computer resource, and data theft. Ransomware and distributed denial-of-service (DDoS) attacks are new cyberspace crimes that have caused people a fortune in money (Parker, 1978)

This chapter will help you understand the concept of cybercrime, the classification of cybercrimes, and the procedure for reporting cybercrime. The chapter also suggests standards to improve the reporting method of cybercrimes.

DOI: 10.4324/9781003517290-12

Cybercrime

Indian law does not describe cybercrime explicitly. Although the Information Technology Act 2000 (IT Act 2000) defines various cybercrimes such as tampering with computer source code documents, computer-related offences, identity theft, and cyberterrorism, it does not define cybercrime.

The first cybercrime law of South Africa, that is Electronic Communications and Transactions Amendment Bill 2012, defines cybercrime as follows: *"cybercrime" means any criminal or other offence that is facilitated by or involves the use of electronic communications or information systems, including any device or the Internet or any one or more of them.*

Professor S.T. Viswanathan has given three definitions in his book *The Indian Cyber Laws with Cyber Glossary*:

1) Any illegal action in which a computer is the tool or object of the crime, that is any crime, the means or purpose of which is to influence the function of a computer.
2) Any incident associated with computer technology in which a victim suffered or could have suffered loss and a perpetrator, by intention, made or could have made a gain.
3) Computer abuse is considered as any illegal, unethical, or unauthorized behaviour relating to the automatic processing and transmission of data (Viswanathan & Naidu, 2001).

Typology of Cybercrime

The use of Internet evolves as a new dimension of information that is known as infotainment, where we can use the Internet as a source of entertainment, and at the same time we can learn and gather information from the same source. Due to the increasing technology and ease of services, about 800 million people use the Internet in India. But, very less of them are aware about the careful use of services, and a large number of people are victims of crime in the virtual world. In the virtual world, we can categorize some cybercrimes as–

1) Cybercrime against computer resources
2) Cybercrime against individuals
3) Socio-economic cybercrimes

1) **Cybercrime against Computer Resources:** Targeting computer resources was the first-ever cybercrime committed in the history of humankind. Computer resources include all hardware and software of the machine, including data. If a perpetrator tampers with any hardware or software and renders it malfunctioning, such an act is considered a cybercrime. These can be further classified as (i) tampering with computer resources, (ii) data theft, (iii) cybercrimes relating to intellectual property rights (IPRs), and (iv) piracy. Examples of such crimes include hacking, data theft, data breach, software piracy, and violation of IPRs (Rao, 2004).

2) **Cybercrime against Individual:** This category of cybercrimes is similar to traditional crimes and more or less can be classified similarly, such as

    a. **Offence against the reputation of an individual:** For example cyber-defamation, identity theft, personation, and posting obscene material
    b. **Offence against women:** For example cyber-stalking, pornography, posting obscene material, prostitution, and sexual harassment
    c. **Offence against an individual's property:** For example cyber-vandalism, cybersquatting, piracy, IPR violation, salami attacks, phishing, embezzlement, DDoS attack, ransomware, and credit and debit card fraud (Fatima, 2016)
    d. **Offence against mental health:** For example cyber-bullying, harassment, child pornography, drug trafficking, account hacking, and online trolling
    e. **Cyber-extortion:** Generally, cyber-extortion is defined as threatening to disable any service or compromise the security of a computer resource and thereby asking for money for abstaining from doing such an act. But the ambit of cyber-extortion is quite vast. Surprisingly, our legislature had not even thought about it. Unknowingly we all have been a part of cyber-extortion. I hope all of us had put up a display picture supporting a cause or posted a status with hashtags. We tend to form opinions before verdicts of honourable Supreme and High Courts and express them through social media, which is like media trials and should be considered extortion.

3) **Socio-economic Cybercrime:** For example cyber corporate espionage, embezzlement, fraud, and cheating
4) **Offence against State:** For example cyberterrorism, cyber espionage, and cyber lobbying

Reporting of Cybercrime: Existing Legal Framework

According to the social contract theory of state origin, the state came into being by a contract between individuals and society. Through one contract, the individuals pledge to obey the orders of the state (*Pactum Subjectionis*); in turn, the state must protect its subjects (*Pactum Unionis*). Therefore, the state has a duty to protect its subjects from any type of crime (Sasan, 2021).

In a country like India, which is the second-most populous country, the state cannot provide a watchdog to every citizen. Therefore, reporting crime by the citizen becomes a vital step and a necessity to curb crime. Reporting of crime sets the criminal machinery in motion, and as soon as the authorities respond to a crime, it becomes easier to bring it to justice.

According to the study "Non-Registration of Crimes: Problems and Solutions" conducted by the Tata Institute of Social Sciences (TISS), Mumbai, almost 75% of crimes are not reported because people are unhappy with the behaviour of the police and how they treat a complainant. The study claims that the police are reluctant to file first information report (FIR) due to political influence (Chauhan, 2017). Traditional crimes are usually reported at the police station, and each state has developed an online mechanism to file e-FIR. Before devolving into how to report a cybercrime, let us discuss the need to report a cybercrime.

Need to Report Cybercrime

People these days are reluctant to report crimes. The reasons are discussed above. There can be many other reasons, such as social stigma, retaliation from criminals, belief that authorities are not competent, and procedural hindrances. The same is the case with cybercrimes. The main reason for the non-reporting of cybercrimes is the lack of awareness. People don't want to report cybercrimes because they feel it is inevitable and the loss done cannot be recovered. They might be valid to some extent, but they should report cybercrimes for the following reasons:

1) **To provide input:** Reporting a cybercrime can help authorities understand the nature and ways used by the criminal. These inputs can help the authorities develop standard operating procedures (SOPs) to deal with cybercrimes.
2) **To ensure other people are aware:** When one reports a cybercrime and authorities have dealt with it, it can be developed into a case study. Such case studies can help people be aware of cybercrimes and ways to prevent them.
3) **To strengthen the cybercrime reporting mechanism:** Cyberspace crimes are a novel addition to criminology. In addition to this, cybercriminals can devise new ways to commit cybercrimes. Such dynamic crimes need an active approach. Hence, more cases mean more ways to curb crime.
4) **To deter criminals**: Criminals don't indulge in crime because the punishment has set a deter. Cybercriminals think they are privileged, and due to the anonymity of place and identity, no one can trace them, which is true to some extent. Non-reporting of cybercrimes adds the cherry on top. As soon as they are caught and are punished, it creates fear in the minds of criminals. The deter cannot be established without the first step of reporting a crime.
5) **The only solution:** Cybercrime does not have the element of the traditional crime concerning the relationship between the criminal and the victim because both are distant, facing their respective screens. In comparison, traditional crimes occur in a physical medium and are easily detectable by the public and the police to a certain extent. That is not the case with cybercrimes. Cybercrime is detected by authorities only when the victim reports it. This is the grey area in the field of the cybercrime justice system.

Existing Legal Framework to Report Crime

Under the Code of Criminal Procedure, 1973, offences are divided into two categories: cognizable offences and non-cognizable offences. Cognizable offence is defined under Section 2(c) of the Code, which states that ". . . *in which a police officer may, in accordance with the First Schedule or under any law for the time being in force, arrest without warrant*". Non-cognizable offence is defined under Section 2(l) of the Code as offence ". . . *in which, a police officer has no authority to arrest without warrant*".

Cognizable offences are to be reported in accordance with the provision provided under Section 154.[1] An informant can approach the officer in charge of a police station with a written complaint or can inform the officer orally. Oral information must be reduced to writing by such officer and read over to the informant. Each information, whether given in writing or reduced in writing by an officer, must be signed by the person giving it and entered into a book. One thing must be noted here: if the information involves an offence committed against a woman and the informant is the woman victim, then such information must be recorded by a female police officer. This clause was inserted as a result to the judgement of the Christian Welfare Society.[2] If a police officer refuses to record information, then the aggrieved person can approach the superintendent of police (commonly known as SP), and he can cause to record the information and depute an investigating officer to investigate the matter. The information recorded under Section 154 of the Code is commonly known as the First Information Report or FIR.

Section 155[3] provides that non-cognizable offences can be reported in the same way, but as the definition under Section 2(l) provides, such offences cannot be investigated except by an order by the court.

Another way of reporting a crime is provided under Section 190(1)(a),[4] which states that the court can take cognizance of a case upon receiving a complaint of facts that constitute offence. These cases are called complaint cases and are dealt accordingly under the Code.

There is also a mechanism to file an e-FIR through State Police Application and website.

The Supreme Court in the case of *Lalita Kumari*[5] gave various guidelines regarding registration of FIR. The Constitution Bench headed by P. Sathasivam gave eight guidelines, which are as follows:

1) Registration of FIR is mandatory under Section 154[6] if the information discloses commission of a cognizable offence, and no preliminary inquiry is permissible in such a situation.
2) If the information received does not disclose a cognizable offence but indicates the necessity for an inquiry, a preliminary inquiry may be conducted only to ascertain whether cognizable offence is disclosed or not.
3) If the inquiry discloses the commission of a cognizable offence, the FIR must be registered. In cases where the preliminary inquiry ends in closing the complaint, a copy of the entry of such closure must be supplied to the first informant forthwith and not later than 1 week. It must disclose reasons in brief for closing the complaint and not proceeding further.
4) The police officer cannot avoid his duty of registering offence if cognizable offence is disclosed. Action must be taken against erring officers who do

not register the FIR if information received by him discloses a cognizable offence.

5) The scope of preliminary inquiry is not to verify the veracity or otherwise of the information received but only to ascertain whether the information reveals any cognizable offence.
6) As to what type and in which cases preliminary inquiry is to be conducted will depend on the facts and circumstances of each case. The category of cases in which preliminary inquiry may be made are as under:

    a) Matrimonial disputes/family disputes
    b) Commercial offences
    c) Medical negligence cases
    d) Corruption cases
    e) Cases where there is abnormal delay/laches in initiating criminal prosecution, for example, over 3 months of delay in reporting the matter without satisfactorily explaining the reasons for delay.
    The aforesaid are only illustrations and not exhaustive of all conditions that may warrant a preliminary inquiry.

7) While ensuring and protecting the rights of the accused and the complainant, a preliminary inquiry should be made time bound, and in any case, it should not exceed 7 days. The fact of such delay and the causes of it must be reflected in the General Diary entry.
8) Since the General Diary/Station Diary/Daily Diary is the record of all information received in a police station, we direct that all information relating to cognizable offences, whether resulting in registration of an FIR or leading to an inquiry, must be mandatorily and meticulously reflected in the said Diary, and the decision to conduct a preliminary inquiry must also be reflected, as mentioned above.

Most of the cybercrimes are governed by the IT Act, which is a special Act. Section 5[7] provides that if a procedure is provided under any other law, then that procedure must be followed instead of the Code of Criminal Procedure. Although the IT Act does not provide any specific procedure to report cybercrime, the government of India has developed a portal to report the same.

Procedure to Report Cybercrime

A victim can register his complaint to (i) the Online Cybercrime Portal, (ii) helpline number(s), (iii) the nearest police station, and (iv) cybercrime police station. A complete procedure along with flowcharts is discussed below.

i. Report to the Online Cybercrime Portal

The government has developed a mechanism to report cybercrime. The Ministry of Home Affairs has a dedicated website to register complaints online: *www.cybercrime.gov.in*.

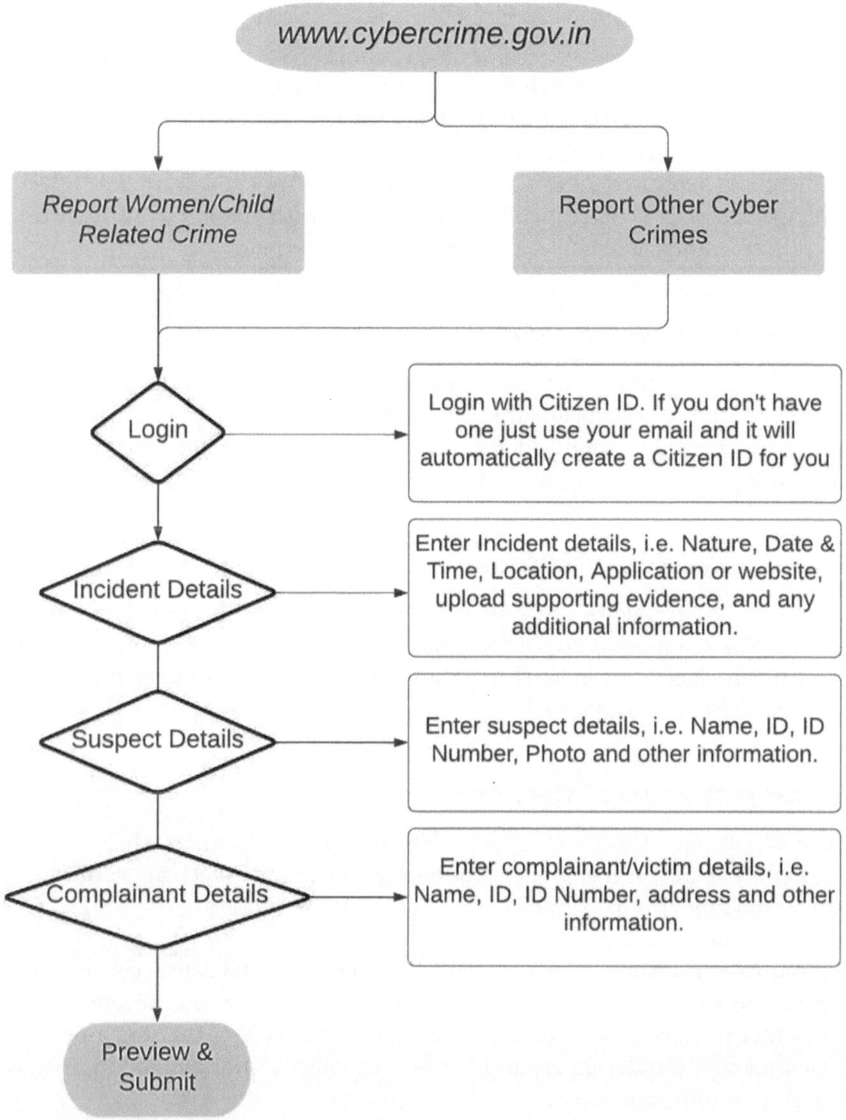

Figure 9.1 Flowchart of crime reporting procedure through the portal

Source: Authors have created the chart themselves

There are two options to file a cybercrime complaint: "*REPORT WOMEN/ CHILD RELATED CRIME*" and "*REPORT OTHER CYBERCRIME*". Women- and child-related crimes include online harassment. Cyber offences related to women can also be reported anonymously. Here is a flowchart with easy steps to file a complaint through the portal.

ii. Report to Helpline Numbers/Call Centre

Another way to report cybercrime is to report it to the helpline numbers. There are two dedicated helplines to report women-related offences: 181 and 1090. The difference is that 1090 has police personnel dealing with calls, whereas at 181, there are private counsellors.

There is a dedicated 24x7 toll-free number, that is 1930 (earlier 155260), to report financial cybercrime. This is launched with the intent of reporting cybercrime immediately in cases involving financial fraud.

iii. Report at a Nearby Police Station

Not tech-friendly victims can also report cybercrime to their nearest police station. The victim or complainant should provide a complete statement of facts along with the supporting evidence. The complaint is like any other ordinary police complaint.

iv. Report to Cybercrime Police Station

There is a cybercrime police station in every range of the respective police division. For example there are 18 zones in Uttar Pradesh. Only a cybercrime involving an amount of more than INR 1 lakh is to be reported to the respective cybercrime police station.

Lacunae in Reporting Cybercrime

There is nothing perfect – everything has some innate lacunae, which renders it less effective and at maximum impotent. Similarly, the mechanism of cybercrime reporting also has some lacunae, which are as follows:

1) **No uniform system:** There is no uniform system for reporting cybercrimes, for example, if a cybercrime or fraud happens. The victim is puzzled about whether to report to the local police or the cyber cell, or call someone. The victim keeps wandering around banks and police authorities and ultimately becomes more aggrieved.
2) **Unawareness about the cybercrime reporting mechanism:** The data collected during the doctoral research of Sandeep reveals that 95% of people believe that police is the right authority to report cybercrime, and 97% of the people were not aware of the whereabouts of the nearest cyber cell. These data show that people are unaware of the complaint authority.
3) **Insufficient police personnel:** The district cyber cell is constituted of two police officers of constable rank who function under subordination of the in-charge of the cyber cell who is of inspector rank. The whole district cyber cell is usually situated in the command house, that is the official residence of the SP. The SP has the command of the whole police force of the district

and, therefore, is busy. That leaves it to the in-charge and constables of the cyber cell. Constables are usually not well-educated persons. All knowledge they have is through their training, which is also not enough suited to the conditions. Although the in-charge is qualified enough, he/she cannot become a lone ranger to curb cybercrime.

4) **Unqualified police personnel:** Although they have received formal training, the police personnel are generally underqualified than the criminals. Criminals are usually IIT graduates or highly qualified.
5) **Jurisdiction issues:** Sometimes there are circumstances in which the police are confused about the jurisdiction, and there is a delay, which gives ample amount of time to the offender to escape.
6) **Unwillingness of the police to register an FIR:** The police are not willing to register a cybercrime case due to the hardships in the investigation.
7) **Lack of awareness among people:** The data collected by researchers also reveals that people do not have knowledge of many crimes, so they don't treat the offenders as criminals; they don't feel it necessary to report them.

Conclusion and Suggestions

Today almost 90% of the cybercrimes go unreported. The criminals think they are invincible and can keep committing such acts. The main contention here is people are not aware of cybercrimes as to which act is a crime and which is not. Anything that does not feel right is cybercrime and should be reported accordingly. People, especially the female population, are reluctant to file a complaint. The suspected fear is true to some extent. Although the police take the necessary precautions, somehow the information is leaked, which discloses the whole scenario along with the personal information of the victim, which leads to further hardship for the victim. Here, the responsibility is on us and the media houses that we avoid sharing such content which involves victims' personal information.

So far, we have discussed cybercrime and its classifications, the whole procedure of reporting cybercrime, and the shortcomings of the mechanism. Before concluding the chapter, here are some suggestions that can be adopted to strengthen the cybercrime reporting mechanism.

1) An ordinary person does not know about the cyber cell and where it is situated. A police circular proposing three wings of the cyber police/cyber team has been proposed. One is at the zone level as zonal cybercrime cell (ZCC), the second is at the district level as district cyber cell (DCC), and the third is in every police station as cybercrime team (CCT) (Director General of Police, U.P. – C. O. – 12/2020). But it is ironic that there is only one cyber cell in each district that has been working at the district level, which makes it tough to report cybercrime. One cyber cell in every police station should be established to prevent and control cybercrime. Easily reachable cyber police is an excellent attempt to report crimes, and undoubtedly, that will help.

2) People are not aware of all forms of cybercrime; they are not willing to register such violations. They think a fake SMS or call is petty and do not report it, which later turns fatal. Most people are not unaware of the mechanism and appropriate authority for reporting cybercrime.
3) There is no mandatory requirement to register an FIR in cases of cybercrimes. However, in traditional crimes, there is a mandate that an FIR must be registered, as observed by the Supreme Court in the *Lalita Kumari* case.
4) Time is of the essence in controlling cybercrime. If the perpetrator gets enough time to erase the footprint, the police will never be able to catch him. So there must be attempts made to minimize the delay. The SOP to curb cybercrimes should be tested and be foolproof. The government should establish a cyber branch or cyber cell in each police station. The cyber cell is endowed with the mandatory duty to register an FIR and get in touch with the concerned bodies, such as banks, to take action at their level. Then a reference should be made to the cyber cell, which should proceed further on the technological level.

In a populated country like India, mishaps are bound to happen, but through a joint effort, we can make cyberspace safer and free from crime. Let's do it . . .

"Failure to report may prove fatal."

Notes

1 Section 154 of the Code of Criminal Procedure, 1973.
2 *Christian Welfare Society v State of Maharashtra* (2004) AIR SC 7.
3 Section 155 of the Code of Criminal Procedure, 1973.
4 Section 190(1)(a) of the Code of Criminal Procedure, 1973.
5 Para 111 of the *Lalita Kumari v Government of Uttar Pradesh & Others* (2014) 2 SCC 1.
6 Section 154 of the Code of Criminal Procedure, 1973.
7 Section 5 of the Code of Criminal Procedure, 1973.

References

A Brief History of the Internet. (n.d.). Retrieved June 23, 2023, from https://www.usg.edu/galileo/skills/unit07/internet07_02.phtml.
Chauhan, N. (2017, November 8). 75% of people do not report crimes as cops are unfriendly. *The Times of India*. https://timesofindia.indiatimes.com/india/75-of-people-do-not-report-crimes-as-cops-are-unfriendly/articleshow/61569006.cms
Christian Welfare Society v State of Maharashtra (2004) AIR SC 7.
Director General of Police, Uttar Pradesh – Circular Order- 12/2020 data gathered through Right to Information Act, 2005. vide application dated August 20, 2021.
Fatima, T. (2016, January 1). *Cyber crimes* (2nd ed.). Eastern Book Company.
Parker, D. B. (1978, March 1). *Crime by computer* (1st ed.). Scribner Paper Fiction.
Rao, S. V. (2004). *Law of cyber crimes & information technology law*. Wadhwa and Company.

Sasan, J. M. V. (2021, July 1). The social contract theories of Thomas Hobbes and John Locke: comparative analysis. *Shanlax International Journal of Arts, Science and Humanities*, *9*(1), 34–45. https://doi.org/10.34293/sijash.v9i1.4042
Viswanathan, S. T., & Naidu, N. C. (2001, January 1). *The Indian cyber laws with cyber glossary*. Bharat Law House.

Part 4

Cryptocurrency and Cybersecurity

10 The Intersection of Cryptocurrency and Cybersecurity

Challenges and Opportunities

Garima Kohli and Saloni Devi

Introduction

Blockchain is the latest advancement in digital technology. It is a decentralized, indirect, safe-keeping structure that licenses the expansion of innovative alphanumeric stages and facilities through this emerging expertise. Blockchain skill is thoughtful of a spread-out distributed ledger technology (DLT). It is a pool of chunks, where each chunk brings a batch along with period engraved cardinal statistics, which is the sole identifier. Instead of relying on a single centralized authority to maintain the authoritative record, the Blockchain allows all participating parties to maintain their own copy of the distributed and replicated archive. The notion added a portion of courtesy as soon as it remained castoff for the cryptocurrency Bitcoin in 2009. Blockchain, unlike belongings, has the aptitude to suggestively support the investment sector. This blockchain offers a high level of security by preventing fraudsters from conducting transactions more than once. The blockchain know-how espoused in expanding cryptocurrency has shocked the financial segment, administration, investors, shareholders, and all associated with it. The rapid increase in the popularity of cryptocurrencies, starting with the introduction of Bitcoin in 2009, has greatly impacted the market. In the current situation, cryptocurrency is reflected as impending coinage that can swap the existing paper money across the globe. Cryptocurrency is an arithmetical or automatic technology or Internet legal tender that helps cryptography for safety. Cryptocurrency has generated unparalleled variations in the fiscal economy, showing together confident and adverse offerings. The concept of cryptocurrencies may be difficult to grasp, but it is easy to use. Cryptocurrency transactions have minimal to no transaction costs, in contrast to the fees associated with transferring funds from a digital wallet to a bank account. You can make transactions at any time, and there are no limits on purchases and withdrawals. Anyone is free to use cryptocurrency, unlike setting up a bank account, which requires documentation and other paperwork. International cryptocurrency transactions are faster than wire transfers too. Wire transfers take about half a day for the money to be moved from one place to another. With cryptocurrencies, transactions take only a matter of minutes or even seconds.

DOI: 10.4324/9781003517290-14

Furthermore, cryptocurrencies are also blockchain technology as they have topographies that include protection, decentralization, and no prerequisite of the third revelry. Bitcoin was created in the wake of the 2008 worldwide economic crunch to activate external financial institutions, governments, and central banks. Most of the cryptocurrencies were conventional, and the most eminent and popular was Bitcoin, which has created blockchain technology (Ghosh et al., 2020).

Bitcoin was produced in 2009 as open-source software. With blockchain know-how, Bitcoin permits handlers to mark transparent connected dealings. Every customer can see these communications; however, they are fortified over the procedure inside the blockchain. Although the whole world can perceive the matter, only the Bitcoin holder can decode it with its key that is agreed to by each proprietor. Distinct from a financial institution, there is no fundamental expert witness character in Bitcoin. Bitcoin customers regulate the conveyance and reception of currency, which consents for unidentified dealings to take place throughout the world. The Bitcoin blockchain might be hand-me-down to yield a ground-breaking composition solution. Despite the fact that the Bitcoin blockchain technology was first designed with a specific use case in mind, its initial design allows for a diverse range of experimental relationships (Prybila et al., 2020). Blockchain was created to serve as the distributed ledger for Bitcoin. Emerging blockchains that support Bitcoin incentivize encryption, resulting from the growing focus on Bitcoin (Islam et al., 2019). In the mandate to craft innovative blockchains, Bitcoin makers have reformed and heightened the imaginative Bitcoin technology.

Blockchain is a decentralized book of accounts that records the transactions on several systems at a similar point in time (Abramova & Böhme, 2016). Blockchain is also referred to as the next-generation Internet, "the modern foundational technology" with the capability to reorganize monetary transactions, which may impact the way humans correlate the wealth of the nation, which may bring modifications to the economy (Zachariadis et al., 2019). Blockchain has thus proved to be a game-changing digital innovation that has engrossed the interest of associations and the government sector worldwide. During this intellect, the construction of a novel Altcoin may be observed as a break in society. Furthermore, the sequence of Bitcoin's native geometric shapes and structure has undergone changes and concluded within a specific timeframe (Nerurkar et al., 2021). Thus, the utilization of cryptocurrencies in average businesses and pecuniary bionetworks is gradually growing. As cryptocurrencies continue to cultivate, there are chances that they might substitute the character of outdated money in cash and coins and develop progressively. However, some trials stretch out further, hindering the vast executions of cryptocurrencies as an argument for mediocre cost and a foundation of revenues, which will be discussed in the succeeding section.

Hence, the objective of the study was to examine the challenges and opportunities of cryptocurrency and cybersecurity.

Review of Literature

In the present era, cryptocurrencies and blockchain have gained the attention of academicians and practitioners. cryptocurrencies such as Bitcoin are automated money that uses digital technology and cryptography to relieve safe and unidentified dealings. During the worldwide financial disaster of 2008, an unidentified individual, crowd, or an association working under "Satoshi Nakamoto" popularized a digitally connected structure situated on the cryptocurrency Bitcoin (Nakamoto, 2008). Bitcoin is a distributed digital ledger that was popularized in 2008 and utilized at the commencement of 2009 and uses blockchain technology (Rejeb et al., 2021). Furthermore, Briere et al. (2013) stated that cryptocurrencies, particularly Bitcoin, are innovative monetary instruments and are an investment option with diversified perquisites. In the words of Trautman (2014), cryptocurrencies are a division of electronic money that may be dependent upon a decentralized set of connections or have central institutions. Thus, as explained by Duque (2020) and Hudson and Urquhart (2019), cryptocurrencies are the latest form of digital currency that is formed from cryptographic algorithms, using protocols, and are exchanged through smart technology, for example peer-to-peer networking (Nakamoto, 2008). Cryptocurrencies are situated based on the use of multifaceted cryptographic approaches, which help the customers with a safe and protected mode of exchange (Bulut, 2018). Most cryptocurrencies are constructed to establish fresh innovative units of currency with a minimum total sum (Baur et al., 2015). Contrary to it, cryptocurrencies that are issued by the state are not administered by well-known legal terms but are driven by automation (Dodd, 2018). Consequently, it proves cryptocurrencies are a modern innovative technique that is dissimilar from the conventional medium of exchange. The arrival of cryptocurrencies has generated an advanced area in the banking and financial field, which needs awareness from both the academic and general public at large (Aslan & Sensoy, 2020; Baumöhl, 2019; Cerqueti et al., 2020; Corbet et al., 2019; Platanakis et al., 2018, Vidal-Tomás et al., 2019). The cryptocurrency market is worth over US$500 billion (Chang et al., 2020). An important momentum following the establishment of cryptocurrencies was an urgent demand to develop a system that permitted speedy and economical transactions exclusive of the intermediation of some reliable sources such as banks (Bação et al., 2018; Chapron, 2017; Kfir, 2020; Kolber, 2018; Sudzina, 2018). Thus, eminent researchers, future academicians, and participants from the financial sector believed Bitcoin to be a modernized forward-looking medium for state-issued currency (Bouri et al., 2018; Bouri et al., 2017; Hong, 2017); (Rejeb et al., 2021).

Approximately 1,600 cryptocurrencies were operational with the launch of Bitcoin (Wilson, 2019). Apart from its publicity, cryptocurrencies are presently used as a medium of exchange to purchase merchandise and services in the actual world (Dostov & Shust, 2014; Guadamuz & Marsden, 2015). Cryptocurrency has made a drastic shift from its design, administration, and regulation as a whole (Shahzad et al., 2018). The digital expertise behind the production of cryptocurrencies is blockchain (HashemiJoo et al., 2019; Lu et al., 2019; Searing & MacLeod, 2019). In the present era, the blockchain market has developed rapidly across the globe, and by 2025, it is further expected to reach new heights in the business sector, amounting to US$39 billion. This exponential growth of the emerging technology is because of its attributes such as transparency in digital transactions, faith, and a platform for multi-stakeholders (Yli-Huumo et al., 2016; Iansiti & Lakhani, 2017; Bohme et al., 2015). Thus, future researchers believe that blockchain is an institutional technology (Iansiti & Lakhani, 2017) and is also referred to as the backbone of cryptocurrency (Zhong et al., 2019).

The application of blockchain to the problem of cybersecurity has been a major concern in present times (Salman et al., 2018). The problems and objections connected through the utilization of protection services in the private structural design in different application sectors offer an inclusive analysis of current blockchain-enabled programs for safety service operations regarding its confidentiality, verification, seclusion, information, access control and resource attribution, and assurance of reliability in scattered networks. Thus, this modern technology has attracted substantial awareness from financial institutions and worldwide retail banks (Dashkevich et al., 2020; Polasik et al., 2015). Several banks take advantage of blockchain to set up financial digital technology, also known as FinTech startups, to control blockchain in providing monetary services and supporting cryptocurrencies (Milne, 2018). The studies mentioned earlier respond to queries associated with the broader utilization of blockchain technology; however, they have not observed its usage in developing cybersecurity solutions. Thus, blockchain technology has a brief history in the field of research and development and is gradually gaining momentum.

Hence, the study's originality lies in providing a reasonable and more comprehensive perception of the challenges and opportunities brought by the tradition of cryptocurrencies in financial management. The present study fills up the existing gap in the review of studies related to the shortage of widespread investigation of cryptocurrencies through the financial scenario. Besides, finance and commerce academicians are still not familiar with the latest opportunities of these budding electronic financial instruments that are offered to business units, individuals, and financial institutions (Charfeddine et al., 2020). The present study also acknowledged an inadequacy of literature highlighting the challenges and opportunities of cryptocurrencies in the financial sector. The study also aimed to study the functioning of cryptocurrencies in reshaping and disrupting present monetary systems.

Research Methodology

The present study is completely grounded on an extensive review of the literature. Researchers explore and cite several bases such as newspapers, journals, websites, articles, and other statutory annual reports.

Challenges

The practice of cryptocurrencies is not unrestricted from monetary glitches and safety apprehensions. Investigators examined numerous readings and cryptocurrency stages and similarly perceived cryptocurrency as vending mediums in command to discover trials that happen in such cybernetic occurrences. The key difficulties of these virtual currencies include the following:

Safety bullying: Hackers and malevolent operators will be able to make as abundant as they need from effective exchange if they halt the scheme and identify the monotony of simulated currency growths. This project resulted in the possibility of producing authentic counterfeit currency or low-cost processor-generated transactions by simply manipulating the financial records. For example, the act of selling computer-generated items and real-world currency within the game is a direct violation of World of Warcraft (WoW) rules and regulations. Consequently, numerous individuals access WoW Gold trading platforms in order to buy virtual currency in order to acquire various items they require. Many World of Warcraft gold vending websites lack reliability and are vulnerable to fraud. Additionally, many of these businesses are reluctant to provide refunds for either non-existent or counterfeit virtual currency.

Failure apprehensions in cryptocurrency structures: The infinite distribution of cybernetic coinage in computer-generated communities will clue to pecuniary snags. Meanwhile, its supply is not built on the claim and hoard. It is possible for particular benefactors such as Next Lifecycle to subject boundless Linden Dollars and surge their effective amounts in the direction of advancing further existing profits. Additionally, it addresses the issues of inflation and financial concerns that are significant factors contributing to the decline in the virtual trading system.

Influence on tangible financial structures: Ever since certain computer-generated exchange arrangements are associated through actual domain regulatory classifications; they may mark the loads and stock amenities of factual realm dough. For illustration, permitting operators to get hold of virtual and tangible things and facilities with fundamental money in some platforms may lessen the burdens on existing money. Subsequently, selected stands empower handlers to interchange their cybernetic money with material notes, and this will advance the loads on actual domain cash. This variation will upshoot the actual monetarist arrangements.

Gilt agricultural threats: In China and other developing economies, Gilt agri-business is a buzzword. Gold agronomists are groups that show communal events such as World of Warcraft to increase gold, which is replicated through exchange of the game, and then move it for physical money. The battered procurers are the players who do not partake in an adequate interval to show and strive on behalf to purchase practical cash. Moreover, an enormous money stream is spawned after the gold unindustrialized procedure which needs to be maintained and standardized.

Instability in computer-generated coinage worth: Computer-generated coinage is quite unstable. Various researchers have stressed that recently, the recognition and value of a simulated currency have dropped.

Currency laundering: Coinage laundering is an exclusive threat that is exactly feasible to mount with the tradition of virtual currency, particularly with panels that authorize trainers to trade off cybernetic money with physical cash.

Unlimited individuality hazards: Gamers and operators can create supplementary through unfamiliar individualities and practice them for illegitimate dealings. It has been difficult to differentiate the foundation of creating or cashing out cybernetic exchanges. This is an indication of miscommunications in the circumstances of money laundering doubt. Moreover, the weird individuality will permit crooks to get compensated with computer-generated currency for their misconduct.

***Dark marketplace for cryptocurrency*:** The economic situations of nearly civic events such as Next Life and World of Warcraft are established to form a dark marketplace for procurement and marketing of their cybernetic currency. The growing endorsement of replicated currency in reachable locations has headed towards a thriving black market for distributing virtual currency with real money. For example, when a gamer selects to release from a game, he/she may want to hawk the controlled practical currency by impacting them in the game's mediums. The technique of getting the expenditures is perilous as countless spiteful users may not broaden the reimbursement or disparity after giving them.

Opportunities

Being a fairly new product, the prospects of cryptocurrency appear to be auspicious. Moreover, having intensified in terms of its value and cost, the upcoming occasions are still required.

No restrictions: Digital currency systems are insupportable to break. Its money is difficult to forge and can be paid in doubles. Many companies dealing in online businesses admit that BTC is growing, which reflects the system's trustworthiness.

Diminutive Bitcoin procedure price: Bitcoin cryptocurrency aids the aim of e-commerce. There have been zero payments to banks and other organizations. The key amount of such a procedure is arithmetic, which does not want money. This approach directly alerts users to access Bitcoin miner's wallets.

Devolution: In this system of cryptocurrency, there is no leading expedient professional in the mesh; the system is dispersed to all members, and each computer taking out Bitcoin is subordinate to this system. This means that the dynamic expert does not influence verdict directives for holders of Bitcoins, and if some part of the web goes detached, the compensation edifice will persist to instigate probable.

Secrecy: Any organization can generate an infinite number of Bitcoin addresses, regardless of its location, address, or any other form of evidence. Therefore, absolute confidentiality is upheld.

Transparency: Blockchain technology has been utilized in all Bitcoin transactions. The blockchain preserves evidence of nearly all transactions or data records. If a firm publicly discloses its Bitcoin address, then anyone can ascertain the amount of Bitcoin owned by the company. The entire system is characterized by transparency.

No chances to use some personal data for fraud: Bitcoin transaction happens with two keys, public key and private key, which will work through arithmetic function. So, there are fewer chances of fraud and misuse of personal data in BTC network transactions.

No inflation: Neither political stakeholders nor corporate firms can induce inflation in this Bitcoin system. Furthermore, the maximum number of coins is strictly limited to 21 million.

Peer-to-peer cryptocurrency network: A peer-to-peer cryptocurrency network is responsible for all operations. In such networks, there is no master server that is responsible for all operations. Information is exchanged between 2 and 3 or more software clients. Bitcoin transactions are done by hundreds of distributed servers.

Unlimited possibilities of transaction: Unlimited transactions are possible with a Bitcoin wallet, no matter where the Bitcoin wallet is located in the world. Each of the wallet holders can pay anyone, anywhere, and any amount.

Speed of transaction: The speed of transaction after the Bitcoin network processes the payment has been faster than that of any other mode of transaction.

Cryptocurrency Scenario in India Concerning Cybersecurity

Cybersecurity helps sustain the reliability of data through the Blockchain using the encrypted infrastructure and the public–private system of keys, which have an affirmative role in the verification and permission processes, safety and security of data, and privacy. The experience of cyber risks is at the top because of the option to admit data from numerous devices, but the blockchain is based on a highly developed quantum computing scheme that is difficult to bust. The cybersecurity solutions presented by blockchain technology are connected to encrypted data and the use of hashing functions to avoid cyberattacks, which are more in trend in the current years. Cybercriminals are paying attention to advanced digital techniques of pilfering personal detection of data or other precious information, such as intellectual property or financial statements.

Future Scope of Cryptocurrency in India

Cryptocurrency and the guidelines of the executive Digital Currency Bill 2021 are likely to be released in the winter assembly session of the parliament. It is a bill that would legalize cryptocurrency in India. On December 7, 2021, Finance Minister Nirmala Sitharaman purported that the projected Central Bank Digital Currency will not enhance cryptocurrency in India.

Futurists think that by the year 2030, cryptocurrencies will engage 25% of nationalized currencies, which means a momentous portion of the globe would consider cryptocurrency as a means of transaction. It is going to be progressively more acknowledged by merchants and consumers, and it will continue to have an impulsive nature, which means prices will persist to vary, as they have been doing in ancient times.

Conclusion and Recommendations

Cryptocurrency is anticipated to become the predominant medium for currency exchange in the future, due to the abundance of cryptocurrency available in various forms. However, handlers have not implemented the entire architecture for cryptocurrency. Many existing cryptocurrency systems lack the confidence of the general public at present. While Bitcoin is being effectively regulated, people must still take precautionary measures when using this vital form of cash, which remains a significant risk for cybersecurity. The potential of Bitcoin is promising and enlightening, as it provides many platforms for hopeful fluctuations in the development and advancement of e-payment and e-business sectors. Due to the rapid development of digital technology, cryptocurrency will continue to advance. Large merchants are obtaining expenses through varied categories of cryptocurrency, and countless citizens are now more conscious of the opportunities and potentials that cryptocurrency can suggest. Advanced patterns of computer-generated currency have likewise appeared and expanded everywhere around the globe in recent times. M-Pesa is a cryptocurrency protocol that offers safe payment services. It gained popularity in Kenya in 2007 and has since been adopted in several Asian (including India), African, and European nations, establishing itself as a widely accepted payment system. An in-depth analysis from multiple angles is necessary to understand the correlation between the practical economic regulations and the governmental framework for establishing cryptocurrency projects. In addition, the level of acceptance and responsiveness also necessitates careful consideration and extensive analysis using large-scale models. Confidence and assurance are significant aspects that need to be considered when expanding and swapping cryptocurrency forms. Furthermore, the scope of the study can be stretched to the emerging areas for applications of cryptocurrency across diverse divisions in India.

References

Abramova, S., & Böhme, R. (2016). Perceived benefit and risk as multidimensional determinants of bitcoin use: A quantitative exploratory study. In *37th International Conference on Information systems*, Dublin, Ireland. https://informationsecurity.uibk.ac.at/pdfs/Abramova2016_Bitcoin_ICIS.pdf

Aslan, A., & Sensoy, A. (2020). Intraday efficiency–frequency nexus in the cryptocurrency markets. *Finance Research Letters*, *35*, 101298. https://doi.org/10.1016/j.frl.2019.09.013

Bação, P., Duarte, A. P., Sebastião, H., & Redzepagic, S. (2018). Information transmission between cryptocurrencies: Does Bitcoin rule the cryptocurrency world? *Scientific Annals of Economics and Business*, *65*(2), 97–117.

Baumöhl, E. (2019). Are cryptocurrencies connected to Forex? A quantile cross-spectral approach. *Finance Research Letters, 29*, 363–372. https://doi.org/10.1016/j.frl.2018.09.002

Baur, A. W., Bühler, J., Bick, M., & Bonorden, C. S. (2015). Cryptocurrencies as a disruption? empirical findings on user adoption and future potential of Bitcoin and co. In M. Janssen, M. Mäntymäki, J. Hidders, B. Klievink, W. Lamersdorf, B. van Loenen, & A. Zuiderwijk (Eds.), *Open and big data management and innovation* (pp. 63–80). Springer International Publishing.

Bohme, R., Christin, N., Edelman, B., & Moore, T. (2015). Bitcoin: Economics, technology, and governance. *Journal of Economic Perspectives, 29*(2), 213–38.

Bouri, E., Gupta, R., Lau, C. K. M., Roubaud, D., & Wang, S. (2018). Bitcoin and global financial stress: A copula-based approach to dependence and causality in the quantiles. *The Quarterly Review of Economics and Finance, 69*, 297–307.

Bouri, E., Molnár, P., Azzi, G., Roubaud, D., & Hagfors, L. I. (2017). On the hedge and safe haven properties of Bitcoin: Is it really more than a diversifier? *Finance Research Letters, 20*, 192–198. https://doi.org/10.1016/j.frl.2016.09.025

Briere, M., Oosterlinck, K., & Szafarz, A. (2013). *Virtual currency, tangible return: Portfolio diversification with bitcoins ULB–UniversiteLibre de Bruxelles.* Working Papers CEB, 13–031.

Bulut, A. (2018). Cryptocurrencies in the new economy. *Journal of International Trade, Logistics and Law, 4*(2), 45–52.

Cerqueti, R., Giacalone, M., & Mattera, R. (2020). Skewed non-Gaussian GARCH models for crypto currencies volatility modelling. *Information Sciences, 527*, 1–26. https://doi.org/10.1016/j.ins.2020.03.075

Chang, V., Baudier, P., Zhang, H., Xu, Q., Zhang, J., & Arami, M. (2020). How blockchain can impact financial services: The overview, challenges and recommendations from expert interviewees. *Techno Logical Forecasting and Social Change, 158*, 120166.

Chapron, G. (2017). The environment needs crypto governance. *Nature News, 545*(7655), 403–405.

Charfeddine, L., Benlagha, N., & Maouchi, Y. (2020). Investigating the dynamic relationship between cryptocurrencies and conventional assets: Implications for financial investors. *Economic Modelling, 85*, 198–217.

Corbet, S., Lucey, B., Urquhart, A., & Yarovaya, L. (2019). Cryptocurrencies as a financial asset: A systematic analysis. *International Review of Financial Analysis, 62*, 182–199. https://doi.org/10.1016/j.irfa.2018.09.003

Dashkevich, N., Counsell, S., & Destefanis, G. (2020). Blockchain application for central banks: A systematic mapping study. *IEEE Access, 8*, 139918–139952.

Dodd, N. (2018). The social life of Bitcoin. *Theory, Culture and Society, 35*(3), 35–56. https://doi.org/10.1177/0263276417746464

Dostov, V., & Shust, P. (2014). Cryptocurrencies: An unconventional challenge to the AML/CFT regulators? *Journal of Financial Crime, 21*(3), 249–263.

Duque, J. J. (2020). State involvement in cryptocurrencies. A potential world money? *The Japanese Political Economy, 46*(1), 65–82.

Ghosh, A., Gupta, S., Dua, A., & Kumar, N. (2020). Security of cryptocurrencies in blockchain technology: State-of-art, challenges and future prospects. *Journal of Network and Computer Applications, 163*, 102635.

Guadamuz, A., & Marsden, C. (2015). Blockchains and bitcoin: Regulatory responses to cryptocurrencies. *First Monday, 20*(12). https://doi.org/10.5210/fm.v20i12.6198

HashemiJoo, M., Nishikawa, Y., & Dandapani, K. (2019). Cryptocurrency, a successful application of blockchain technology. *Managerial Finance, 46*(6), 715–733.

Hong, K. (2017). Bitcoin as an alternative investment vehicle. *Information Technology and Management, 18*(4), 265–275. https://doi.org/10.1007/s10799-016-0264-6

Hudson, R., & Urquhart, A. (2019). Technical trading and cryptocurrencies. *Annals of Operations Research*, *297*, 191–220. https://doi.org/10.1007/s10479-019-03357-1.
Iansiti, M., & Lakhani, K. (2017). The truth about blockchain. *Harvard Business Review*, 1–11. https://enterprisersproject.com/sites/default/files/the_truth_about_blockchain.pdf
Islam, A. N., Mantymaki, M., & Turunen, M. (2019). Why do blockchains split? An actor-network perspective on Bitcoin splits. *Technological Forecasting and Social Change*, *148*, 119743.
Kfir, I. (2020). Cryptocurrencies, national security, crime and terrorism. *Comparative Strategy*, *39*(2), 113–127. https://doi.org/10.1080/01495933.2020.1718983
Kolber, A. J. (2018). Not-So-Smart blockchain contracts and artificial responsibility. *Stanford Technology Law Review*, *21*, 198. https://heinonline.org/HOL/Page?handle=hein.journals/stantlr21&id=198&div=&collection=
Lu, Q., Xu, X., Liu, Y., Weber, I., Zhu, L., & Zhang, W. (2019). uBaaS: A unified blockchain as a service platform. *Future Generation Computer Systems*, *101*, 564–575.
Milne, A. (2018). Cryptocurrencies from an Austrian perspective. In A. Godart-van der Kroon, & P. Vonlanthen (Eds.), *Banking and monetary policy from the perspective of Austrian economics* (pp. 223–257). Springer International Publishing.
Nakamoto, S. (2008). *Bitcoin: A peer-to-peer electronic cash system*. www.bitcoin.org.
Nerurkar, P., Patel, D., Busnel, Y., Ludinard, R., Kumari, S., & Khan, M. K. (2021). Dissecting bitcoin blockchain: Empirical analysis of bitcoin network (2009–2020). *Journal of Network and Computer Applications*, *177*, 102940.
Platanakis, E., Sutcliffe, C., & Urquhart, A. (2018). Optimal vs naïve diversification in cryptocurrencies. *Economics Letters*, *171*, 93–96.
Polasik, M., Piotrowska, A. I., Wisniewski, T. P., Kotkowski, R., & Lightfoot, G. (2015). Price fluctuations and the use of Bitcoin: An empirical inquiry. *International Journal of Electronic Commerce*, *20*(1), 9–49. https://doi.org/10.1080/10864415.2016.1061413
Prybila, C., Schulte, S., Hochreiner, C., & Weber, I. (2020). Runtime verification for business processes utilizing the Bitcoin blockchain. *Future Generation Computer Systems*, *107*, 816–831.
Rejeb, A., Rejeb, K., & Keogh, J. G. (2021). Cryptocurrencies in modern finance: A literature review. *Etikonomi*, *20*(1), 93–118. https://doi.org/10.15408/etk.v20i1.16911
Salman, T., Zolanvari, M., Erbad, A., Jain, R., & Samaka, M. (2018). Security services using blockchains: A state of the art survey. In *IEEE communications surveys & tutorials*. IEEE. https://doi.org/10.1109/COMST.2018.2863956.
Searing, J. M., & MacLeod, D. (2019). Cryptocurrency gift strategies for not-for-profits: Here's what organizations should consider as they ponder whether and how to accept donations of virtual currency. *Journal of Accountancy*, *227*(2), 34–36.
Shahzad, F., Xiu, G., Wang, J., & Shahbaz, M. (2018). An empirical investigation on the adoption of cryptocurrencies among the people of mainland China. *Technology in Society*, *55*, 33–40. https://doi.org/10.1016/j.techsoc.2018.05.006
Sudzina, F. (2018). Distribution of foreign aid in cryptocurrencies: Initial considerations. *International Advances in Economic Research*, *24*(4), 387–388.
Trautman, L. J. (2014). Virtual currencies; bitcoin & what now after liberty reserve, Silk Road, and Mt. Gox? *Richmond Journal of Law and Technology*, *20*(4), 1–108.
Vidal-Tomás, D., Ibáñez, A. M., & Farinós, J. E. (2019). Weak efficiency of the cryptocurrency market: A market portfolio approach. *Applied Economics Letters*, *26*(19), 1627–1633. https://doi.org/10.1080/13504851.2019.1591583
Wilson, C. (2019). Cryptocurrencies: The future of finance? In F-L. T. Yu & D. S. Kwan (Eds.), *Contemporary issues in international political economy* (pp. 359–394). Springer.

Yli-Huumo, J., Ko, D., Choi, S., Park, S., & Smolander, K. (2016). Where is current research on blockchain technology? – a systematic review. *PLoS One, 11*(10), e0163477.

Zachariadis, M., Hileman, G., & Scott, S. V. (2019). Governance and control in distributed ledgers: Understanding the challenges facing blockchain technology in financial services. *Information and Organization*, *29*(2), 105–117. https://doi.org/10.1016/j.infoandorg.2019.03.001

Zhong, L., Wu, Q., Xie, J., Guan, Z., & Qin, B. (2019). A secure largescale instant payment system based on blockchain. *Computers & Security, 84*, 349–364.

11 Unveiling Cryptocurrency

Unfolding the Hubbub around Cryptocurrency

Pradeep Kumar Singh and Sandeep Mishra

Introduction

Money is the most powerful tool in the present time. It can literally buy anything. Money has been used as weapon to settle wars and seal unethical deals. In olden times, currency, that is money, had various shapes and sizes. Throughout the history of mankind, it transformed from metal plates to papers, and now to zeros and ones in this digital age, that is digital currency. The transformation of currency was aimed at solving various problems, and one such problem was procuring change and handling the money. Getting the change[1] for larger denominations back in the time was pretty tricky. One used to search for change from one vendor to another. Another issue one faced was that hard cash was easy to steal and hard to handle during commute. During travel, one family member used to take care of all the valuables, including cash. Then, the automated teller machine, popularly known as "ATM", was introduced. ATMs were portable cash counters for us, and we could withdraw money from our account anytime, anywhere. ATMs solved the problem of carrying cash, but chasing the change persisted as one could not find the exact denominations he wanted, and he had to look for the change all the same. Then, the unified payment interface (UPI) was introduced, a bold step of the government in a country like India, where access to the Internet was such a big issue, and more than half of the population was tech illiterate in terms of use. Except in metro cities, paying through UPI is also an issue in India as the population is reluctant that others might rob their accounts, but it has solved the problem of change. Now, one could pay in any denomination up to two decimal places.

In recent days, cryptocurrency is in vogue; everyone wants to buy it and get rich in a year or two. Everyone knows it is a digital currency; it works on the blockchain; one can use any wallet available, on either Play Store or IOS Store; it has grown in the past years like a mammoth; and it is like a stock market. In this chapter, we will strive to understand the concept of cryptocurrency, how it is valued, what blockchain is, and the legal aspect. In addition to these, the study will provide an understanding of whether one should buy it or not. Should it be legalized or not? Is the recent move of the government of India to tax cryptocurrency at 30% correct, and what would be the future decision of the government?

DOI: 10.4324/9781003517290-15

This chapter will simplify the concept of cryptocurrency. Along with this prime objective, you will know the following at the end of the chapter:

1) The idea of cryptocurrency and blockchain
2) Working of the blockchain
3) Valuation of cryptocurrency
4) The current legal framework for cryptocurrency in India
5) Comparative study of the regulation of crypto taken so far by various countries around the world
6) The results if India adopts crypto

Barter to Cryptocurrency: An Evolution

The financial systems we observe today evolved from the simple system of exchange of things. We already discussed the "problem of change". Let us look at the evolution of money from another perspective. During primitive periods, there was no concepts such as money, ownership, or possession. The communities were in small groups; most were hunters and gatherers. Gradually, the communities moved towards settlements, which forced them to reside in a particular area. These areas were abundant in most necessities but could not fulfil all wants. This need to acquire things from others gave birth to the barter system.

Barter System

Simply put, barter is an exchange of things for things, services for things, things for services, or services for services. It can also be termed commodity money. This method evolved gradually and was practised over the centuries. Around the 11th century BCE, Chinese people started using tokens, which represented things to be exchanged by it. Only those things could be exchanged that were represented by the token. It solved the problem of people carrying heavy goods.

Currency

With the evolution of civilization and increase in intelligence, coins were made to replace the concept of tokens. The first coins were used by Lydians[2] (present Turkey) around 500 BCE. They were made of electrum and silver. Furthermore, coins were developed, and other metallic coins such as silver, copper, zinc, and nickel coins were issued. The coins had a fixed value, and a certain number of things or services could be exchanged for a coin.[3]

Paper Money

China was a pioneer in introducing paper money. Around 700 CE, the Chinese started using "paper money". It was also associated with flying cash as it was made of paper and prone to fly. Later, flying cash was introduced in Europe, and banks started to issue paper money as well. During the Colonization era and American Civil War, the flow of money increased.

Plastic Money

Plastic money refers to the debit/credit cards that are made of plastic. "Charg-it" was the first actual bank card and was issued in 1946. The card was invented by John Biggins, a banker in Brooklyn. However, only local purchases could be made (*Blog – Cashco Financial*, 2024).

Virtual Money

The 21st century, often referred to as the "Digital Age", gave rise to digital transfer of money from one account to another. This added another feature to the portability of money. Now, one does not need anything – just his mobile and a particular application, such as BHIM or PhonePay, to make payments or send money to friends and family. Digital payments such as Internet banking and UPI transactions were a huge breakthrough in the banking era.

Virtual money, on the other hand, refers to a currency to which everyone has access irrespective of citizenship. This currency is neither minted nor printed. It actually has no physical form. One can say that it is the abstract form of money or completely electronic money because it is not controlled by banks or governments. The first virtual currency of the world is Bitcoin (BTC), which was introduced by Satoshi Nakamoto [a pseudonym used by the creator(s) of BTC] in 2009.

Cryptocurrency: Genesis and Kinds

BTC is a decentralized virtual cryptocurrency that uses peer-to-peer network and works on blockchain technology and validates itself by a proof-of-work or consensus system. As the abstract of Bitcoin whitepaper reads: "*A purely peer-to-peer version of electronic cash would allow online payments to be sent directly from one party to another without going through a financial institution*" (Nakamoto, 2009), which reveals the true intention of Nakamoto, the creator of BTC. A decentralized currency means a currency that is not controlled by any intermediary, that is banks generally. It is virtual in the sense that there is no mint which mints the BTC notes or coins. In fact, BTC was created to introduce electronic cash without any controlling authority. BTC is considered a currency in the sense that it is being widely used around the globe as currency to pay for daily expenses and income tax.

Blockchain: According to Euromoney, "*Blockchain is a system of recording information in a way that makes it difficult or impossible to change, hack, or cheat the system*" [What is blockchain?, URL: https://www.euromoney.com/learning/blockchain-explained/what-is-blockchain]. In simple terms, blockchain is a digital ledger that records every transaction done within 10 minutes, and the transactions done after 10 minutes will be recorded in a newly formed block. Therefore, to record the transactions done in an hour, the BTC blockchain requires 6 blocks. These blocks are assigned with a complete random number called nuance and are time-stamped. It also has the hash code of the previous block.

Peer-to-peer network: Peer-to-peer (P2P) networking is 2 or more computers connected with equal permission and responsibilities for processing data. In the BTC network, every person using BTC downloads a wallet to transact in BTC. All such people and their mobiles form a network and have equal rights to create, store, and access the blockchain data.

Proof of work: Proof of work (PoW) is a form of cryptographic proof in which a person (prover or miner) claims to another (verifier) that he has solved a particular puzzle to find the correct nuance, therefore adding a valid block to the blockchain. It helps BTC to come to a consensus, i.e., agree on records of the blocks of the blockchain. The process of adding blocks to the blockchain is called "mining". The concept was invented by Cynthia Dwork and Moni Naor in 1993, and the term PoW was coined by Markus Jakobsson and Ari Juels in 1999 (Nevil, 2023).

Cryptocurrency being the child of technology is surrounded with a lot of technological stuff. There is a ton of it around crypto, but the theme of chapter does not allow me to dive further into the science. Now, let us dig into the functional and working mechanism of cryptocurrency.

Cryptocurrency: Function and Working Mechanism

After discussing the technology behind cryptocurrency, let us move on to more behavioural part of the cryptocurrency, that is to learn how one can buy, sell, and use crypto. If one needs goods, he visits the market or searches goods online. Similarly, if one needs to buy cryptocurrency, he needs a market that sells it. There are various applications, available at Android and IOS platforms, that act as a medium of exchange. These applications are similar to stock exchange. Today, a considerable population is investing in, transacting through, and sending information using crypto and blockchain. [As one sends crypto from his wallet to another, he can embed a small text into the transaction, which will be private information for the parties and spam to the rest of the world.] Therefore, we need to know the basics of it, which are covered in the following.

Availing Cryptocurrency: Procedural and Technical Takeaway

According to *Forbes* (Tretina, 2022), one can buy cryptocurrency in four steps:

Step 1: Choosing Point of Sale/Exchange Point

If one wants to buy crypto, he has to choose from various applications or websites that act as the point of sale (PoS) for various crypto, for example WazirX,

Unocoin, CoinDCX, ZebPay, CoinSwitch Kuber, Bitbns, and Krypto. Before choosing the PoS for the desired crypto, one must keep in mind the following things.

Is the desired cryptocurrency listed within the application you are choosing? Actually, there were more than 5,000 cryptocurrencies available in 2022, and usually an application lists 100–500 cryptos. Next thing to keep in mind is what fees or brokerages are being charged by the PoS provider. You can compare prices among all or few applications, as per your convenience. Last but not the least, the application you are choosing must have an integrated wallet where you can store crypto and transact from. Integrated wallets provide security and hassle-free experience during transactions.

Step 2: Selecting Method of Transaction

Once you have finalized the PoS for the crypto, you must find a suitable transaction method. There might be some options that are on discount or charging less.

Step 3: Placing an Order

The last step to buy a cryptocurrency is to place the order after you have selected the desired crypto from the listed cryptos.

Step 4: Storing Cryptocurrency

Almost all the applications at PoS provide an integrated wallet to store the crypto in order to transact in future. There are two types of crypto wallets to store crypto: "Hot wallet" and "Cold Wallet". Hot wallets are those that are constantly connected to the Internet and available online and are protected by the providers. Integrated wallets are hot wallets. Cold wallets are the ones that remain disconnected from the Internet and only connected at the time of transaction, for example a pen drive. Cold wallets are considered safer than hot wallets as they are distant from the Internet, and it is not easy for a hacker to gain access to your crypto. On the other hand, a hot wallet is connected to the Internet 24x7 and has a higher chance of a hacker breaching into the wallet. The only drawback of the cold wallet is if you lose the access code somehow, it will be impossible for you to gain access to your crypto, while if you lose the access code of your hot wallet or it is hacked, the provider will help you regain the access.

Cryptocurrency Transactions

Transaction in cryptocurrency works fluently like any UPI application. All you need is the receiver's crypto address. The address is attached to a wallet in which the crypto amount is to be paid. Taking the example of ZebPay, all you need to do is open the app > click on the cryptocurrency you want to send >

click send > enter address (you can send to pre-added addresses) > enter the amount > enter PIN, and it is done. Given below is the simple walkthrough to send crypto. (*How to Trade in Crypto–Crypto and Crypto–INR Pairs on Exchan(India)*, n.d.)

4.2.1 Selecting Currency: First, the user needs to select the currency and the application itself converts it into BTC.

4.2.2 Entering the Receiver's Address: The user needs to enter the BTC address of the receiver.

Finalizing the Transaction: Furthermore, the user needs to enter his security PIN that he had created while signing up.

Similarly, you can receive crypto using your QR code or by giving out the address.

Valuation of Cryptocurrency

Demand and supply are two terms that decide the value of goods in the market. The BTC is similarly valued. Today, there are only 21 million BTCs, that is limited supply, but the demand to own it is ever increasing. Therefore, the value kept rising since its launch. Another reason that affects the price of the BTC is the major events, for example the collapse of MtGox in 2014–2015, the COVID-19 pandemic in 2019–2021, and the decisions of various governments to regulate it.

BTC first started with a negligible value of $0.003 per coin in 2009, which rose from $1 to $32 in 2011 and $1,163 in 2013. It became bearish in 2015, but by 2020 it touched $29,096 and stands at $73,805 in 2024 (India, 2024; Edwards, 2024).

Regulation of Crypto: Indian Commitments

I'm sure you have heard about countries like El Salvador legalizing BTC as parallel currency in the country. India is the second most populous country, and if people indulge in cryptocurrency, then the government must intervene to regulate the transactions. Here are some updates on the regulation of cryptocurrency by the Indian government and its regulatory bodies.

RBI Circulars

The first information shared by the Reserve Bank of India (RBI) was in 2013 through a press release (*Reserve Bank of India – Press Releases*, 24 C.E.) to create awareness among citizens of the disadvantages of virtual currencies such as Bitcoin, Litecoin, BBQcoin, and Dogecoin. It created awareness among users of possible security threats during transaction, storing crypto in e-wallets, illicit and illegal use, and about no fixed value.

On April 6, 2018, RBI issued another circular prohibiting dealing in "virtual currencies" (VCs) (*Reserve Bank of India – Notifications*, 2018) citing various risks, banned the dealing in VCs with immediate effect, and gave a 3-month period to withdraw all the entities dealing in VCs. This circular was challenged in the *Internet and Mobile Association of India (IMAI) v Reserve Bank of India*[4] on the following grounds:

1) The RBI does not have the power to regulate VCs as it does not come under the legal tender.
2) Various countries have tried and tested the VCs and found it to be free of flaws. The Security Exchange Board of India (SEBI), the Department of Economy Affairs of Government of India, and the Central Board of Direct Tax and Securities also did not find any concerning issues regarding VCs.
3) The circular prohibits dealing in VCs, which violates the fundamental right u/A 19(1)(g).[5]

The Supreme Court observed that the circular is unenforceable and unlawful and, therefore, quashed the RBI circular banning the VCs.

Ministerial Committees

A committee was constituted on November 2, 2017, to study various issues pertaining to VCs and to propose specific actions, under the chairmanship of

1) Subhash Chandra Garg, Secretary, Department of Economic Affairs, Ministry of Finance
2) Ajay Prakash Sawhney, Secretary, Ministry of Electronics and Information Technology
3) Ajay Tyagi, Chairman, SEBI
4) B.P. Kanungo, Deputy Governor, RBI, as members

The committee recommended about DLT,[6] which replaces the traditional ledger system and allows recording, sharing, and transfer of data. It further recommended the use of DLT in the entire financial system and was regulated by various regulatory bodies, such as RBI, SEBI, IRDA, PFRDA, and IBBI. The committee also recommended that the VCs must be distinguished from fiat money as VCs are not legal tender and not backed by the RBI. The committee, although focused on studying the benefits of VCs in terms of technological advancements and efficiency, also focused on non-backing of VCs by governments and misuses of VCs, which are later discussed in this chapter. The committee under Chapter 3 of its report suggested to issue central bank digital currency (CBDC), which is also discussed in detail later in this chapter.

Parliamentary Discussions

In the budget session of the Indian Parliament of the year 2022, the Union Government declared that it would tax all the income generated by crypto trading. The bill also defines VCs comprehensively to cover all VCs including non-fungible tokens (NFTs) and cryptocurrencies, for example Bitcoin and Dogecoin. The features of the Bill can be summarized as follows:

1) Clause 3(b) inserts Clause 47A in Section 2 of the Income Tax Act, which defines "virtual digital assets".
2) Clause 16 amends Section 56 of the Income Tax Act to add VCs as property.
3) Clause 28 of the Bill inserts Section 115BH in the Income Tax Act, which imposes a flat 30% tax effective from April 1, 2022. An important thing to note here is that Section 115BH provides that *no set off of any loss shall be allowed.* That means income is to be taxed irrespective of profit or loss.
4) Clause 59 of the Bill inserts Section 194S in the Income Tax Act, which provides for 1% Tax Deducted at Source (TDS) on each transaction above INR 10,000 or different transactions adding up to INR 50,000 done through VCs. This clause further strives to regulate the transactions in VCs.
5) The government has also introduced CBDC, that is rupee as digital currency based on the blockchain technology by 2023.

Regulation of Crypto: International Commitments

United Kingdom

In the United Kingdom, cryptocurrency is not legal tender, which means it does not have similar status as sterling pound, but it is legal to transact in VCs subjected to registration with the Financial Conduct Authority (FCA). After January 10, 2021, all crypto asset firms must register with the FCA. Such firms must comply with anti-money laundering (AML) and counter-terrorist financing (CTF) reporting and customer protection guidelines. They must also comply with money laundering laws and Terrorist Financing and Transfer of Fund (Information on the Payer) Regulations (2017). In 2020, the Financial Crimes Enforcement Network (FinCEN) issued a notification to observe the "Travel Rule" in crypto transactions.

United States of America

VCs, including cryptocurrency, do not enjoy legal status in the US economy, but transacting in VCs is not illegal in the United States. Although cryptocurrencies are not considered legal tender, crypto exchanges are money transmitters and come under tax guidelines. The position of crypto in the United States is somewhat similar to that in the United Kingdom. In the United States, crypto service providers must be registered with FinCEN and come under the Bank Secrecy Act's scope. The US Securities and Exchange Commission (SEC) considers VCs as securities; therefore, security laws apply to the transaction, e-wallets, etc.

Although the federal government has merely regulated the cryptocurrency, the states of the United States have adopted different measures regarding crypto, for example the state of Colorado has started accepting cryptocurrency for paying taxes. Similarly, California has also begun taking crypto to pay for government services.

El Salvador

El Salvador had introduced BTC as legal tender alongside its original currency dollar. The Salvadoran government has bought 550 Bitcoins worth US$26 million and infused it into its economy. The Salvadoran government also established "*Banco de Desarrollo de la República de El Salvador*" (Development Bank of the Republic of El Salvador) and allocated a 150-million-dollar fund to back BTC transactions. It has also installed 200 BTC ATMs across the country to ease up the use of BTC. Data from Coin ATM Radar shows that El Salvador has the third highest number of BTC ATMs across the world, behind the United States and Canada. These ATMs are manufactured by Chain Bytes, a US-based company. In order to use BTC, one needs to download El Chivo wallet in his smartphone and buy some credit in the form of BTC. The wallet acts as a platform to perform all functions related to BTC transactions, such as converting dollars to BTC and vice versa, and day-to day-transactions. The Salvadoran government is also promoting the use of BTC among its citizens by giving $30 as a welcome bonus on downloading the wallet.[7]

Central African Republic

On April 27, 2022, the Central African Republic (CAR) became the second country in the world and the first country in Africa to legalize BTC. It is to be noted here that the CAR is not following El Salvador in adopting BTC, but it merely adopted it as reference currency, that is the primary investing currency for stock players ["Central African Republic Clarified That It Accepted Bitcoin as a Reference Currency" (*Central African Republic Clarified That It Accepted Bitcoin as a Reference Currency*, 2022).

China

Cryptocurrency is completely banned in China. In 2017, China imposed ban on investing and trading in crypto. In 2021, China banned crypto completely. Along with China, almost 40 countries either banned cryptocurrency or restricted its use. Such countries include Nepal, Bangladesh, Qatar, Tunisia, Egypt, Iraq, and Morocco.

Legal Status and Hurdles in Regulation of Crypto in India

When China closed its economical borders to crypto, India became the largest market for crypto. India, the world's largest democracy and the second most populous country in the world, has outgrown China, and the population of India has adopted the new ways of banking. The generation took crypto as natural and started investing in it, without any second thought.

The Indian Stand on Crypto

When Coinbase tried to enter the Indian market with all huff-puff, in April 2022, CEO Brian Armstrong travelled to India to launch services. But the RBI blocked its operations abruptly, hence cutting off access to India's market.

After India imposed a 30% tax on crypto, various crypto exchanges had shifted to countries having friendlier laws. Nischal Shetty and Siddharth Menon, co-founders of WazirX, India's largest crypto exchange by volume, had moved to Dubai with their families. Crypto exchange firms like Zeb-Pay, Vauld, and CoinDCX moved to Singapore. Irrespective of that they have moved to other countries, the firms maintain a headquarter in India to further explore the possibilities.

Recent acts of the government and the possible hints about how India might regulate the VCs and the digital assets have left the industry in oblivion, but Indian investment in crypto keeps increasing.

India does not seem to view the stakes the same way, and its go-slow approach may be vindicated by the recent crash in crypto prices and disasters like the implosion of Terra's UST stablecoin and the ongoing hacks draining funds from DeFi projects. Officials have also signalled that they do not think India can rein in crypto on its own, given the global nature of the technology (Choo, n.d.).

Till now, India has adopted the wait-and-see approach and held back on introducing crypto legislation. "We have also seen that cryptocurrencies are not amenable to definition as a currency, asset or commodity; they have no underlying cash flows, they have no intrinsic value; that they are akin to Ponzi Schemes, and may even be worse", the RBI deputy governor quoted (*Reserve Bank of India – Speeches*, 2022).

Indian Prime Minister Narendra Modi at the World Economic Forum in Davos stated that crypto is "an example of the kind of challenges we are facing as a global family with a changing global order" and called for collective and synchronized action of the governments of the world (Baruah, 2022).

During her budget speech in 2022, Indian Finance Minister Nirmala Sitharaman stated that India will take a considerate decision on regulation around VCs. During her speech at Stanford University, she emphasized that the Indian government is going to take a more cautious approach to crypto regulation, saying that "it can't be rushed" and that more information is needed (*India to Take a Considered View on Crypto: Finance Minister Nirmala Sitharaman*, 2022).

Furthermore, India taxing the crypto income is a balanced move, but imposing high rates of tax shows the reluctancy to adopt the new mechanism. Talks are being held that a 28% GST might be imposed on crypto payments. Several Indian parliamentarians have called for crypto to be taxed at 50% because it is like casino and lottery earnings (Helms, 2022).

Moreover, the Indian stand on crypto is not like that of El Salvador or the CAR but more like that of the United States and United Kingdom. Although there are contentions that India is mistaken about cryptos and it does not have a mobile market like the United States', but the Indian economy and tech framework are different from those of the United States. So, it is obvious to have different policies from that of the United States and United Kingdom.

Conclusions and Suggestions

As the Indian market of crypto is facing some ups and downs, many Indian users have moved to other exchanges. Some have moved to decentralized exchanges because they don't collect know-your-customer (KYC) data with the intention to avoid taxes, the *Times of India* (*ToI*) quoted. Such users might face hardships while converting their crypto holdings to INR and tax might be imposed at that time.

Calling the Indian government opposed to the VCs is not true, as the Indian government announced that it will introduce a CBDC by 2023. Basically, the Indian government is introducing a digital rupee (₹) based on the blockchain technology. The RBI's annual report published on May 26, 2022, revealed a step-by-step structured approach to launch the digital rupee. Below is the timeline as pointed by the *ToI* (*RBI Proposed to Adopt a Graded Approach to Launching the Country's CBDC*, 2022).

1) The introduction of CBDC has been announced in the Union Budget 2022–2023 and an appropriate amendment to the RBI Act, 1934, has been included in the Finance Bill, 2022.
2) The Finance Bill, 2022, has been enacted providing a legal framework for the launch of CBDC.
3) The report preceded the details about the CBDC's work by explaining the disruption of technology with the advent of fintech.
   - It has halted and disrupted the banking sector, financial services, and insurance in the way of product structuring, back-end analytics, and delivery of services, the report explains.
   - Such an innovation necessitates the regulators and authorities to step in to regulate the space to nurture the innovation in a sustainable manner and to also mitigate any associated risk.
4) The bank is currently exploring the pros and cons of introducing a digital rupee in India.
5) The design of CBDC should be in accordance with the stated objectives of monetary policy, financial stability, and efficient operations of currency and payment systems.
6) The required and appropriate design elements of CBDCs that could be implemented with little or no disruption are being examined.

Furthermore, India is moving towards a healthy crypto ecosystem. As pointed out by Ajay Seth, secretary of the Finance Ministry's Department of Economic

Affairs, "Our consultation paper is fairly ready. We have gone into a deep dive into this," and the paper will be put forth after discussing it with the International Monetary Fund (IMF) and the World Bank. According to *Economic Times*, it is expected to come out in August. However, the law on cryptocurrencies will take some more time as India is waiting on global consensus.

Adopting crypto as the national currency or even a parallel currency, like El Salvador, would be a step too far. It will be like giving away the control to the holders of that crypto. Like every change takes time, it will too.

Notes

1 Change of money: act of exchanging denominations of money.
2 Alyattes I had issued the first metal coin made of electrum, an alloy of gold.
3 Fun fact: Spanish dollar, also known as "Piece of 8", was literally a conjoint coin and can be cut to provide a change.
4 2020 SCC Online SC 275, Equivalent citation: MANU/SCOR/18084/2018, (03.07.2018 – SC Order).
5 Article 19(1)(g) of the Constitution of India.
6 DLT is a blockchain-based digital system that stores itself on various servers, making it a distributed ledger. DLT stores basic information such as transaction and customer details.
7 This is available only to Salvador citizens.

References

Baruah, R. (2022, January 18). *PM Modi calls for global action on crypto at virtual Davos meet | Mint*. Mint. Retrieved June 30, 2022, from https://www.livemint.com/economy/pm-modi-calls-for-synchorised-global-action-on-cryptocurrency-at-world-economic-forum-11642438173783.html

Blog – Cashco Financial. (n.d.). *Cashco financial*. Retrieved June 8, 2022, from https://cashcofinancial.com/2016/01/the-history-of-plastic-money/

Central African Republic clarified that it accepted Bitcoin as a reference currency. (2022, May 2). *The Times of India*. Retrieved June 21, 2022, from https://timesofindia.indiatimes.com/business/cryptocurrency/bitcoin/central-african-republic-clarified-that-it-accepted-bitcoin-as-a-reference-currency/articleshow/91251526.cms

Choo, L. (n.d.). India's taking a go-slow approach to crypto. *Protocol*. Retrieved June 5, 2022, from https://www.protocol.com/fintech/india-crypto-regulation-tax

Edwards, J. (2024, March 14). Bitcoin's price history. *Investopedia*. Retrieved April 12, 2024, from https://www.investopedia.com/articles/forex/121815/bitcoins-price-history.asp

Helms, K. (2022, April 7). Indian parliament member insists crypto is like gambling–wants to tax at 50%. *Bitcoin News*. Retrieved June 30, 2022, from https://news.bitcoin.com/indian-parliament-member-insists-crypto-is-like-gambling-wants-to-tax-at-50/

How to trade in crypto–crypto and crypto–INR pairs on Exchan(India). (n.d.). *ZebPay*. Retrieved January 20, 2023, from https://help.zebpay.com/support/solutions/articles/44001971011-how-to-trade-in-crypto-crypto-and-crypto-inr-pairs-india-

India, F. (2024, April 10). Bitcoin's price history: 2009–2024. *Forbes India*. https://www.forbesindia.com/article/explainers/bitcoin-price-history/92523/1

India to take a considered view on crypto: Finance Minister Nirmala Sitharaman (Press Trust of India, Interviewer). (2022, April 27). *The Indian Express*. Retrieved

June 30, 2022, from https://indianexpress.com/article/india/india-to-take-a-considered-view-on-crypto-nirmala-sitharaman-7890452/

Nakamoto, S. N. (2009). Bitcoin: A peer-to-peer electronic cash system. *Bitcoin*. Retrieved June 8, 2022, from https://bitcoin.org/bitcoin.pdf

Nevil, S. (2023, May 27). What is proof of work (PoW) in blockchain? *Investopedia*. Retrieved April 12, 2023, from https://www.investopedia.com/terms/p/proof-work.asp

RBI proposed to adopt a graded approach to launching the country's CBDC. (2022, June 1). *The Times of India*. Retrieved June 30, 2022, from https://timesofindia.indiatimes.com/business/cryptocurrency/blockchain/rbi-proposed-to-adopt-a-graded-approach-to-launching-the-countrys-cbdc/articleshow/91926536.cms

Reserve Bank of India – Notifications. (2018, April 6). Retrieved June 21, 2022, from https://www.rbi.org.in/Scripts/NotificationUser.aspx?Id=11243

Reserve Bank of India – Press releases. (24 C.E., December 24). Retrieved June 21, 2022, from https://rbi.org.in/Scripts/BS_PressReleaseDisplay.aspx?prid=30247

Reserve Bank of India – Speeches. (2022, February 14). Retrieved June 30, 2022, from https://m.rbi.org.in/Scripts/BS_SpeechesView.aspx?Id=1196

Tretina, K. (2022, April 8). How to buy bitcoin instantly in India (April 2024). *Forbes Advisor INDIA*. Retrieved May 10, 2022, from https://www.forbes.com/advisor/in/investing/how-to-buy-bitcoin-in-india/

Part 5

Data Localization Policy and Online Dispute Resolution

12 Policing Virtual Reality and Promising Cyber Peace: An Impending Need for Integration of Cybersecurity

Madhuri Irene

Introduction

The advent of the new millennium has been an admixture of tremendous technical innovations and gorgeous trade wheel rotation in addition to unpredictable financial, health, and environmental pandemonium. While the evolution of the Fourth Industrial Revolution moved from mechanics to 'Artificial intelligence', the emergence of destructive technologies permeated into human life, vetted all aspects of life – men and machines, and remained ubiquitous and unrivalled. Modern man inundated under technological tenor and tenure started breathing in virtual reality (VR) instead of virtuous virility. Relations are construed and constructed online in social, economic, and professional planes, and human business, trade, and commerce are determined and dissolved online. The exponential growth of modern trade and commerce on regional and global levels diminished the presence of parties, and the conclusion of contracts was accomplished online virtually. "Online dispute resolution (ODR)" has become a handy and hilarious instrument in the settlement of disputes of human business and commercial complexities.

As ODR hovers in VR, more so in the post-pandemic period, it is naturally afflicted with the discomforts of technological operations and human aberrations such as fraud, cheating, and stealing of resources of economic worth. Digital reality is not a sanctimonious shelter to protect all human interests and rights in the commercial world, and the world of assumptive VR is sought to be protected and strengthened with an enduring technical and legal framework. The fountain of cybercrimes is found to be jetting out enigmatic problems in human and trade relations, warranting credible security in the cyber world. Business transactions are reportedly victims of cyberattacks every 11 seconds. The global initiative to encompass robust cybersecurity measures sparked through the "Protocol on Cyber Security, 2020" rekindled the hopes of the business world to meet the needs of the upsurge in "ODR". The ODR should be ensured and emboldened to counter and inhibit potential hackers from deciphering and accessing sensitive information and to armour the

DOI: 10.4324/9781003517290-17

integrity, confidentiality, and availability of arbitration and dispute settlement in the cyberspace world.

Fictional reality hoisted a hilarious and enticing world for active generations – infants, young, and, to some extent, tired and retired. Life is becoming too mechanical; machine-driven intelligence controlling the human race and natural humans is being developed by "artificial intelligence (AI)". The traditional and age-worn concepts of contracts, property, persons, criminality, and liability may be constrained to be redefined and jurisprudence reformulated. Of course, law is not parochial to defy change in human attitudes and lives but shall be restrictive when the change in technical civilization tends to annihilate the very core of humanity and human values and human rights philosophy. It may be preposterous to construe human life as a commercial product, and if metallic robots claim rights of love, sex, reproduction, and sovereignty against their very creator, that is human beings, then the survival of human race will certainly be at stake and nears extinction. The subtlety between aspiration and ambition may evaporate, and the rationality of mind and conscience may go berserk.

A totally virtual experience is one in which nothing perceived is real. While VR substitutes a synthetic environment for the real one, augmented reality (AR) enriches the actual physical environment with superimposed virtual objects. Users remain immersed in real space as AR seamlessly integrates visual information such as virtual objects or tools to help users perform actual tasks (Malhotra, 2021). "AI" -based products may initially be non-invasively seen on the human body but subsequently devices implanted internally, which we are gleaning through three-dimensional engineering.

The virtual morality of the contractual nexus between absentia parties and online trade reality appears to be invisibly beyond depiction or description. Mortal man may be disguised in virtual fantasy, but moral principles of contracts, contacts, and relationships cannot be disguised by manoeuvrability and expediency – be in the virtual world or virtuous, that is physical world. Moreover, with the fast-evolving social VR where the right to privacy may have to be traded off, the hustle between anonymity and familiarity becomes a matter of investigation and research (Divine et al., 2020). However, the grace of liberal familiarity (self-disclosure) provisions in social VR might be incompatible with the defined legal framework pertinent to online trading platforms.

Knowingly or unknowingly, we are ushering into "instrumentarian society", which may be understood as a society in which individuals are herded as machines operating collectively under the control of algorithms. Shoshana Zuboff, a harsh critic of the digital industry's agenda to programme humans as machines, says that "automated machine processes not only know our behaviour but also shape our behaviour at scale. With this reorientation from knowledge to power, it is no longer enough to automate information flows about us; the goal is to automate us" (Zuboff, 2019).

Caveat to the human race, the mirth and might of machinated magnificence and the delirium of simulated virtual realism may become menacing malevolence as the splinters of "AI" substituting and overpowering the natural intelligence are scaring even the scientists and experts to caution that we are slowly nearing extinction when human race is turned into fodder of "AI" and humans traded off both online and offline. Whether "AI" is an angel or apocalypse is a new topic of high debate among scientists and other intellectuals.

Literature Review

A "systematic literature review on virtual reality and augmented reality" in terms of privacy, by Singh Aditi, Nirat Bhatnagar, Siddhant Damani, Charles Hobbs, Nehal Sarda Dalberg Advisors Accelerating the Adoption of ODR in India Could Transform How Disputes Are Resolved in an Overburdened System 2022 further P. SAMUEL JONATHANAI, 'machine learning will change the way we live' especially on Virtual cloud technology will ensure seamless connectivity and data storage, Bharath Visveswaraya, article on Justice-as-a-Service: India's "Online dispute Resolution" Movement at an Inflection Point, and also Mark Eggleton Cybersecurity desperate for people power May 25, 2022 who mentioned on Cybersecurity issues and matters of digital economy is taken from Business Jargons Digital Economy: https://businessjargons.com/digital-economy.html

Artificial intelligence matters taken from Garg Deepak, Potential AI risks for humanity: Speculative scenarios, https://timesofindia.indiatimes.com/blogs/breaking-shackles/potential-airisks-for-humanity-speculative-scenarios/ Sharma et al. "Security and privacy in Virtual Reality: and literature review (Al-Kofahi et al., 2021)". A systematic literature review on Virtual Reality and Augmented Reality in terms of cybersecurity by Patel & Trivedi (2022), Virtual Reality and Cyber Security: A Systematic Literature Review by Khan et al. (2021), Cybersecurity Threats and Karuppannan Jaishankar, International Institute of Justice and Police Sciences, International Journal of Cyber Criminology Vol 1 Issue 1 January 2007, systematic literature review of Jewkes, Y., & Yar, M. (2010). Introduction: The Internet, cybercrime, and the challenges of the 21st century. In Y. Jewkes & M. Yar (Eds.), Handbook of Internet crime). Willan Publishing, Kashettar Swathi 'Nano robots Will Help Humans Achieve Immortality by 2030 April 4, 2023 and also Sharma Navneet & Sethi Kritika 'Online Dispute Resolution' platforms can ease case burden on courts 2020

Methodology

The methodology of this chapter is based on doctrinal research. To identify the key legal rules and principles that apply to VR and cybersecurity, I analysed a variety of legal sources, including primary sources like statutes, cases, and regulations. I also considered secondary sources such as law review articles and treatises.

Result and Discussion

Translucent Technology and Laggard Legislation

By the end of the 20th century, willy-nilly science and technology had transformed natural human life and existence into machine-oriented business and mechanical intelligence. Technology has been taking the lead and rapidly permeating into all aspects of human and business life and spreading its tentacles into medical, educational, agricultural, trade, and commerce spheres, particularly with the explosion of high-powered technologies, including AI and machine learning.

Technology is not a mere dream but a product of dreams of innovation, inventions, and human intelligence, and its interrelationship with human life, society, and the environment is inextricable. Technology is the solicitation of scientific knowledge for the benefit of individuals, industry, and society to strengthen the economic prosperity of the state. Of course, the profuse use of technology brings with it the virus of crimes, as could be seen in cases of cybercrimes such as hacking, identity thefts, malware installation, and phishing (Abhishek, 2022).

The impact of technology on society is inexplicable and has both positive and negative results. Positively, technology makes the resources and means easily accessible for a happier life for individuals and society, such as good communication facilities, well-developed technical education, and potential use in the mechanized agricultural sector and health sector. To cite negative impacts, we may refer to the increase in unemployment, environmental pollution, health and mental concerns, and cybercrimes, as well as cultural changes and conflicts.

The Fourth Industrial Revolution has ushered in aggressive changes through information technology, nanotechnology, AI, and machine learning, leaving their footprints on the social, economic, and cultural aspects of human life. The assertion and transformation of disruptive technology (most of the technology that displaces an established or traditional technology or any brand-new product measured ground-breaking in that it creates a completely new industry) or destructive technology for the transformation of human health, education, trade and industry, and prosperity is no doubt an accepted fact of the later part of the 20th century and the present run of the 21st century. From steam engine to smart computers, the impact of break-through technologies on economic bloom so profoundly proclaimed is also tainted with the fissiparous tendencies and discriminatory divisions in social segments.

In the second decade of the 21st century, we stand on the cusp of the Industry 4.0 (Fourth Industrial Revolution) paradigm with a core of industrial revitalization, transformation, and development. Industrial Revolution 4.0 or Industry 4.0 is the combination of the cyber and physical worlds through the introduction of new technologies in the industrial fields that are empowering India. We all know that the digital revolution became the firm ground with the amazing interconnectivity of the Internet of Things (IoT) and machine-to-machine communication (M2M), which allows for self-observing smart machines that can evaluate and diagnose without human intervention. The emergence of smart factories that access real-time data to boost productivity and efficiency goes one step further in some cases, where organizations are utilizing AR and AI for further development (Gupta, 2021).

Science travels in Sputnik and Law limp with caged cavalry. Science and technology and law are not distant and disconnected islands but species with the consanguinity of observation, experimentation, and proven factual matrix. For reasons better known to the scientific world, the distilled declaration of "proved fact" appears to sound all of a sudden, whereas the declaration of fact in law comes after prolonged discussion, debate, and verification on the touchstone of legality. Although both science and law have a common object, that is service to the human race, science is awarded with the hundred percent objectivity, but legal results are often attributed subjectivity. Furthermore, science until its bloom is not restrained or refrained by either society or the state, and its early fabulous benefits are garnered by a selected and privileged group of people, that is mostly investors and researchers or inventors, and modern technological innovations are especially free from the complexities of the legal dragnet. No doubt, technological inventions are of Goliath stature, but the law could not become David before the technology. While science armed with incredible innovative technologies pierce through space and bewildering black-hole notches, augmenting corporate earnings at unpredictable heights and treading tax-less lawns, the state regulatory mechanism and legal control appear to be at a laggard snail pace.

Trade Online and Dispute Resolution

Trade prosperity exerts a tremendous impact on national economic prosperity and is reflected in global economic viability. According to the Global Trade Outlook of 2023, the world's merchandise trade volume was anticipated to grow 1.7% in 2023 before reaching 3.2% in 2024. However, geopolitical tensions, food insecurity, potential financial instability stemming from fiscal policy tightening, and growing levels of debt may tilt the balance of expectations.

Again, the trade capacity growth in 2022 was slower than expected at 2.7% following a fourth quarter slump but was still stronger than worst-case scenarios due to the Ukraine war. The value of world stock trade rose 12% to US $25.3 trillion in 2022, inflated in part by high global commodity prices, and the value of world commercial services trade increased 15% in 2022 to US$ 6.8 trillion. Digitally distributed services exports were worth US$3.82 trillion in the same year (Embargo, 2023). The share of online trading in India in the fiscal year 2018 accounted for nearly 30% of overall trade, showing an increase of 12% over the previous year, and Internet trading has become mainstream in the country today, with many new customers entirely using online financial services companies (Rathore, 2022). According to the Trends & Landscape Report, 2021, India's $14 billion online trade was affected by the COVID-19 pandemic in several sectors, forcing companies to shift towards digitization to stay operational and competitive ("GCC Intensity Index", 2021). India's e-commerce market is one of the fastest growing in the world. The value of Indian e-commerce was $46.2 billion in 2020 and is likely to grow at 18.29% to $136.47 billion by 2026, catalysed by digital payments.

There is enough sarcasm in depicting the duration of litigation in India, and in commercial cases, the parties should spend over 4 years in the portals of courts and spend more than 1/3 of the claim value on the court and advocacy fee. Land disputes have a longer gestation of 20 years or more. The negative impact of inefficient courts on access to justice, governance, and ease of doing business is undisputable since nearly 67% of the prison population is under trial, and a staggering $20 billion infrastructure projects are stuck in pending litigation. Although India made good strides in ease of doing business, it ranks 163 out of 190 countries with respect to contract implementation (Visveswaraya & Musthafa, 2020). Alternative judicious systems of dispute resolution are not the gremlins of modern industrial and technological revolutions but are considered the rabid offspring of judicial delays, laxity, and complacency in disposing of cases before the courts and judicial institutions.

With 4.5 million cases pending in high courts, 31 million in district courts, and 350,000 in the 5 central tribunals, we are in need of ODR platforms to come up to the rescue. The ODR mechanism is simple and effective and thus carries enormous potential to become the mainstream dispute resolution system, the acceptance of which cannot be called into question (Sharma & Kritika, 2023). According to the National Centre for Technology and Dispute Resolution, the use of ODR will play a major role in easing the burden of courts. According to the latest data, more than 3,600,000 cases in India have been resolved through ODR since 2020. The private ODR institutions are instrumental in making ODR processes reachable to parties. This will generate a large number of employment prospects for arbitrators, mediators, and advocates.

According to the 2017 UNCITRAL's Technical Notes, "'Online dispute resolution' is a mechanism for resolving disputes through the use of electronic communications and other information and communication technology". In other words, ODR is a process to resolve disputes outside courts, combining technology and alternative dispute resolution (ADR) mechanisms (UNITED NATIONS, 2017). ODR is a breakthrough in the arena of dispute resolution across different sectors comprising finance and e-commerce. It is a process to settle disputes outside courts, combining technology and ADR mechanisms. A research report of the Dalberg Team comprising Aditi Singh, Charles Hobbs et al. observed that a wider adoption of ODR might improve access to inexpensive, cost-effective, and just dispute resolution in India that would unlock $26.5 billion in economic assistance annually, which might greatly improve the well-being of marginalized populations and the elevation of enterprises to augment and buttress the national economy (Dalberg Implement).

Moreover, the non-filing of ODR cases during the COVID-19 pandemic period due to the dysfunction of courts may push the stability of the Indian economy back to a decade. India distinguished with its technological leadership globally backed by relevant legislation such as the Information Technology Act and the Data Protection Bill, and with the increase of ODR cases, an active dispensation of cases online, particularly related to trade and commerce, would brighten the economic viability, reducing the delay in settlement of disputes. Furthermore, the NITI Ayog Report titled "Designing the Future of Dispute Resolution" exhorted to deal with challenges such as bringing awareness about ODR in the public, secure technical and other infrastructure, attending to security concerns and cultural and linguistic subtleties, and constructing an effective legal framework that ensures trust, accessibility, and fruitful implementation.

Having taken note of the significance and importance of the adoption of ODR techniques, it is heartening to note that the government of India has made laudable efforts, such as the National Centre for Dispute Resolution, the Online Consumer Mediation Centre (OCMC), the Digital India flagship programme, the Samadhan Portal, the National Internet Exchange of India (NIXI), the e-Courts Integrated Mission Mode Project, and e-Lok Adalats, to extensively promote ODR. Investing in ODR and using more advanced second-generation technology can assist India in stirring towards a more revolutionary justice system. India's capacity and resource potential should not be questioned in applying second-generation technology in dispute resolution, and it should also rely on institutional will and personal integrity (LEXPEEPS- 2021).

Complementing the ideological implementation of governments, the private sector has also shown appreciable initiatives to promote and expeditiously enforce the scheme of ODR, and many legal and technological experts in coordination with social and business leaders launched the E-ADR Challenge in 2019 to welcome innovation to the field of law and build an alternative dispute resolution platform that could accelerate the process of dispute resolution with the help of advanced technology. ODR platforms in India, including ODR ways, Presolv360, and SAMA, have been actively working to popularize ODR ways.

The notion of "quick and painless justice" propagated through the ODR mechanism may no doubt be alluring, but the dispensation of justice under this umbrella is mostly dependent upon technically related cooperation and expertise, and any failure in the perpetual partnership of technology may directly impact the very purpose and efficacy of alternate dispensation of justice. Due to the enormous data and information relating to the public on the Internet, the uninterrupted dread of information disclosure falling into the hands of unscrupulous criminals, and the lack of an effective and timely preventive and punitive mechanism, there is an imminent need to design a fool-proof policing wing – manual and technological – to guard against cybercrimes and technological terrorism. Talking about the need for a "mindset shift" in regard to dispute resolution, Justice Chandrachud articulated that "we need look upon dispute resolution not as relatable to a place, namely, a court where justice is administered, but as a service that is availed of". The stars seem to be aligning, and India seems ready to encircle ODR (Visweswariah & Mustafa, 2020).

Legal and Regulatory Measures

Keeping aside the voluminous regulatory mechanism of corporations, there are few statutory provisions touching online trade and e-commerce, such as

a) Income Tax Act, 1961
b) Consumer Protection Act, 1986
c) Information Technology Act, 2000
d) Foreign Exchange Management Act, 2000
e) Payments and Settlement Systems Act, 2007
f) Companies Act, 2013
g) Laws related to GST

In July 2020, the Ministry of Consumer Affairs, Food, and Public Distribution published the Consumer Protection (E-Commerce) Rules, 2020. The rules define how to display the country of origin of products and services, the labelling of goods with expiration dates, and information about returns, refunds, exchanges, warranties, and guarantees. In June 2021, the ministry recommended additional amendments to the rules, including alteration of the definition of an e-commerce entity, mandatory registration of e-commerce entities, establishment of a grievance redressal mechanism, a ban on what the Indian government alleges to be the manipulation of e-commerce search results, and a ban on flash sales.

Moreover, there are no specific laws that administer the use of consumer data and privacy, although the IT Act of 2000 and the Indian Contract Act of 1872 touch upon these issues. With the proliferation of the digital ecosystem in our country, the Data Protection Bill, 2019, was designed to address personal data protection and privacy after deliberation before the Joint Parliamentary Committee was improvised and introduced in the parliament, recently ensuring a comprehensive legal framework on the subject. Beyond that, the RBI has issued new policies for payment gateways and payment aggregators that prohibit them from storing credit card data. Foreign companies must form an Indian goods and services tax (GST)-registered entity or partnership with an Indian distributor or trader when doing business in India. The Ministry of Trade and Industry regulates online sales in the Indian market.

In 2019, the Indian government issued a draft National E-Commerce Policy to regulate this sector. This policy focuses on cross-border data flows, intellectual property, and competition. The government of India allows 100% FDI in B2B e-commerce businesses and 100% FDI in B2C e-commerce under the "automatic route", without prior approval of the RBI or central government.

The e-commerce policy also addresses topics in the Draft Non-Personal Data Governance Framework and National Cybersecurity Strategy 2020.

Thus, we can see that the rate at which political and legislative control emerges does not correspond to the rate of technological development and that state executives and institutions must prepare to shrink the gap between technology and law to meet the progress of society.

Are ODR platforms a viable alternative to cybersecurity?

With the recent proliferation of ODR cases, ODR platforms operate complex software that allows them to manage multiple simultaneous file downloads in real time. To meet the needs of emerging security in the event of a cyber threat, the platform has taken painstaking measures by adopting technologically advanced security measures and demonstrating a number of exceptional features powered by various cybersecurity tools, including Protocol 2020 and international standards (ISO). To prevent potential hackers from decrypting and accessing sensitive information and ultimately compromising security, reliability, or accessibility ("CIA triad"), the following measures are generally applied:

1) Multifactor authentication (MFA): Access Controls under Principle 7(b) of the 2020 Protocol
   Two-step confirmation is a noticeable feature of many ODRs that limits the potential for data exposure. This feature provides an additional layer of security so that only authorized individuals can access sensitive information.
2) Encryption of data: Principle 7(c) of the 2020 Protocol
   Encryption is a cybersecurity measure that protects information by using extremely complex and unique codes that blend up data and prevent unauthorized users from deciphering sensitive information. It helps prevent the discovery of confidential information, including trade secrets, financial information, and personal distinguishable information.
3) Collecting and storing information: Asset management encapsulated in Principle 7(a) of the 2020 Protocol
   "Asset management" is another important standard in the process of collecting and storing all sorts of information during the case supervision of arbitral proceedings, which is encapsulated in Principle 7(a) of the 2020 Protocol.
4) Managing breach incidents: Principle 7(h) of the 2020 Protocol – Information Security Incident Management
   During the COVID-19 pandemic, despite robust security measures, there has been a notable spike in fishing attacks, mal-spams, and ransomware attacks. To ensure the recovery of lost or stolen information, Principle 7(h) is applied, and through repetitive platform audits to perform a studied plan of action to respond to an incident and to detect new security vulnerabilities or potential threats, breach occurrences are managed. In doing so, stakeholders shall take proactive steps in adopting tailored automatized safeguard tools that encompass essential security measures, such as multitiered

authentication, encryption, secured collection, and storage, as well as in managing breach incidents to minimize the risk of a security breach during online proceedings (Gonzales & Masumy, 2020).

"Man-in-Loop" (Artificial) Intelligence: Friend or Foe!

The sudden spring of AI is being greeted with both bouquets and brickbats. Even expert scientists, philosophers, and progressive thinkers of the day are apprehensive of unforgivable perils and upheavals that may endanger the very existence of human race. On the one hand, AI is credited with bringing astounding results and amazing benefits of technological revolution, positively impacting social, economic and cultural fronts, and on the other hand, AI is accused of being a harbinger of doomsday for human existence. AI systems may be integrated with quantum computing systems, distributed systems, and cloud servers. Such robust computing capacity can affect spectacular brain power that can unleash the secrets of humanity, mortality, and the ways to go beyond humanly possible boundaries. It can get to know the secrets hidden in the outer space, potential alien life, and God element (Garg, 2023).

According to Ray Kurzweil, a former Google scientist with an insightful predictive sense, nanorobots will help humans become immortal in just 7 years. Nanobots are tiny 50- to100-nm broad robots that are now utilized in research as DNA probes, cell imaging tools, cell-specific delivery vehicles, etc. Kurzwell's prediction of robots defeating chess players was realized. Reconnecting the brain and spine, AI can make paralysed patients move (Kashettar, 2023). Virtual cloud technology will ensure seamless connectivity and data storage, and AI and machine learning will change the way of life in this modern era (Jonathan-2021). Stephen Hawking said, "The development of full 'Artificial intelligence' could spell the end of the human race". Elon Musk claims that AI is humanity's "biggest existential threat" (Kelsey, 2021). AI is also charged for accelerating the cybercrimes emerging from information technology. For half a century, Geoffrey Hinton, a pioneer in AI, nurtured the technology at the heart of chatbots like ChatGPT. Now he worries it will cause serious harm and warns of the probable dangers ahead, and the threat of A.I. would be more urgent than climate change.

Deepak Garg, director of leading india.ai and NVIDIA Bennett Research Center on AI, observes that AI development is going beyond the boundaries of human ethics, morality, and safety. He states that there will be a loss of human autonomy since the new generation is becoming overdependent on AI-enabled systems, which can lead to the weakening of human agency and decision-making capabilities and make the human race vulnerable and agile before these powerful technologies. The endless use of AI will result in enormous cultural change, the benchmarks of morality and ethics may have to be redefined, and it will become difficult to distinguish between AI and non-AI systems and species (Garg, 2023).

Furthermore, it is predicted that AI may see the emergence of sects devoted to the worship of AI. The latest generation of AI-powered chatbots, trained on large language models, has left their early users awestruck – and sometimes terrified – by their power. These are the same sublime emotions that lie at the heart of our experience of the divine, and the rise of AI may give rise to new religions (McArthur Neil, 2023). Unscrupulous use of AI with regenerate capabilities and embedded systems used as swarm drones and arms and ammunitions in warfare may result in catastrophic damage to the human society. Nanorobots created with malicious intent have numerous scenarios that cause lethal impacts on individuals. AI is rapidly becoming embedded around us, hidden but ubiquitous. Science fiction that depicts AI in the form of conscious beings has fuelled popular misconceptions of AI and done some disservice by trivializing the imminent AI revolution. Fantastic narratives have generated lively speculation and debate regarding the consciousness of machines. People often confuse intelligence and consciousness. Intelligence exists in many forms and can be conscious or unconscious. Human intelligence is only one kind of intelligence (Malhotra, 2021).

AI: Friend or Foe

AI, having come into existence, will continue to exist, perpetuate, and hold a predominant position over other disruptive technologies, and we cannot annihilate such a wondrous scientific and technological power and energy from the realm of industrial and individual life. Insofar as trade disputes and the resolution of trade conflicts are online, its basic and essential features and knowledge of its operation are inevitable requirements to conclude all trade and commercial differences or disputes. Trade and commerce have become coextensive with AI, and the law of trade and commerce is required to move along with the principles and law of virtual reality. Very strangely and disquietly, the law of AI has not yet crossed the threshold of deliberations.

To compare AI with natural intelligence in terms of definition, ambit, scope, and purpose would be a Herculean task or an imprudent casualty. From the viewpoint of common sense, natural intelligence ennobles us to realize that the principles of nature are inherently embedded not only in the hearts of humans but also in all living creatures. Natural intelligence admits the need to respect nature, its grant, and benevolence for all living and non-living beings, not to deplete or dent nature, to move with beings with a sense of equality, fraternity, and liberty. It is an organic evolution felt and experienced palpably by humans.

AI, on the other hand, is an inorganic experience caused by machine intelligence and a simulation of purported intelligence originating from a mechanical process or endeavour. Unfortunately, the birth of AI is concealed or hidden from disclosure for a long time until the innovation is declared in public, but its growth runs with unpredictable speed beyond human imagination and control. That is why law could not simultaneously take birth and growth with AI. It is ironical that natural intelligence loses or diminishes its glow and intellectual value with the active play of AI.

Change is the law of life. We cannot prevent or stultify the innovations and development in human history, so AI should be allowed to live its life to comfort and complement the needs and services of human beings. A constructive and positive utility of AI cushions human prosperity, and nefarious and inimical application of AI may end in counterproductive results. In fact, for any calamity due to the application or operation of AI, we should not accuse the science of AI since such a hazardous direction emanates from the natural intelligence of the human mind only.

We love robots to function as assistants or attendants but not to be sensitized with human love and reproductive desires. We may accept ChatGPT for limited academic consultations but not to multiply reformed copy scripts. Honesty of the human mind may succeed with AI, and dishonest minds and thoughts may mislead AI to devastate human nature. Punish the offender and not the knife used in the commission of offence.

Unwieldy Cyber Criminology vis-à-vis Amorphous Security Cordon

> *"Intelligence is not only the ability to reason; it is also the ability to find relevant material in memory and to deploy attention when needed."*
> – Daniel Kahneman, Thinking, Fast and Slow, Macmillan Publishers, NY

Humans are the most incorrigible polluters of space, both physical and virtual. We have converted pristine space into a storehouse of fragmented rocket debris, and in the information age, we have criminalized the virtual space with cybercrimes committed on planet earth; both the natural environment and virtual environment are sullied. Social scientists and legal doyens are awestruck to find the traditional criminology bloated by the new extension – cyber criminology – overshadowing the conventional concepts of crime and its constituents. Thus, cyberspace has become an exciting frontier for criminologists. Virtual reality and computer-mediated communications challenge the traditional discourse of criminology, introducing new forms of deviance, crime, and social control (McKinsey & Co 2019).

Many renowned academic experts, such as Loader and Thomas (2000), Littlewood (2003), Yar (2005), and Douglas Thomas observed how cyberspace has emerged as a new locus of criminal activity. In fact, criminology has been remiss in its research into the phenomena of cybercrime and has been slow to recognize the importance of cyberspace in changing the nature and scope of offending and victimization; paradoxically, some of the most marginalized and neglected debates facing criminologists and other scholars interested in cybercrime, deviance, policing, law, and regulation in the 21st century are yet to be disseminated for the benefit of the public (Jewkes & Yar, 2010).

Cyber criminology is a radical and evolving discipline for social scientists and computer wizards to crystallize research on many aspects of the interface between computer science, Internet science, and criminology (Jaishankar,

2007). Cyber criminology may be defined as "the study of causation of crimes that occur in the cyberspace and its impact in the physical space" (Jaishankar, 2007). McAfee used an alternate word, "virtual criminology", in their report published in 2006 (Indian Institute of Astrophysics). There is a need to identify the differences between cyber criminology and cyber-forensics. Cyber-forensics deals exclusively with the investigation of cybercrimes, whereas cyber criminology deals with the causation of cybercrimes.

There is a great need for leveraging knowledge from the past to address the future, and the discipline of cyber criminology approaches the future, facing the dire need to document the literature in this rapidly changing area, which has become more important than ever before. Moreover, the fields of Internet science, computer science, and criminology remained compartmentalized without an interdisciplinary approach, and as such, cyber criminology would coordinate the work of Internet and computer scientists, communication specialists, and criminologists for such an interdisciplinary approach to cybercrime, cybercriminal behaviour, cyber victims, cyberlaws, and cyber investigations.

Needless to say, cybercrime constitutes the nucleus of cyber criminology. In a broader sense, cybercrime may be understood as any criminal activity that involves the use of information technology illegally and includes unauthorized accessing information, intercepting data, damaging or deleting data, interfering with the functioning of a computer system, and identity theft. In the absence of proper and effective security measures, cybercrimes affect all levels of business, government transactions, and public privacy, and in view of the enormous use of the Internet, cybersecurity has become the crux of the problem for all individuals, institutions, society, and states. Today, "in computers" (computer illiterate individuals) are at a disadvantage more than normal illiterate individuals. However, cybercriminals are not part-time amateurs or script kiddies but state-sponsored adversaries and professionals. It is pertinent to refer to an observation of Halliday on the nexus of cybercrimes and Internet made in 2011 producing evil effects on society:

> As urban disturbances spread across numerous English cities, politicians and mass media claim that new social media had been used by participants as a means of disseminating information about incidents in real time and utilized as a means of social coordination to facilitate rioting and to better evade the police. The U.K. Prime Minister, David Cameron, suggests that barring "trouble-makers" from using such media may be desirable in the interests of public order.

Cybercrime

Computer-related "cybercrime" can be classified as a type of crime rather than a specific crime. For example "hacking/cracking" involves unauthorized entry into the computer systems and databases of another person or entity, stealing information and money in routine transactions; piracy of newly created or disseminated forms of intellectual property in cyberspace; pornography created and transmitted over the Internet; and the use of the Internet to bully or harass others. The consequences of cybercrime are the same as those of traditional crimes, except that different methods are used. An increasing number of people are becoming vulnerable due to the transnational nature of the Internet and the increasing access of criminals to more victims.

Cybercriminals may target an individual's private information or corporate data for theft and resale.

Cybercrime usually does not occur in a vacuum; in many ways, they are distributed in nature. In other words, cybercriminals often rely on other actors to commit crimes, for example malware creators use the dark web to sell code, illegal drug distributors use crypto brokers to hold virtual currency, or state threat actors rely on cryptocurrencies. Technology contractors steal intellectual property (IP).
Online extortion:

A crime involves an attack or threat of attack along with a need for money to stop the attack.

Cryptocurrency mining:

An attack that uses scripts to mine cryptocurrency in the browser without the user's consent. Cryptocurrency attacks can involve downloading cryptocurrency mining software into the victim's system.

Identity theft:

An attack occurs when an individual accesses a computer to collect a user's personal information, which they then use to impersonate that person or gain access to valuable accounts or their value, such as credit and debit cards.

Cyber espionage:

Crime involves cybercriminals breaking into a system or network to gain access to confidential information held by a government or other organization. Attacks can be motivated by profit or ideology.

Cybercrime is a multibillion-dollar industry that makes cybercriminals rich, with an annual income of approximately US$1.5 trillion, and 43% of victims are small businesses, mainly through scams. Software piracy:

An attack involving the illegal copying, distribution, and use of software programs for commercial or personal use.

Phishing campaigns, credential attacks, credit card fraud, exit scams, malware infections into systems and networks, illegal gambling, sale of illegal items – such as weapons, fake gases, drugs, or products – and soliciting, manufacturing, possessing, or distributing children for pornographic content.

Cybercrime

Cybercrime statistics present a frightening scenario. According to the US FBI Internet Crime Records, approximately 422 million people were affected; 800,944 claims were registered in 2022. It is expected that some 33 billion accounts could be hacked by 2023, causing nearly $8 trillion in losses. Cybercrime losses are expected to reach $10.5 trillion by 2025, up from $6 trillion in 2022. An estimated 80% of reported cybercrimes are typically due to attacks.

Thirty-three billion accounts were estimated to be hacked by 2023, corresponding to 2,328 victims per day or 97 victims of cybercrime per hour. A total of 8,00,000 cyberattacks were recorded, and there was an average hacker attack every 39 seconds. It is estimated that 2,328 cybercrimes occur every day. Over the past 21 years, from 2001 to 2021, cybercrime claimed the lives of at least 6.5 million victims, with an estimated $26 billion in damage during the same period. Phishing accounted for approximately 16% of all data breaches, causing an estimated $4.91 million in damage.

Cybercriminals are very hard-hearted, have little or no respect for human morality and values, and do not hesitate to deal even with corpses. During the war in Ukraine, scammers and malicious attackers embezzled money from a generous and innocent public by launching fraudulent fundraising appeals such as "Help save Ukraine's children", and Slavic-language phishing emails increased sevenfold. The attackers installed malware on Ukrainian systems. Cybersecurity culture

The cybercrime statistics mentioned above call for immediate remedial action – at the national, regional, and international levels – and underline the importance of cybersecurity. All government and business leaders are encouraged to develop and adopt the necessary policies, create a strong cybersecurity culture, and take preventive actions by establishing a cybersecurity hedge.

The results of joint research by the IBM Institute for Business Value and the University of Oxford Research Unit paint a compelling picture of the evolution of cybersecurity into an important strategic capability. 66% of respondents view cybersecurity primarily as a revenue enabler. Rethinking security through a lens of value instead of as a budget line item can lead to transformative growth.

Prof. Lesley Seebeck advocates that cyber skills should be embedded in us as a life skill. The war for talent in the space is a global one as organizations not only find it difficult to fill positions in the field but also struggle to retain staff long term. Prof. Seebeck further says that cybersecurity is the flip side of the digital world. "We live digitally on our phones, but the flip side of that is we're constantly being monitored and tracked, so cyber skills should be embedded in us as a life skill that's taught from the early days of primary school", she says (Mark Eggleton 2022).

It appears that all the users of cyber connectivity, individual or institutional, might not be provided with effective and foolproof cybersecurity systems. Moreover, the day-to-day evolution of information technology and Internet services and other technological inventions can hardly be checked or controlled despite cogent and vigilant security cordons in view of the nature of technical developments with the advent of AI and machine learning. New kinds of crimes emerge every day and hour beyond the imagination of human brains. The cyber network in some aspects is amorous and amorphous. Thus, cybersecurity has become a part of the regular functioning of the cyber business world.

Benefits of Digital Economy

The limitations of the digital economy are discussed as follows:

1) Cybersecurity: Increasing digitalization has resulted in an increasing number of cyber threats and crimes in the recent past, and unless cybersecurity effectively counters cybercrimes, a safe and trusted environment exists, and the cyber economy cannot strengthen the national economy.
2) Disruptions in labour markets: Recent changes in digital transformation and the rise of the cyber economy have resulted in the loss of jobs and deleterious labour market changes that have widened income inequality and unrest in labour and manual workers.
3) Strong infrastructure requirement: It requires strong infrastructure concerning Internet, telecommunication, and mobile industry penetrating even suburban and rural areas with sound Internet connectivity (Business Jargons).

Threat actors are winning in the cyber economy, seizing on the expansion of organizations' overall attack surfaces and increased vulnerabilities introduced by society's reliance on connected services. Cybercriminals are damaging and disturbing cyber peace, making a deep dent on the cyber economy or digital economy. It is time for operation leaders to flip the equation – not by matching dollars lost with increased spending but by changing how they think about cybersecurity. Cyber peace ensures a good cyber economy. The camaraderie of cyber peace and cyber economy is the need of the hour and a clarion call for a sustainable future.

Conclusion and Policy Recommendation

The amazing developments brought about by information technology have churned economic development in many fields, such as education, health, industry, agriculture, and business. The transition to Industry 4.0 and the subsequent ubiquitous digitalization and integration of AI into the economic system have set the stage for a fundamental change – one towards forming a cyber-economy: a type of economy in which humans are economic subjects who interact with or are confronted with AI (Alexander et al., 2021).

The term "cyber economy" refers to those parts of the economy that are fundamentally based on the application of digital information and communication technologies in their value creation, transaction, allocation, distribution, and benefit creation, that is an economy based on the Internet or an economy in cyberspace. The terms "digital economy" and "cyber economy" are synonymously and widely used and are also known as the "Internet economy", "online economy", and "network economy". This economy emerges consequent to the digital revolution, that is digital information and communication technologies in the course of digitalization; consequently, there is a change in the structure and functional logic of technical, economic, social, and political systems and processes. Digital transformation impacts the shift in essential economic processes in the digital info-sphere (Lengsfeld, 2019).

The digital economy results from billions of everyday online connections among people, businesses, devices, data, and processes. The backbone of the digital economy is hyperconnectivity, which means the growing interconnectedness of people, organizations, and machines that results from the Internet, mobile technology, and the IoT. The digital economy gradually undermines conventional notions of business structure, consumer services, information, and goods. Professor Walter Brenner of a university in Switzerland stated that the aggressive use of data is transforming business models, facilitating new products and services, creating new processes, generating greater utility, and ushering in a new culture of management (Heath and Micallef, 2021).

Technology defines to a great extent the possibilities that companies have at their disposal for strategy reframing. The influence of the Internet and computer communications does not stop at the outer boundaries of technical computer communications but spreads through history as we move towards increased use of online tools to accomplish e-commerce, information acquisition, and community operations. To make security a critical enabler of successful transformation and growth, organizations are shifting their focus from risk exposure to cyber resilience (IBM Institute for Business Value, 2023). Rather than living in a state of perennial defence, where attention is focused on mitigating threats and surviving to fight another day, leaders need to recognize security as an essential common thread that ties together the organization's business and technology strategies. Technology-enabled business transformation is no longer about investing in individual areas simply to achieve functional maturity. Instead, it must be about combining technologies and capabilities to unlock larger pools of value, aligning operations to achieve greater efficiencies, and collaborating more effectively to deliver better business outcomes. Policing cyberspace and virtual reality is an incessant and inevitable need to safeguard the cyber economy.

References

Abhishek, L. (2022). *Notes.* https://www.geeksforgeeks.org/impact-of-technology-on-society/

Alexander, C., Vladimir, M. F., Julia, V. R., Elena, G. P. (2020). *The cyber economy opportunities and challenges for 'artificial intelligence' in the digital workplace(2019).* Springer International Publishing

Business jargons digital economy. https://businessjargons.com/digital-economy.html

Damian, H., & Ludwig, M. *What is digital economy? Unicorns, transformation and the internet of things.* https://www2.deloitte.com/mt/en/pages/technology/articles/mt-what-is-digital-economy.html

Divine, M., Zamanifard, S., & Guo, F. (2020, November 1–4). Anonymity vs. familiarity: Self-disclosure and privacy in social virtual reality. In *26th ACM symposium on virtual reality software and technology (VRST '20)*, Virtual Event, Canada. ACM, New York, NY, USA. https://doi.org/10.1145/3385956.3418967

Eggleton, M. (2022, May 25). *Cybersecurity desperate for people power.* https://www.afr.com/technology/cybersecurity-desperate-for-people-power-20220522-p5anja

Embargo. (2023). *This publication is under embargo until 14.00 Geneva time on 5 April 2023.* chromeextension://efaidnbmnnnibpcajpcglclefindmkaj/https://www.wto.org/english/res_e/booksp_e/trade_outlook23_e.pdf

Emergence & future of online dispute resolution in India post covid-19 by: Lexpeeps. (2021, December 2). https://lexpeeps.in/emergence-future-of-online-dispute-resolution-in-india-post-covid-19/https://www.nasscom.in/knowledge-center/publications/gcc-india-landscape-2021-beyond

Garg, D. (2023, May, 7). Potential AI risks for humanity: Speculative scenarios. *The Times of India.* https://timesofindia.indiatimes.com/blogs/breaking-shackles/potential-airisks-for-humanity-speculative-scenarios/ ('GCC Intensity Index', 2021).

Gonzales, W., (CyberArb), & Masumy, N. (2020). https://arbitrationblog.kluwerarbitration.com/2020/09/25/online-dispute-resolution-platforms-cybersecurity-champions-in-the-covid-19-era-time-for-arbitral-institutions-to-embrace-'Online dispute Resolution's/

Gupta, P. (2021). *Key trends Industrial Revolution 4.0 in India.* https://www.eletimes.com/key-trends-of-industrial-4-0-revolution inindia?gclid=%20CjwKCAjwvJyjBhA-pEiwAWz2%20nLXnw5vOR6DavhZCqsWvvEUQb1vO9SnhwNSCUvCbiSzKU-WQPwRChjhoCtXwQAvD_BwE

Heath, D., & Micallef, L. (2021). *What is digital economy? Unicorns, transformation and the internet of things.* Deloitte. https://www2.deloitte.com/mt/en/pages/technology/articles/mt-what-is-digital-economy.html (accessed on 22.09.2022)

IBM. (2023). *IBM institute for business values prosper in the cyber economy.* https://www.ibm.com › case › YLGDAMVR

Indian Institute of Astrophysics, Bangalore. chromeextension://efaidnbmnnnibpcajpcglclefindmk aj/https://www.ifap.ru/pr/2008/n081212b.df

Jaishankar, K. (2007). Establishing a theory of cyber crimes. *International Journal of Cyber Criminology*, *1*(2), 7–9.

Jewkes, Y., & Yar, M. (2010). Introduction: The internet, cybercrime, and the challenges of the 21st century. In Y. Jewkes & M. Yar (Eds.), *Handbook of internet crime.* Willan Publishing.

Jonathan, P. S. (2021, September 15). *'Machine learning will change the way we live': Virtual cloud technology will ensure seamless connectivity and data storage, says SRM Pro V-C.* https://www.thehindu.com/news/national/andhra-pradesh/ai-machine-learning-will-change-the-way-we-live/article36464676.ece

Kashettar, S. (2023, April 4). *Nano robots will help humans achieve immortality by 2030.* https://www.analyticsinsight.net/latest-news/nanorobots-will-help-humans-achieve-immortality-by-2030

Kelsey, J. (2021). *Reconciling Tax and Trade Rules in the Digitalised Economy: Challenges for ASEAN and East Asia*. Economic Research Institute for ASEAN and East Asia.

Khan, A., Krishnan, S., & Dhir, A. (2021). Electronic government and corruption: Systematic literature review, framework, and agenda for future research. *Technological Forecasting and Social Change, 167*, 120737.

Lengsfeld, J. (2019). *Digital era framework*. https://philpapers.org/rec/LENDEF-3

Littlewood, J. (2003). *Cyber security desperate for people power*. https://www.afr.com/technology/cybersecurity-desperate-for-people-power-20220522-p5anja

Loader, B. D., & Thomas, D. (Eds.). (2000). *Cybercrime: Law enforcement, security and surveillance in the information age* (1st ed.). Routledge. https://doi.org/10.4324/9780203354643

Malhotra, R. (2021). *'Artificial intelligence' and the future of power – 5 battlegrounds* (p. 22). Rupa Publications India Pvt. Ltd.

McArthur, N. (2023). *Gods in machine? Rise of 'artificial intelligence' may lead to new religions*. https://www.ndtv.com/science/gods-in-machine-the-rise-of-artificial-intelligence-may-result-in-new-religions-3871893

McKinsey & Co. *Perspectives on transforming cybersecurity*. https://www.mckinsey.com/~/media/McKinsey/McKinsey%20Solutions/Cyber%20Solutions/Perspectives%20on%20transforming%20cybersecurity/Transforming%20cybersecurity_March2019.ashx

Patel, P. D., & Trivedi, P. (2022). A systematic literature review on Virtual Reality and Augmented Reality in terms of privacy, authorization and data-leaks. arXiv preprint arXiv:2212.04621.

Rathore, M. (2022). *Share of online trading in overall trading volume India 2012–2018*. Published by July 21, 2022. https://www.statista.com/statistics/1056671/india-share-of-online-trading-turnover/

Sharma, N., & Kritika, S. (2023). *'Online dispute Resolution' platforms can ease case burden on courts*. https://www.policycircle.org/economy/industry/online-dispute-resolution/

Singh, A., Bhatnagar, N., Damani, S., Hobbs, C., Dalberg, N. S. (Advisors). *Accelerating the adoption of ODR in India could transform how disputes are resolved in an overburdened system*. https://dalberg.com/our-ideas/accelerating-the-adoption-of-odr-in-india-could-transform-how-disputes-are-resolved-in-an-overburdened-system/

United Nations New York. (2017). https://www.policycircle.org/economy/industry/online-dispute-resolution/https://uncitral.un.org › sites › files › UNCITRAL

Visveswaraya, B., & Mustafa, T. (2020, August 11). *Justice-as-a-service: India's 'online dispute resolution' movement at an inflection point*. https://www.omidyarnetwork.in/blog/justice-as-a-service-indias-online-dispute-resolution-movement-at-an-inflection-point

Yar, M. (2005). The novelty of "cybercrime": An assessment in light of routine theory. *European Journal of Criminology, 2*, 407–427.

Zuboff, S. (2019). *The age of surveillance capitalism: The fight for human future at the new frontier of power*. New York Publications.

13 A Primer on Data Localization Policy in India*,**

Anjali Tandon and Devender Pratap

Introduction

Digitalization is fast becoming an economic reality in operationalizing e-business and e-commerce through electronic data interchange. Recent times are increasingly characterized by the paperless transfer of information and content via telecommunication, media, and entertainment industries, giving fast rise to "big data". The resulting accumulation of mass data, on the one hand, creates opportunities for business firms, and on the other hand, creates privacy issues for end-users of the data-related products and services. Consequently, governments tend to statute laws for data protection which govern the process and purpose of data collection, processing, transfer, and storage ensuring the privacy/rights of subject data. Taking a step in this direction, the Indian government has recently enacted the first data privacy law – Digital Personal Data Protection (DPDP) Act, 2023. Notwithstanding several deliberations over the past years, the novelty of the DPDP Act and the lack of prior experience to guide future regulatory developments necessitate a scrupulous approach.

One aspect of data protection relates to the data localization requirements through which the governments mandate data storage, transfer, and processing within local/designated territories. Apropos the DPDP Act takes a modest approach to the data localization requirement by stating that the government may restrict cross-border data flows by notification. However, the localization requirements as introduced earlier by sector-specific agencies such as the Reserve Bank of India (RBI) will continue in effect. While the DPDP Act has indeed cleared away the longstanding uncertainty around the data localization requirements for business firms by taking a more pragmatic approach, it remains to be seen how the firms translate this into their business, and the implications on data protection (Burman, 2023). At the same time, the Act retains adequate control for the government to grant exemptions for the state functions, thereby leaving scope for revisions and experimentation in response to imperatives of the Act over data protection and data businesses in India. It is important to take note that even though beyond the purview of the DPDP Act, the evolving framework of laws regulating the companies that operate various social media platforms, and the providers of IT services and business

DOI: 10.4324/9781003517290-18

firms also have the potential to influence how the regulations around data protection develop in the country. Therefore, the imposition of data localization requirements by other sector-specific regulators cannot be precluded in the future to protect the interests of the end-users if the need arises. It is with this background that the present chapter provides evidence to guide future regulations around data localization policy in India by presenting an assessment of the likely outcomes in terms of key economic indicators under simulated scenarios.

The impact assessment of a data localization policy has indeed been challenging even for countries with data protection regulations in place for some time now. Part of the challenge is due to the dynamic digital technology frontier, which has constantly moved upwards with the introduction of newer products and services, increased data volume, and emerging risks. Also, the task is arduous due to the inability to predict with certainty the economic value of the likely damages from stricter data restrictions, or the compliance failure due to the scope which may well be inclusive of the personal, national/government, and business losses.

In the Indian context, a study on data localization and restrictive flow of data is critically linked to India's digital services – a key performing sector, further adversely impacting the national income due to its higher digital service elasticity of GDP (CUTS International, 2020). This also impacts investment that is primarily centred in services, the related welfare and innovation, and the start-ups that are highly correlated with exports of digital services. Another study based on limited evidence from India shows the highest costs of data localization for sectors such as communication and financial services (Kathruia et al., 2019). However, a study in the context of data localization, specifically at a sector level identifying the policy sectors, has critical significance. The present chapter is an effort to fill the gap in this direction. These policy sectors tend to further impact business activity in the remaining sectors of the economy due to their use as inputs, thus creating economic externalities. The endeavour is to provide a direction on the likely impact of India's data localization policy which, if introduced in the future, will influence through the channels of digital transactions, e-commerce activity, and the data localization mandate for data firms taking into account various interactive forces operating in the economy.

The underlying approach is to provide a primer by conducting an economic assessment of the likely impact in a computable general equilibrium (CGE) framework. The model is comparative static in nature. This is in the form of designing alternate scenarios to evaluate the direction and magnitude of the economy-wide changes that are likely to occur under a relatively restrictive regime mandating data localization. In the process, hypothetical scenarios are designed with and without accompanying changes in policy to support the concerned domestic industry, which is presently in its infancy. Using the Global Trade Analysis Project (GTAP) model, we simulate the economic impact of a stricter data regimen requiring the localization of data to see if there exist trade-offs on select performance indicators in the economy at the macro and sector levels. We attempt to provide insights that are representative of the direction and proportional in magnitude to the change in the policy regimen ceteris paribus so that more information is available to guide future policy. The approach is through a self-assessment (of India) against a benchmark.

The rest of the chapter is organized as follows. Section 2 explains data localization requirements. The overview of the broader dimension of the data protection policies practised across regions and countries of the world is given in Section 3. Section 4 explains the data protection policy in India. Section 5 presents the formulation of the problem and the underlying methodological details. Results are discussed in Section 6, followed by summing-up in Section 7.

Data Localization Requirements: Genesis and Experience

The accumulation and analysis of data in large pools offers a huge advantage for business firms through developing new products, improved targeting, monetizing content, etc. The ensuing big data technology simultaneously necessitates data storage and processing. Its characteristic volume (exponential size), variety in source and form (such as audio, video, and image), velocity (frequency of generation), and variability (inconsistency) are correlated with additional difficulties and rising costs. Firms overcome the limitations by achieving scalability by transferring data to locations with competitive options to minimize storage and operational costs.[1] The resulting arrangement delimits the geographical boundaries on data while transferring the possession of an intangible, yet critical, asset in an economy – its data. The data firms further champion the analysis of personal and organizational information contained in large and complex data by augmenting data through tracking with public data sources and government statistics, the latter often being the source of sensitive information. This results in a conflict of interest between the data firms optimizing the costs, taking advantage of the large-scale data and the governments concerned with the security and confidentiality of information. The cost competitiveness of data-related operations and the security issues bring in the concept of data locations as the preferred choice for activities such as hosting and processing of data, and the related restrictions in the form of data localization requirements as exercised by nation(s) to address the concern for privacy of data.

The subject has attracted significant attention in the emerging policy debates around the issues of (i) civil protection; (ii) external surveillance at various levels – government, organizational, and individual – posing a challenge to national sovereignty; (iii) economic power (i.e. monopoly) accrued from the access to data; and (iv) misuse of data for undeclared purposes. The concerns arise due to the possible damage from the leak of personal information of clients (e.g. bank account and patient details), employees, etc. A theft/leak of personal information such as social security numbers and banking information can result in fraud in the name of the victim, further raising a legal issue against the inflicted individual. The concerns are common across developed and developing countries.

These risks have led countries to introduce regulations on data that govern the ownership, transfer, storage, and process of data. Governments attempt to control the jurisdiction over data by imposing restrictions that can be absolute, relative, or partial. The data localization requirement is one of the various regulatory measures adopted. It essentially mandates that data generated within a territory are stored, transferred, and processed locally or within a jurisdiction. Although regulations in the form of data localization *per se* do not necessarily guarantee the privacy and security of data, they can prove instrumental by providing assured, unconditional, and protected access to data relating to the individuals/nation as indispensable information during sensitive times. Evidence is the European Union (EU)'s management of the fundamental right to privacy while contact tracing during the COVID-19 pandemic, attributed to the security-related measures adopted by the business firms and organizations mandated under the General Data Protection Regulation (GDPR) (Ventrella, 2020).[2] The GDPR specifies technical standards and requirements for handling territorial data, resulting in de facto localization requirements for data (Parekh et al., 2022). During the pandemic, the European Commission reportedly liaised with eight European telecommunications operators for access to anonymized geolocation data for coordinating measures to track the spread of COVID-19 (OECD, 2020). This gave the EU Commission access to meta-data on hundreds of millions of mobile phones of natives while maintaining privacy standards. The telecom carriers were obliged to service the desired information under the GDPR obligations (Scott et al., 2020). Furthermore, governments tend to minimize the risk of international surveillance and attempt to secure personal/national information by mandating the storage, process, and use within compliant jurisdictions where adequate protection measures have been in place.

The extent of restrictions through data localization is observed to range from mandatory local storage and processing of data (e.g. China), to the conditional transfers subject to meeting the criteria that have been laid before (e.g. the EU). Also, the scope of restrictions can be limited to specific sectors (e.g. health data in Australia). Although countries differ in approaches, and the level of restrictions, there has been a cost attached to regulating the data. A study on the EU notes that data restrictions introduce an extra cost to the firm equivalent to 8% of its profits and 2.2% of its sales (Presidente & Frey, 2022). The fines imposed for non-compliance can potentially cost the firm 4% of its global revenue (Anant et al., 2020).[3] At the same time, mandatory compliance with the data regulations introduces additional costs from maintaining multiple/duplicative data centres. The additional costs are likely to be passed to consumers through increased prices of goods and services, ultimately impacting consumer utility. Since both compliance and non-compliance have associated costs, a comparative analysis would be helpful to address the related concerns of the firms. Interestingly, a study based on the response of multinational enterprises to the GDPR implementation in the EU suggests it pays to invest in compliance through audits, enabling technologies, and expert staffing (Ponemon Institute LLC, 2017). However, the costs are unwanted for the associated business as they detract from the attractiveness of business operations. The likely reciprocation from the multinational corporations is another important consideration. This will have a profound implication on India's booming service exports, primarily under Mode 1 service trade – accounting for more than 60% of India's service exports – which are extensively dependent on information and communication technologies in an ever-increasingly digitalized world.[4] The significance of digital service exports, as illustrated by the GDP elasticity of 0.02, further underscores the critical link with data flows for a developing and service-led economy, such as India (CUTS International, 2020).

Regional and Country-Level Initiatives for Data Protection

Regulations aiming at data protection are enforced in the form of privacy, protection, and localization, while also having significant overlaps within. The gravity of data-related concerns is reflected in the increasing number of controls exercised by countries. The number of countries having data localization controls has increased by 77% in a short span between 2017 and 2021 (Devane, 2023). The number of countries imposing data localization controls has increased from 35 to 62 during the period. Even more notable is the increase in the number of such controls, which has more than doubled over the period from 67 during 2017 to as much as 144 during 2021, suggesting that countries have further added to their existing controls. A substantially higher proportion of countries having some form/level of data localization requirements is a fair indication of the concerns that broadly arise in the context of privacy, leakages/thefts, and the loss of opportunity and jobs in the local economy (UNCTAD, 2023). A significant proportion (71%) of the countries in the world have existing data protection legislation in place, while another 9% have draft legislation. Countries without legislation on data protection account for 15%, and another 5% of countries have no data. As many as 95 laws have comprehensive coverage, and 12 are sectoral or constitute a subset of another regulation (e.g. on e-commerce or related to consumer protection). Across regions, Europe leads with the highest proportion of comprehensive data protection policies; the African region has the highest proportion of draft data protection laws. The partial or sectoral data protection laws are prevalent in western Asia, South East Asia, Central and East Asia, and Africa (UNCTAD, 2016). Quite often restrictions for the protection of data are enforced in varied forms including residency requirements (mandating a geographical territory for storing data), privacy requirements (relating to the laws and regulations governing the data, at its place of storage), and localization requirement (demanding that data generated in place remains within the border).

Upfront examples of region-level initiatives towards protecting data include the initiatives in the EU, Asia-Pacific Economic Cooperation (APEC), African Union, Commonwealth, and the Trans-Pacific Partnership. The GDPR in the EU is the earliest and among the most comprehensive data protection law. Data such as the profile of an individual, employment, finance, health, and payment are mandated to be stored within the territory. Transfer of data, whether for storing or processing, is permitted only to locations with equivalent privacy protection. In the APEC region, a privacy framework with nine principles – preventing harm, notice, collection limitations, uses of personal information, choice, integrity of personal information, security safeguards, access and correction, and accountability – was developed and finalized in 2005. The APEC also has a system for consolidating complaints within the APEC jurisdiction. The more recently introduced Cross-Border Privacy Rules in the APEC system in 2015 encourage firms to voluntarily adopt privacy measures for cross-border data flows. In Africa, the African Union Convention on Cybersecurity and Personal Data Protection was adopted in 2014 to establish a framework for personal data protection, electronic transactions, and cybersecurity. At the subregional level, the East African Community Framework for Cyberlaws was adopted in 2010 recommending member countries to design regulations on data protection. Another subregional initiative has been the Economic Community of West African States Supplementary Act A/SA.1/01/10 with recommendations on the content of laws governing data privacy. It also requires member countries to establish a data protection authority.

At the country level, the Russian case is complex with a combination of laws that protect data in all sectors. In the UAE, third-party transfer of personal data within and outside the country is permitted subject to the consent for the transfer, except for the financial data which has to be retained within borders. Restrictions also exist in the telecommunication industry in the form of prior consent before sharing subscriber information. Through the Cybersecurity Law of Vietnam, the government controls the flow of information instead of data privacy rights. China is noted as a strict enforcer of data localization. Even though data remain within the border, customer consent to store and process data is required. In exceptional cases, where data are transferred beyond the border, the overarching cross-sector Personal Information Protection Law, 2021, mandates prior approval from the Cyberspace Administration of China.

The restrictions, though impacting the competitiveness of the business, give an edge to the firms that oblige. As countries attempt to exercise their control over data, the data firms face the challenge of benefiting from scalability that is constrained since they are required to invest in separate territorial hard and soft infrastructure, organization structure (hiring local expertise), physical assets (land and building), and technical infrastructure (hardware and software such as AI applications). On the other hand, the conduct of a data firm's operation in a manner compliant with domestic data regulation offers a competitive edge through the digital trust of the customer. This not only contributes to improving firms' reputation even in other locations but also expands their domestic market through greater customer traffic due to assured privacy and ethics. In addition, firms with a compliant past also benefit from improved market valuations and better prospects for mergers and acquisitions in the future (Parekh et al., 2022).

There also exist non-commercial considerations, which tend to make the laws stricter. The civil society perspective has received attention with the rising number of high-profile data breaches and instances of surveillance. This makes the linkages between consumer rights and data protection stronger. Traditional consumer protection was designed to cover transactional stages of direct marketing, arrangements in the contract, payment process, and post-sales processes. However, the emergence of digitalization has brought in the need to reform and expand the coverage. Data protection regulations attempt to safeguard consumer rights and privacy by imposing transparency and fairness for an informed decision by the consumer, while also minimizing the instances of potentially fraudulent activity.[5] In this regard, the regulating governments hold the view that territorial control over localized data is vital to ensuring the privacy of the consumer. Other important motivations also include the (i) prevention of monopolies that may arise from the restrained access to data within the firm (e.g. in the case of aggregator firms), (ii) "infant industry" argument in a fast-changing and dynamic environment with continuously evolving technologies, and (iii) benefits from job creation, skill development, and investment in the local economy.

Data Protection in India

The chronology of India's legalization in the IT sphere dates with the proposal of the Information Technology Act of 2000 to deal with e-commerce and cybercrime. The Act came into force with effect from October 17, 2000, to take action against contraventions involving a computer, computer system, or computer network in India, with an extraterritorial applicability. Under the Act, activities such as data theft, hacking, pornography, defamatory content in messages, and spreading viruses are recognized as criminal offenses. Also stipulated under the Act are the rules for due diligence by the Internet Service Providers. India's e-transaction laws are also governed under the United Nations Commission on International Trade Law (UNCITRAL) Model Law on Electronic Commerce (1996) and UNCITRAL Model Law on Electronic Signatures (2001).

Later in the year 2012, the erstwhile planning commission established a committee under the chairmanship of Justice A P Shah to make suggestions on national privacy principles. The Shah Committee report recommended an over-arching law to protect privacy while enlisting nine guiding principles. The recommendations of the report have stayed relevant since then. In 2017, the Telecom Regulatory Authority of India released a consultation paper on privacy, security, and ownership of data in the telecom sectors for comments from the stakeholders.

Over the years, the expanding digitalization of the Indian economy and a range of digital initiatives under the Digital India Mission have contributed to generating an increasing volume of data with a potential value of $1 trillion in the digital economy by 2025 (Ministry of Electronics & Information Technology, 2018). With faster digitization, the need for a system of governance has been noted to leverage the available data for the benefit of the nation and its citizens through the use of data by the government and private sector for socio-economic benefits.

In India, personal data are regulated under the basic framework in the form of Information Technology (Reasonable Security Practices and Procedures and Sensitive Personal Data or Information) Rules, 2011.[6] The Rule primarily ensures that personal data activities, such as collection, processing, storage, handling, retention, transfer, and disclosure, occur only with the consent of the subject to the corporations. It has been argued that the rule lacks a comprehensive approach to address the challenges that have arisen over time, while there also have been areas of ambiguity. In 2017, the petitions on Aadhaar sensitized the privacy rights over data. Consequently, the government constituted a committee chaired by Justice B N Srikrishna to formulate the legal framework for a free and fair digital economy. The committee known as the Srikrishna committee submitted a white paper for public comments in 2018. The emerging concerns around data privacy were endorsed in the landmark judgement of the Supreme Court of India of 2018, recognizing the right to privacy as a fundamental right. Following the developments, the Ministry of Electronics & Information Technology presented a revised version of the Srikrishna Committee report to the parliament, called the Personal Data Protection Bill, 2019. Following the consultations of the Joint Parliamentary Committee, a revised draft was published in December 2021, called the Data Protection (DP) Bill, 2021, which was set to become law. The bill sought data localization for companies, mandating storage and processing within national territory. The proposed text received resistance from big-tech firms due to the expected increase in business costs and due to intensive compliance requirements. However, in August 2022, the DP bill was withdrawn by the government at a stage when it was nearly set to turn into a legal existence with the expectation of a revised version in the future.

Interestingly, the government also set up another committee, the Gopalakrishnan Committee, for a framework on non-personal data. The proposed bill sought to address jurisdictional issues with cross-border data flows by bringing all firms processing data on Indian personnel under the data protection law. Suggestions included the enforcement methods for cross-border offences such as imposing penalties based on global turnover, restriction of market access, mutual legal assistance treaties, mandatory establishment of a representative office, and making the subsidiary/related entity liable for damages.

In the interim, the RBI separately issued a circular for the payment firms on the "storage of payment system data", demanding that all data about payments be stored in servers within India. In case data processing takes place outside India, this should be done within one day of the transaction, and details stored overseas are required to be deleted. The RBI also issued the Guidelines on Regulation of Payment Aggregators and Payment Gateways regulating the activity of digital payment aggregators and providing technology-related recommendations for payment gateways. Following a few extensions on the timelines for enforcement, the guidelines came into force on October 1, 2022. A key provision in the guideline prevents payment aggregators and payment gateways from storing customer card data and related financial data, also mandating that previously stored data are purged. This is an attempt to prevent fraud and personal information leakages that may occur during card transactions, with a clear message from the enforcement of the guidelines that data privacy will not be compromised and that legal jurisdiction will be governed by Indian law.

In the following month of November 2022, a fresh draft of the DPDP Bill, 2022, was introduced by the government for public consultations. The DPDP Act passed in August 2023 was significantly based on this draft, which is considered to have reduced obligations for business firms and offer protection for consumers through a simpler regulatory structure (Burman, 2023). However, the government maintains discretionary powers for exceptional cases and circumstances suggestive of its command over remedial actions as necessary. Particularly in the context of the data localization requirements, a reversal on the course of past versions of the bills is noted through a balanced approach where firms are not mandated for data localization requirements while continuing to uphold the mandates of sector-specific agencies such as the RBI. There is also scope for intervention in the future as interpreted from the possibility of imposing restrictions by notification from the government.

An earlier study by Bauer et al. (2014) quantified the effects of the proposed or enacted legislation of data localization in seven major countries, including India.[7] The results suggested relatively lower losses for India in the state of adopting partial data localization measures. However, the losses will increase manifold if India opts for stricter data localization measures. The stricter compliances add to business costs, as discussed earlier in the context of the EU. There also exists evidence suggesting that the cost of compliance is lower than that of non-compliance. Thus, there arises a clear need for more recent estimates on the cost and benefit of bringing in data regulation in India through a mandatory localization requirement. In the absence of such estimates, the best approach would be to assess the likely changes from the potential impact under hypothetical scenarios.

The DPDP Act creates safeguards through obligations on the collection and processing of data as mandated. The resulting enforcement will lead to the development of minimal standards of behaviour and compliance among the business firms that collect data, which are likely to evolve contingently upon the enforcement of the law. The timing of the Act, which is in its early stage of implementation, makes it opportune to learn from the legal frameworks of other countries, understand the prerequisites that were underlying the regulations, and also make an impact assessment of a restrictive (or alternately liberal) data regulation through their implications on economic activities. More importantly, the impact is likely to spill beyond the digital economy, covering other spheres such as the industry at the second stage, reflecting upon the performance of goods and other services. Against this background, we make a modest attempt to study the impact of data regulations on key indicators of economic performance.

Formulation of the Problem and Methodological Approach

The problem at hand is to understand the impact of a change in the policy ex-ante, thereby necessitating the need to simulate the existing/base-year conditions in the economy. Given the possibility of a simultaneous impact on multiple sectors of the economy and the assessment of different performance indicators, a CGE-based approach is preferred over the econometric modelling, where the effects on other sectors are expectedly significant. Therefore, the present analysis makes use of a computable general equilibrium model, namely the GTAP, which is a multi-country and multi-sectoral model fully documented in Hertel and Tsigas (1997).[8] The GTAP model is extensively used in analysing the impact of policy instruments that have implications on activity, factor use, and international trade. The theoretical formulation of the model is well established in terms of its computational simplicity in providing numerical solutions. The model assumes perfect competition in product and factor markets, constant returns to scale in all production and trade activities, profit-maximizing behaviour by firms, and utility-maximizing behaviour by households. The model is simulated to assess the impact of alternative hypothetical scenarios corresponding to a change in policy. This is executed by introducing a perturbance in the system through policy-relevant variables and/or by making a change in the standard closure.[9] The standard closure of the model fixes all technical change variables, the rates of taxes and subsidies, and the level of factor endowments. The latter effectively allows the prices of factors to vary within a region. Capital and labour (skilled and unskilled) are perfectly mobile between industries of a region.

The present exercise is concerned with the impact of a change in policy on the sector output and factor markets, indicators relating to macroeconomic performance, and investment, while also allowing capital inflows in the policy sectors. This is achieved through tweaks in the standard closure through a swap on the capital stock, which effectively allows capital to grow despite the comparative static nature of the underlying model. The consequent generation of the capital endowments can be considered as capturing the dynamic effect of the capital shock. An additional swap permits to capture the effect of real investment. While India hosts a large number of unskilled workers, we introduce a closure swap to capture the effect on employment by fixing the real wage and allowing employment to grow under this category.

Model and data: The analysis makes use of the GTAP model and GTAP database version 10.1, which is fully documented in Aguiar et al. (2019). The database covers 147 countries across the world, which have been aggregated to 19 countries/regions with India as a separate country. The remaining 18 countries/regions include Australia, Brunei Darussalam, Indonesia, Japan, Korea, Malaysia, New Zealand, the Philippines, Singapore, Thailand, the United States, Vietnam, China, EU36, the United Kingdom, other ASEAN members, SAARC nations, and rest of world.[10] The underlying 65-sector GTAP data are aggregated into 19 broad sectors. These are grains and crops, livestock and meat products, mining and extraction, processed food, textiles and clothing, light manufacturing, heavy manufacturing, computer, electronic and optical equipment, electrical equipment, machinery and equipment nec., utilities and construction, transport and communication, trade, accommodation, food and service, business services nec., communication, financial and insurance services, education, and other services.[11]

Identifying the policy sectors: The dependence of the digital interphase through the use of the Internet and flow of information is recognized across activities spanning agriculture (e.g. for precision agriculture in an outdoor environment), manufacturing (e.g. for supply chain management), and service (e.g. e-commerce) sectors. However, the cost and impact of data localization may vary across sectors and also between companies within a sector. For instance, opportunity costs of data localization are among the highest in the financial services and communication sectors, and for larger firms in general (Kathuria et al., 2019). Also, few sectors are likely to be more impacted than others primarily due to their international tradability, thereby having direct relevance for a data localization policy. Three sectors, namely business services, telecommunication, and financial and insurance services, are considered significant and direct users of e-commerce and digital flows. These sectors are generators of enormous data. The financial sector is already operating under the localization requirement mandated by the RBI (refer Section 4). Due to their high data intensity, these catalyst (choice) sectors are considered as the policy sectors in the present analysis. In fact, existing studies confirm the highest data intensity for telecommunication, closely followed by IT and other information services, and financial and insurance services (Mucha & Seppala, 2021).[12] A change in data localization policy will directly affect their operations through change (likely increase) in costs of operations from the need for fixed and operational expenditures such as the land and building, and soft and hard infrastructure. This is likely to impact their productivity. Almost all remaining sectors of economic activity are downstream users of their services in some form.

Formulation of the problem: The introduction of stricter/wider restrictions through a mandatory localization of data will increase the cost of services in the policy sectors (Carr et al., 2020). The increase in service costs will further be transmitted to the users, thereby raising the price of even other sectors, whether engaged in production or trading. This results in a decline in productivity; presumably, producing an equal amount of output will require higher expenditure on inputs (electronics, software, manpower, electricity, etc.). This in turn will impact the returns to factors of production, with a consequent crowding out of investment from the policy sectors, in the period immediately following the regulatory regime of data localization in place.

Simulation 1 mimics the impact of a restrictive data storage regime through the increase in the cost of capital as a factor of production, which leads to a decline in the efficiency of operations impacting the supply for the three policy services. The direct and indirect use of these services entails the generation point of a data transaction in the economy. Another impact could be through the likely diminished research and development activity under a constrained data flow contributing to the reduced scale of data generation, in turn reducing the precision of algorithms which advantage from running on a large amount of data (Bauer et al., 2014).

Simulation 2 incorporates the effect of a stimulus through an additional capital allocation at the aggregate level for augmenting the capital stock while ensuring capital allocation for the policy sectors as a support measure. For this, we employ a closure where capital in the earmarked sectors is exogenously fixed rather than endogenously or market-determined.

Another modification incorporated in Simulation 3 follows the literature (Malcolm, 1998; Hertel and Tsigas, 1997) where a market disequilibrium is introduced to have a larger inflow of investment in the country. This is likely to help in mitigating the injuries inflicted on the policy sectors. The scenario is executed through a closure swap on the "investment slack".

The employment implications for unskilled labour are modelled in Simulation 4 by fixing the corresponding wages and allowing for the quantity of labour to adjust.

Economic Analysis of the Hypothetical Scenarios

Simulation 1: Introducing data localization requirements

The impact of introducing data localization requirements as a regulatory measure is being modelled through the associated technical change, which brings about a deterioration in the productivity in the policy sectors. The effect occurs through raising the need for additional inputs and resources, thus leading to increased capital costs in the form of investment for the establishment and operation of a local data architecture. This impacts through a decline in productivity as the same amount of output now requires more input(s) of capital, at least in the medium term. It is appropriate to clarify that the amount of output de-augmentation introduced into the system does not exactly correspond to the rate of productivity change. A notional disturbance (shock) is used to provide a sense of the direction and magnitude of the impact of the productivity changes (deterioration) by 1% relative to the existing rate. Under market-driven conditions, the additional cost of business is passed on to the consumer, who pays higher costs for the same consumption as earlier.[13] The results may, therefore, be interpreted in a qualitative manner rather than for estimation purposes in a more literal sense of the term.

An immediate effect of the adverse productivity shock is through contraction of output, thus lowering the factor income followed by the increase in the price of services. The disruption causes a decline in consumer utility, leading to a welfare loss in the economy (Table 13.1 and Figure 13.1). Effectively, this lowers the available income that can be allocated for aggregate private and aggregate government consumption and in savings. The decomposition of the welfare change indeed confirms a significant negative contribution of the technological (in)efficiency in the three policy sectors. While each of the policy sectors contributes to the overall decline, the relatively stronger relevant technological inefficiencies arising in the financial and insurance services and the other business services are indicative of their sensitivity to the issue. A relatively

Table 13.1 Summary of outcomes under different scenarios in India (% change from baseline)

	Simulation 1	*Simulation 2*	*Simulation 3*	*Simulation 4*
A. Macro-level changes				
GDP	−0.16	0.37	0.45	0.56
Welfare (absolute change, $ million)	−3285	3852	6385	8231
Capital formation	−0.29	0.05	1.00	1.00
B. Sector-level changes				
B1. Output				
Other business services	−1.7	1.07	1.39	1.41
Telecommunication	−1.26	4.11	5.32	5.47
Financial and insurance services	−0.25	0.03	0.02	0.17
B2. Demand for unskilled labour				
Other business services	−0.78	−0.04	−0.61	−0.17
Telecommunication	−0.26	−1.68	−2.56	−2.13
Financial and insurance services	0.74	1.41	1.42	1.79
B3. Demand for skilled labour				
Other business services	−0.64	−0.11	−0.76	−0.72
Telecommunication	−0.12	−1.75	−2.7	−2.66
Financial and insurance services	0.88	1.34	1.26	1.23
B4. Exports				
Other business services	−2.45	1.15	1.54	1.51
Telecommunication	−2.75	9.26	11.77	12.01
Financial and insurance services	−2.65	−4.36	−5.96	−5.56
B5. Imports				
Other business services	0.68	0.53	0.66	0.78
Telecommunication	0.81	−2.08	−2.43	−2.42
Financial and insurance services	1.23	2.50	3.39	3.31

Source: Authors' estimates using the GTAP model

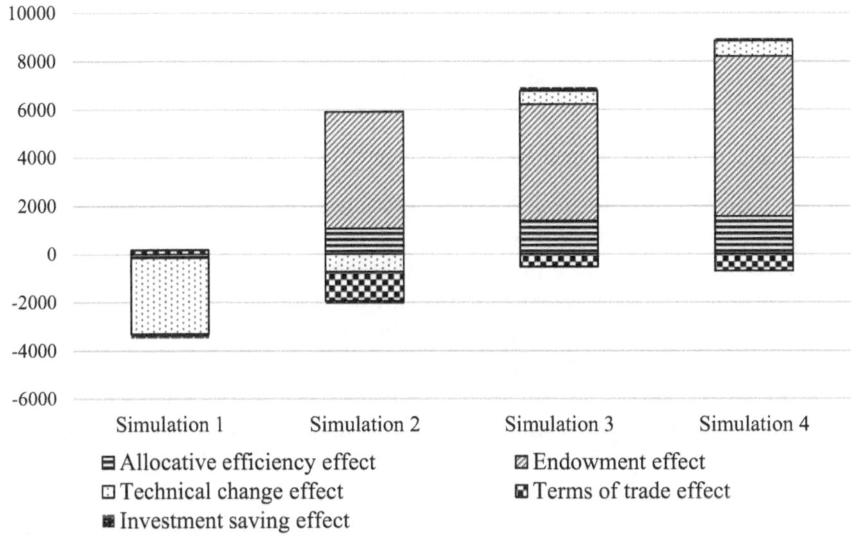

Figure 13.1 Decomposition of welfare change (million dollars)

Source: Authors' estimates using the GTAP model

lower sensitivity of the telecommunication sector to the requirement of data localization is attributed to the presence of large domestic telecom operators that are not dependent on data transfer to other locations. On the external front, given the tradability of the select services, particularly the (export of) business services, the increase in prices is observed to contribute through the improving terms of trade. However, the effect is marginal and, more importantly, inadequate to offset the welfare deterioration due to the technology deteriorating productivity shock. At the aggregate level, real income contracts by (−)0.16%. The decline in overall capital accumulation indicates the need for concerted efforts to improve investment and capital accumulation for improving productivity, an aspect attended to in the following simulations.

While output contracts in each of the three policy sectors, the financial and insurance services are relatively less impacted. The observation is well in order given the significant presence of public sector banks (within the broader financial and insurance services) operating in the domestically owned segment with local data centres, which partially lowers the cost escalation for the sector as a whole.[14] The existence of local data centres in the banking sector validates that local data architecture has not only been established in domestic operations but is also functioning well in a competitive market. Interestingly, while the capital requirement in the other business services and telecommunication sectors is observed to decline, the capital endowments of financial and insurance services increase. The latter is representative of investment in a sector that is well endowed with capital, while also suggestive of the remedial action therein.[15] The higher demand for capital in the sector is also accompanied by the rising demand for skilled and unskilled labour. However, output contraction in the former two sectors displaces labour as observed in the corresponding decline in demand for skilled and unskilled labour. As noted earlier, capital formation declines in the economy at the macro level.

Simulation 2: Capital stimulus for policy sectors

This scenario builds upon Simulation 1 by supporting the three policy sectors by assuring an increase in the available stock of capital for use. The impact of the previous simulation in a general equilibrium model results in the relocation of production factors across sectors of the economy. The attempt here is to provide stimulus to the policy sectors by securing capital for their use to contain the contraction in their output.[16] However, directing the available resources to the choice sectors may create distortions for other sectors and hence cause their contraction. Therefore, an overall capital stimulus of 1% is provided to the overall economy and a preferred sector-level allocation to ensure a 2% increase in capital for the three sectors. The sector-level interventions are observed to contribute to the improvements in the national output through an increase of 0.37% in overall welfare. Notably, the allocative inefficiencies on account of data localization are observed to have been addressed here. Also, the welfare loss on account of technical change has been nearly offset due to the capital augmenting effect. Benefiting from the stimulus, each of the three sectors register an expansion in output. An insignificant increase in capital formation (0.05%) is suggestive of the need to explicitly infuse more investment for productive capacity, leading to the following simulation.

Simulation 3: Getting additional investment inflows

This scenario builds progressively with an allowance for 1% foreign investment.[17] The design of the simulation ensures that even though investment may flow into sectors other than the policy sectors, the latter necessarily benefits from an increase in their capital use. Macro-level performance improves with real GDP growth of 0.45% alongside the increase in capital formation to the order of 1%. This is in contrast to Simulations 1 and 2, which registered crowding out of investment and a contraction and/or insignificant expansion in capital formation, respectively. The consumer utility improves. Each of the three policy sectors register output expansion, with an accompanying employment generation in the financial and insurance services. However, for the other business services and telecommunication, the decline in labour demand with the greater use of capital is suggestive of the possible substitution of capital for labour, therein causing displacement as the management, storage, and processing of data become more automated.

Simulation 4: Endogenizing the level of unemployment for unskilled labour

With generally higher and increasing levels of automation, it is expected that skilled labour will require higher levels of proficiency and talent, although less in number. At the same time, an increasing number of local data centres is likely to create some jobs in the construction sector for temporary and unskilled labour. Also, basic maintenance operations will require unskilled workers for housekeeping activity and security. In this simulation, the impact on labour demand is assessed by additionally fixing the wages of unskilled workers, thereby allowing for their employment to respond. A moderation in the negative effect of unskilled employment is indeed observed, although a complete reversal is outlying. The improved impact on employment of unskilled workers shows up through improvement in real GDP and welfare. The increase in exports of the other business services and telecommunication, as the two major policy sectors, is heartening to note as compared with the base case (Simulation 1).[18,19] The imports of telecommunication are reduced.

Also noted is traction in the manufacturing sectors (computer, electronic and optical equipment, electrical equipment, and machinery and equipment). Although the output expansion is indicative in magnitude, this is perhaps suggestive of the increase in the demand for hardware for creating domestic data architecture.

Conclusion

Our attempt in this chapter is to quantify, although indicatively, the economic effect of data localization policy in India if introduced in the near future. Since a binary discourse of the data localization policy is unlikely to find acceptance by all stakeholders, the analysis attempts to estimate the possible impact by simulating hypothetical scenarios that are relevant as a primer to appraise the possible change in the present policy on data localization. At the same time, a developing economy like India, with a strong commitment to digitalization, needs to reserve some policy space for the development of its infant data architecture industry (Banga, 2021) and for sovereignty concerns. Past experience in liberalizing through lower tariffs without concurrent attention to improving the competitiveness of India's domestic manufacturing has led to sub-optimal outcomes such as import dependency on goods and low levels of indigenous research and development. Of late, domestic competitiveness in manufacturing is being encouraged through initiatives such as the "Make in India" and the more recent Production Linked Incentive (PLI) schemes. Learning from the past, we believe there is a need for domestic readiness before bringing about any change(s) in the existing policy regime. The simulation results show that the observed adversity from the implementation of a data localization requirement could be reversed by bringing in more investments to support the establishment of an indigenous data architecture. The initial disturbance can be disciplined through additional flow of investments to maintain an adequate supply of capital. This will help improve the efficiency of the policy sectors, which will further enhance their competitiveness.

Keeping in mind the welfare loss from the standalone imposition of a data localization requirement, our results are in sync with that of the study reviewed earlier (Bauer et al., 2014). This, however, may not necessarily imply an opinion in favour or against the prospective change in policy. The analysis here is suggestive of the need for groundwork before the policy is revised from its ongoing status. Irrespective of the underlying motivation whether to develop technological independence in an international environment where digital frontiers are dynamic and evolving; address the challenges arising from data monopolies; or protect national sovereignty as an unmeasurable yet determined objective, the analysis underscores the need for better domestic arrangements in place. The initial disturbance in the three policy sectors can be disciplined through a policy supportive for additional investments and supply of capital. An early stage of preparedness in the form of indigenous data architecture and the other related requirements, while ignoring the investment requirements, can have constraining effects on the economy in the short- to medium-term. The data localization will have a limited effect on job creation as well.

In the end, we admit that designing the contours of the policy is complex. Therefore, the results in the chapter are notional and indicative of the direction and magnitude of the likely economic impact. The experience in reality is contingent upon many other factors including geopolitical relationships, democratic outcomes, and human rights and other commercial considerations as they emerge. A discussion on data security is beyond the present scope.

Notes

* Views expressed are those of the authors and in no way reflect the opinion of their affiliating Institutes.

** The guidance received from Prof. Badri N. Gopalakrishnan in formulating the problem is duly acknowledged.

1 Firms tend to select the locations for data centres based on factors such as the availability of large volume of electricity at low prices, green energy sources (due to environmental concerns), proximity to water bodies (such as lakes and rivers for cooling considerations), availability of vast land (for privacy and security), tax incentives, and the distance (of firms) from other existing data centres for fast transfers. In addition, the construction, equipment, and computer costs of a data centre are huge. Thus, setting up a data centre requires a large amount of investments. As a hint, the cost of a Google data centre unveiled in 2007 was estimated at $600 million, according to Googles' earnings reports (Aggarwal, 2014). The tech-giant spent $2.4 billion in its data centres during the same year.

2 The GDPR of the EU is applicable to an entity (including non-EU entities) if they process data on EU personnel or offer goods and services to EU citizens or residents, thereby ensuring appropriate protection of the privacy of the subject.

3 The estimates refer to GPDR regulation in the EU.

4 Based on the trade in services dataset by sector and by mode of supply (TiSMoS).

5 Few of the examples of a consumer exercising privacy on data include the choice to decline cookies when given an opportunity, refrain from accessing a website, use "do not track" options in the software, report wrong information, and access the browser in private mode.

6 Data are often classified into personal and non-personal.

7 The other countries include Brazil, China, the EU, Indonesia, South Korea, and Vietnam.

8 The model is open source and can be downloaded from the official website.

9 A model closure is essentially the definition of endogenous and exogenous variables.
10 For brevity, only results for India are reported.
11 nec.: not elsewhere classified.
12 The estimates of data intensity in Mucha and Seppala (2021) refer to a group of 12 OECD countries. Although the magnitude of data intensity may vary across countries given their level of digitalization, the relative intensities are unlikely to differ substantially.
13 For instance, available estimates suggest that local companies might have to pay additional 30–60% to meet their processing needs under data localization restrictions. The estimates vary with the processing requirements. This is seen in the EU where the estimated cost increases by 10.5% for cloud computing at 4 GB, while no cost escalations are noted for 1 GB and 2 GB requirements (Leviathan Security Group, 2015).
14 The increase in costs from productivity shocks are likely to be lower in future as well. This is majorly due to the localization requirement imposed already by the RBI in 2021.
15 By virtue of the nature of its operations, the financial and insurance services are endowed with a greater amount of capital.
16 However, directing the available resources to the choice sectors may create distortions for other sectors, which can cause their contraction. Therefore, an overall capital stimulus of 1% is provided to the overall economy.
17 The increasing foreign investment mimics the improvement in the price of capital through a disequilibrium in the investment-saving relations for the economy.
18 Decline in exports of financial and insurance services is over a low base due to its relatively low tradable nature.
19 These results are also reported for all preceding simulations.

References

Aggarwal, A. (2014). *How does google store their data?* Retrieved June 8, 2023, from https://www.quora.com/How-does-Google-store-their-data/log.

Aguiar, A., Chepeliev, M., Corong, E.L., McDougall, R., & van der Mensbrugghe, D. (2019) The GTAP data base: Version 10. *Journal of Global Economic Analysis*, *4*(1), 1–27. https://doi.org/10.21642/JGEA.040101AF; https://jgea.org/ojs/index.php/jgea/article/view/77.

Anant, V., Donchak, L., Kaplan, J., & Soller, H. (2020, April). *The consumer data opportunity and the privacy imperative.* McKinsey & Company.

Banga, R. (2021). *Joint statement initiative on e-commerce (JSI): Economic and fiscal implications for the south.* UNCTAD Research Paper No. 58 UNCTAD/SER.RP/2021/1

Bauer, M., Lee-M. Hosuk, Erik, V. D. M., & Bert, V. (2014). *The costs of data localisation: Friendly fire on economic recovery*, ECIPE occasional paper, No. 3/2014, European Centre for International Political Economy (ECIPE).

Burman, A. (2023, October 3). *Understanding India's new data protection law.* Paper, Carnegie India.

Carr, B., French, C., & Lowery, C. (2020). *Data localization: Costs, tradeoffs, and impacts across the economy* (Vol. 19, Issue 3). https://www.iif.com/Publications/ID/4225/Data-Localization-Costs-Tradeoffs-and-Impacts-Across-the-Economy. Institute of International Finance (IIF).

CUTS International. (2020). *Data localisation: India's double-edged sword?* CUTS International.

Devane, H. (2023). *Data localization: A complete overview.* Retrieved June 8, 2023, from https://www.immuta.com/blog/data-localization/.

Hertel, T., & Tsigas, M. (1997). Structure of GTAP. In T. W. Hertel (Ed.), *Global trade analysis: Modeling and applications.* Cambridge University Press.

Kathuria, R., Kedia, M., Varma, G., & Baghchi, K. (2019). Economic implications of cross border data flows. In *Indian Council for Research on International Economic Relations (ICRIER).* https://icrier.org/pdf/Economic_Implications_of_Cross-Border_Data_Flows.pdf

Leviathan Security Group. (2015). *Quantifying the cost of forced localization.* Leviathan Security Group.

Malcolm, G. (1998). *Modeling country risk and capital flows in GTAP.* GTAP Technical Paper No. 13, Center for Global Trade Analysis, Purdue University. https://www.gtap.agecon.purdue.edu/resources/res_display.asp?RecordID=316.

Ministry of Electronics & Information Technology. (2018). *India's trillion- dollar digital opportunity.* Retrieved April 10, 2023, from https://www.meity.gov.in/writereaddata/files/india_trillion-dollar_digital_opportunity.pdf

Mucha, T., & Seppala, T. (2021). Estimating firm digitalization: A method for disaggregating sector-level digital intensity to firm-level. *MethodsX, 8.*

OECD. (2020, April 23). *Tracking and tracing COVID: Protecting privacy and data while using apps and biometrics.* Retrieved June 10, 2023, from https://read.oecd-ilibrary.org/view/?ref=129_129655-7db0lu7dto&title=Tracking-and-Tracing-COVID-Protecting-privacy-and-data-while-using

Parekh, S., Reddin, S., Rowshankish, K., Soller, H., & Strandell-Jansson, M. (2022). *Localization of data privacy regulations creates competitive opportunities.* McKinsey & Company.

Ponemon Institute LLC. (2017). *The true cost of compliance with data protection regulations.* Globalscape. Retrieved May 20, 2023, from https://static.fortra.com/globalscape/pdfs/guides/gs-true-cost-of-compliance-data-protection-regulations-gd.pdf

Presidente, G., & Frey, C. B. (2022, March 10). *The GDPR effect: How data privacy regulation shaped firm performance globally.* CEPR VoxEU Column.

Scott, M., Cerulus, L., & Kayali, L. (2020). *Commission tells carriers to hand over mobile data in coronavirus fight.* Retrieved June 9, 2023, from https://www.politico.eu/article/european-commission-mobile-phone-data-thierry-breton-coronavirus-covid19/.

UNCTAD. (2016). *Data protection regulations and international data flows: Implications for trade and development.* United Nations. https://unctad.org/system/files/official-document/dtlstict2016d1_en.pdf

UNCTAD. (2023). *Data protection and privacy legislation worldwide.* Retrieved June 8, 2023, from https://unctad.org/page/data-protection-and-privacy-legislation-worldwide.

Ventrella, E. (2020). Privacy in emergency circumstances: Data protection and the COVID-19 pandemic, *ERA Forum, 21*, 379–393.

Index